UNDERSTANDING
PRESENTATION
GRAPHICS

UNDERSTANDING PRESENTATION GRAPHICS

MICHAEL TALMAN

SYBEX®

SAN FRANCISCO • PARIS • DÜSSELDORF • SOEST

Acquisitions Editor: Dave Clark
Editor: Marilyn Smith
Project Editor: Barbara Dahl
Technical Editor: Kim Marshall
Word Processors: Ann Dunn, Susan Trybull
Book Designer: Lucie Živny
Typesetter: Stephanie Hollier
Proofreader: David Silva
Indexer: Ted Laux
Cover Designer: Thomas Ingalls + Associates
Cover Photographer: Mark Johann
SYBEX is a registered trademark of SYBEX, Inc.

Library of Congress Card Number: 91-66941

ISBN: 0-7821-1023-1

Manufactured in the United States of America

10 9 8 7 6 5 4 3 2 1

To Blackie Davidman, whose wisdom
and guidance inspired so many of us as
artists and as human beings.

Acknowledgments

Many thanks to my editor, Marilyn Smith, and the staff at SYBEX for their encouragement and support.

Special thanks to:

Paula Toth, who talked me into writing this book and contributed greatly to the early stages of the writing.

Steve Bettcher, John Lyons, Carol Wright, and the incredibly talented staff of Corporate Images, Inc.

William Coggshall of New Media Research.

The many wonderful artists and designers I've worked with over the past 15 years.

Jim Flannery.

CONTENTS AT A GLANCE

TABLE
OF
CONTENTS

PART 2: PRODUCING YOUR PRESENTATION · 63

CHAPTER 5: Organizing Presentation Production · 65

CHAPTER 6: Format Design: Slide Frame Layout · 77

CHAPTER 7: Format Design: Using Color   107

CHAPTER 8: Format Design: Typography and Type Styles 131

CHAPTER 11: Using Illustrations in Your Presentations 263

CHAPTER 12: Producing Your Final Output 297

INTRODUCTION

ORATOPHOBIA: FEAR OF PUBLIC SPEAKING

In 1987, the *San Francisco Chronicle* published a poll in which hundreds of people were asked "What is your greatest fear?" Most of the answers were predictable: death, illness, war, the dentist. There was one answer, however, that surprised even the poll takers. At the top of the list was the one thing people feared the most: speaking in front of a large group of people.

Even the most experienced public speaker occasionally suffers from stage fright before a speech and "flop sweat" (a term used by professional comedians) while speaking. So why do people get up and speak in front of 10, 100, or 1000 strangers? The answer is that each and every speaker wants those strangers to take some *action*: to vote for Joe Blow, to invest in Hypothetical International, to build that new plant or tear down the old one, to save the whales.

The stakes involved in any presentation can be high; professional reputations, million-dollar budgets, and billion-dollar investments can be on the line. But even if you're just giving a short talk to fellow employees about a company benefits package, you can experience "presentation stress."

Adding to the difficulty of giving any presentation are the conditions under which presenters are often forced to work. Most presentations are scheduled with little or no advance warning. The presenter must prepare a speech while still keeping up with his regular workload. Slides are produced quickly, with the company president's name misspelled. There is no time to rehearse. The meeting room is often uncomfortable. The meeting audience is barely awake (morning), half asleep (after lunch), or eager to go home (late afternoon).

Getting those tired, distracted strangers to listen and understand is hard work, but if you start off on the right foot you can make your job a lot easier. With proper planning, you can create an effective, exciting presentation that will motivate your audience and help reduce your own public speaking phobia.

WHAT MAKES A PRESENTATION EFFECTIVE?

There is more to giving a presentation than a few slides and an off-the-cuff speech. A successful presentation is a carefully planned campaign to bring the audience members over to your side. It is designed to convince them that your opinion is the right one and that they should take action.

The key to a successful presentation is that it should be *message driven*. By sticking to a clear, well-thought-out message, you can focus the audience members' attention on what you want them to do. Creating an organized story-like structure for your presentation, with a beginning, middle, and end, enables you to clearly explain your message to the audience. This structure also allows you to control the pace at which the information is provided.

Presenting the right amount of information necessary to clarify your message is essential to good communication. Too much information can often be confusing. Too little will fail to persuade. Visually interesting, well-designed presentation graphics that enhance and clarify information will enable your audience to recall and act on your message.

Most of the work involved in creating an effective presentation happens before you create a single presentation graphic. Organization, planning, outlining, and basic visual design all need to be done before the actual presentation slides or overhead transparencies are created.

WHAT IS A DESKTOP PRESENTATION?

Until recently, a person giving a speech turned over a rough draft of his or her speech and any required charts and graphs to a graphic artist. The artist then prepared storyboards and rough sketches for the slides or overhead transparencies to be used in the presentation. After approval of the storyboards, the slides were produced using either traditional paste-up art and photography or expensive, high-end computer workstations.

Traditional art methods were too slow to allow last-minute changes. They also required a very skilled artist to prepare even the simplest text slide. This labor-intensive process led to one major end result: an expensive presentation.

Computer workstations, such as those manufactured by Genigraphics, Autographix, and Dicomed, solved a lot of the problems associated with traditional art methods. It became quite easy to make last-minute changes. It was also a lot easier to produce a large number of slides in a small amount of time. However, these workstations also required skilled operators, and a single workstation represented an investment of $50,000 to $200,000. Such a large investment in staff and equipment led to the same end result: an expensive presentation.

Like the desktop publishing revolution of several years ago, new developments in the world of personal computers have changed the way presentations are created. The traditional tools for creating presentation graphics have been refined, streamlined, made user-friendly, and moved to your desktop computer. Inexpensive, specialized applications now make it possible for anyone with an IBM PC compatible or Macintosh computer to create professional-looking presentation graphics. The old, expensive, photographic and computer hardware necessary to image slides and overhead transparencies is being replaced by low-cost desktop film recorders and service bureaus that specialize in imaging slides from your computer files. The desktop presentation revolution is here!

Creating a desktop presentation means having control of the entire presentation process from start to finish. You create your own presentation plan, outline, and script. You develop a storyboard and design your own slide or overhead transparency graphics. You print your own handouts and speaker notes. You make decisions about layout, color, and typography. It's a lot of work, but the payoff is that *you* get to make all these elements work together to serve your message.

Desktop presentations can be produced with a wide variety of software. In addition to specialty software such as Microsoft PowerPoint and Aldus Persuasion, virtually any graphics-oriented software can create slides, including drawing, illustration, desktop publishing, page layout, and even spreadsheet programs.

No matter what type of software you are using, there are basic principles of preparation, good design, and well-organized production that will guide you in creating an exciting, effective presentation.

WHO SHOULD READ THIS BOOK?

If you are creating slide shows and other visual presentations using desktop presentation software (or considering it), you will find suggestions on how to make your work more organized, professional, and creative. This book will be valuable to anyone using the following presentation graphics software: Microsoft PowerPoint, Aldus Persuasion, Micrografx Charisma, Harvard Graphics, Lotus Freelance Graphics, Claris Hollywood, CorelDRAW!, MORE, CA Cricket Presents, plus many other illustration, page layout, charting, and presentation graphics programs.

If you are a corporate manager considering switching your slide production from a graphics production company to an in-house operation, you will be able to familiarize yourself with the process and pitfalls of slide making, so you can make an informed, practical decision for your organization.

ABOUT UNDERSTANDING PRESENTATION GRAPHICS

Creating an effective presentation involves much more than sitting down at your computer and knocking off a few slides in Harvard Graphics or PowerPoint. Producing a successful presentation requires planning as well as graphic skill. *Understanding Presentation Graphics* is your guide to the total process of preparing and producing a presentation using your computer. In this book, you will find practical guidelines for every phase of preparing a presentation, whether it is produced as 35mm color slides, black-and-white or color overhead transparencies, computer screen shows, or video.

In most corporate situations, the planning, writing, and graphics production for a presentation are often a team effort. The speaker will prepare an outline and the text of his or her speech, while other people in the organization will create the slides, design and print handouts, and arrange meeting room space and facilities. Although you should pay particular attention to the sections of this book which apply to your specific role, don't neglect the rest of the process. You will find it easier to support the team effort when you understand the part of each person in the group.

If you are flying solo—writer, artist, and speaker all rolled into one—you will create more dynamic, effective presentations by following the guidelines in this book.

Understanding Presentation Graphics follows the presentation production process from beginning to end. Part 1 deals with the pre-production process: production scheduling, planning, outlining, scripting, and creating a storyboard. Part 2 covers the actual process of designing and creating presentation graphics. It includes three chapters on format design: laying out the slide frame, using color, and choosing type styles. The next three chapters deal specifically with the design of slides with text, charts and graphs, and illustrations. The final chapters provide details on methods for final production and preparations on the day of the presentation. Most of the examples are for 35mm slides, but the principles apply to all media.

Appendices include a guide to presentation software; a guide to national, regional, and local imaging service bureaus; and a bibliography.

Each chapter of *Understanding Presentation Graphics* also contains a chapter in a "real-life" story, in which you will meet the management and staff of Hypothetical International. Hypothetical, an unusually diversified holding company, is in the process of issuing some new stock, and the three top corporate officers are preparing a "road show" for presentation to brokers, stock analysts, and institutional investors. They have recently switched to using desktop presentation tools to create their in-house presentations, and this is their first big presentation for an outside audience. Their story shows how the guidelines presented here relate to a typical business situation.

part I

Preparing a Presentation

chapter 1

Creating a Production Schedule

Just as you wouldn't plan a trip around the world without some sort of itinerary, you shouldn't plan a presentation without a production schedule. If there are several people involved in preparing the presentation, it's important to make sure that no one is left waiting for another person's input. A production schedule lets everyone know exactly what is expected of them and when their tasks should be completed.

Even if you're working alone, a simple production schedule will help you avoid procrastination and develop a work flow that will produce the best possible presentation.

SETTING UP A SCHEDULE

A production schedule can vary widely in complexity. For a small presentation, it may be just a series of checkpoints for accomplishing certain tasks during the preceding week. For a three-day conference involving many speakers, it can be like a battle plan for the production team, with overlapping deadlines and goals spanning several weeks before the final meeting.

A plain calendar page is the ideal tool for creating a production schedule. Mark sections for each of the tasks discussed in the following pages. In many cases, these sections will overlap, especially if the presentation will include several speakers. Mark deadlines (such as due dates for final script or imaging) in red to make them stand out.

Estimating production time is a skill which comes with practice, but you can protect yourself from serious scheduling problems by keeping these few things in mind:

- Be practical; set goals that are achievable.
- Always assume any task will take longer than planned.
- Treat all deadlines seriously; don't procrastinate.
- Remember Murphy's Law: If something can go wrong, it will.

BOTTOM-UP PRODUCTION SCHEDULING

The moment a speaker steps up to the podium to begin giving a presentation, there's no longer any time for additions, changes, or repairs to the presentation materials. That date—the day of the presentation—becomes your final "drop-dead" deadline. By working from the bottom up, or backward from the presentation date, you can create a production schedule that will ensure that everything is finished by that day.

Figure 1.1 shows a typical production schedule for a presentation. The time estimates are for a presentation of consisting of from 20 to 100 slides. The actual time necessary for each task depends on your skill level and the amount of time that can be diverted from your regular duties. Remember, everything else in a company doesn't come to a halt just because there's a big presentation coming up.

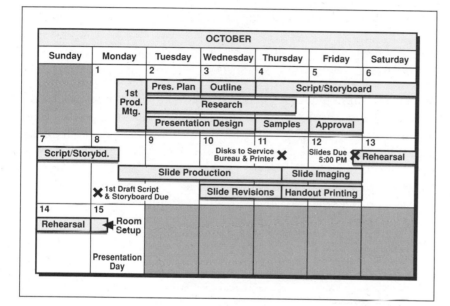

Figure 1.1:

A typical production schedule

Many of the tasks can overlap, making the actual production time much shorter than the sum of its parts. If necessary, you can compress your production time quite a bit if everybody does their part.

The following sections explain the stages of presentation production and how to schedule them, working backward from the presentation date.

PRESENTATION DAY SETUP

The amount of time necessary for setting up the equipment for a presentation can vary widely. Determine when you can first get access to the room where you will be giving your presentation. In general, most presentations can be set up during the morning of the meeting. If you are just giving a short talk in a company conference room, there will actually be very little for you to do besides placing a slide tray on the projector and focusing.

A presentation involving many speakers, multiple projectors, and sound equipment may require considerably more setup time (up to two days).

Don't take chances in preparing the room or rooms for a large meeting. If you are unfamiliar with the complexities involved in such a project, consider using the services of a staging company that specializes in setting up large-scale presentations. You can usually find local staging companies listed in the business section of the phone book (the Yellow Pages) under Audio-Visual Equipment—Renting & Leasing. If possible, contact a few of them for cost and time estimates.

SPEAKER REHEARSAL

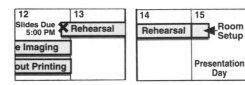

Like anyone else who performs in front of an audience, a presentation speaker needs time to rehearse for the show. In your production schedule, allow a couple of days for the speaker to have a copy of the slides to use in practice sessions.

If you anticipate last-minute changes to a few slides, it may be worthwhile to go ahead and process all the slides so that the speaker can rehearse with them. Then you can redo just the slides that have changes and replace the incorrect slides before the presentation.

PRODUCTION OF HANDOUTS AND OTHER MATERIALS

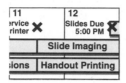

The length of time to be allotted to printing the audience handouts and other materials for the presentation depends on their content. If you are giving a short presentation consisting of mostly text slides to a small audience, materials preparation should not take more than a day.

On the other hand, printing large numbers of handouts containing complicated presentation graphics can take a lot of time (up to three days). Depending on your software, the complexity of your graphics, and the speed of your laser printer, it can take several hours to print just the master copies of the handouts for a 100-slide presentation. To this, add the time required for photocopying (or printing), collating, and binding the materials.

FINAL IMAGING OF SLIDES
OR OVERHEAD TRANSPARENCIES

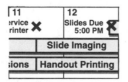

Whether you are producing your slides on an in-house film recorder or using a service bureau, you **must** allow enough time for the final imaging, film processing, mounting, and tray placement of your slides.

Film recorder performance varies widely. Depending on the film recorder model, a single slide file can take from 2 to 20 minutes to image. It also takes time to process the film, mount the slides, and place the slides in trays. When you are producing many slides this way, the process can take up to two days. If you are using an in-house film recorder, check with the person who operates it for an estimate of imaging and finishing times for your project.

Most imaging service bureaus have a normal 24-hour turnaround for 35mm slides. (Large presentations of 100 or more slides may take longer to process.) If you are in a big hurry, they will usually be able deliver your slides in less than 24 hours, but be prepared to pay dearly. Many service bureaus charge up to a 200 percent premium for same-day service.

REVISIONS AND LAST-MINUTE ADDITIONS

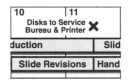

It doesn't matter how much you prepare, or how many times you check and recheck your figures, there will always be last-minute changes to your presentation.

Since changes are unavoidable, plan for them in your production schedule. Allow a day or two for final revisions. You can't predict all the changes that will be necessary, but scheduling them will at least make room for more routine revisions and additions.

The best way to manage revisions is to save up as many changes as you can for a final revision cycle, rather than interrupting the work flow repeatedly for small changes. It is much easier to go back and make all the revisions to your entire presentation at once than to pick at it piecemeal. Postponing the final revisions allows several generations of changes to accumulate, and you will be able to revise each slide in a single session.

SLIDE OR OVERHEAD
TRANSPARENCY DESIGN AND PRODUCTION

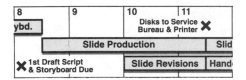

Most of your actual production time will be spent creating graphics for your slides or overhead transparencies. The length of time required to design and produce these items varies from one presentation to another. You may spend two hours creating the slides for one presentation and two weeks producing the ones for another presentation. A number of things can affect the production time of your project:

- Your skill and experience level
- The complexity of your graphics
- The speed and ease of use of your software

Make sure you've allowed enough space in your production schedule to do the job right the first time. Rushed production often leads to typographical and other errors. You are probably familiar with the quote:

> "There is never enough time to do a job right... But always enough time to do a job over."

If you are not sure how much time to allow for slide production, time how long it takes you to create a few slides (simple and complex) and multiply that figure by the appropriate factor for your estimate. For example, if it takes you one hour to produce three slides in a twenty-slide presentation, allow at least seven hours (or a full day) to create all of them. Your ability to estimate production time will grow as you gain experience.

PRESENTATION DESIGN AND APPROVAL

2	3	4	5
Pres. Plan	Outline	Script/Storyboa	
	Research		
Presentation Design		Samples	Approval

Design revisions affect the entire presentation. Although you can deal with last-minute changes to particular slides, changing the basic design of a presentation toward the end of your schedule can be disastrous, especially in a large presentation. You can avoid such catastrophes by scheduling early design decisions and approval.

Take a couple of days to create a design for the format of your presentation, with several examples of text and chart slides as well as a color palette sample. Allow one day to have the color and format samples imaged on film. The processed samples will give you a true idea of how the final slides will look.

Have the people involved in the presentation review the design by viewing the projected imaged samples and get their approval before continuing. You will usually be designing the presentation and getting approvals during the same time the script and storyboard are being prepared.

PRESENTATION PLAN, OUTLINE, SCRIPT, AND STORYBOARD

2	3	4	5	6	7	8
Pres. Plan	Outline	Script/Storyboard			Script/Storybd.	
	Research					
Presentation Design		Samples	Approval			✗ 1st Draft Sc & Storyboa

The presentation plan and outline are the backbone of your presentation, so don't skimp on the time you spend working on them. The more complete they are, the faster the rest of your production will go. Take a day to develop the plan, and write as thorough an outline as possible.

With the help of a good outline, writing the first draft of your speech (the script) should take only a day or two. While you are writing the first draft, make notes on what sort of slides will be necessary to support your topics, using your outline for reference.

Spend one more day creating drafts of your slides, including sketches of any charts you may need. These should be rough drafts, without any embellishments. Include just the basic information you need to create the slides with your presentation graphics software. Some software packages, such as Aldus Persuasion and Micrografx Charisma, can generate the text for your slides directly from your outline.

RESEARCH

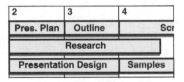

If you already have a great deal of the information you need at hand, most of the research for the presentation can be completed in the course of developing an outline and script. For example, company financial, sales, and production data are usually readily accessible.

However, if extensive research is necessary, allow for it in your schedule. Also include some extra time in the slide-production phase for adding any new information that arrives later in the schedule.

FIRST PRODUCTION MEETING

If your presentation is a team effort, get the members of the team together for an initial production meeting as soon as a presentation date is decided. At this meeting, begin to establish the scope of the project by covering the following items:

- How long will the presentation be?

- How many slides will be needed?

- Where is the presentation to be given?

- Will any special equipment be needed?

If you do not have all the information you need to develop a complete schedule, do the best you can at the initial meeting. Make sure everyone on the presentation team gets the missing information as soon as possible.

PRODUCTION DEADLINES AND CHECKPOINTS

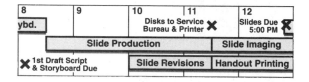

After you have determined a general timetable for your production schedule, mark specific dates for when tasks have to be completed. For example, set deadlines for the speaker to finish the outline and a nearly final script and for delivery of the final diskette(s) for imaging.

Any time one person depends upon another person for information, set a date for when that information will be available.

FUDGE FACTORS

No matter how well you plan your production schedule, a few delays are unavoidable. To compensate for the inevitable, build a "fudge factor" into the schedule. Add a day or half-day to make up for lost time due to missed deadlines, miscommunication, or outright disasters.

ASSIGNING PRIORITIES

In the rush of creating a presentation, it's easy to lose track of your priorities. You can avoid confusion and conflict by frequently reminding yourself of what is most important.

In the early stages of production planning, concentrate on developing a final outline and storyboard. If these are complete and satisfactory, there will be less chance of drastic revisions in the overall presentation later in the production process.

When you're creating slides or overhead transparencies, keep the big picture in mind. Don't hold up production of the whole presentation just because you're missing a few numbers for a chart or graph. Get as much done on the slides as soon as possible. In most cases, you can set up charts or tables in advance, leaving blanks for missing data. You can also create text slides that are incomplete. It's easier to change words or numbers and add text than it is to create an entire slide at the last minute.

If you are working as part of a team, make prompt and accurate communication your top priority. Nothing disrupts the production process more than crossed signals between team members.

Give vendors, such as printers and imaging service bureaus, plenty of advance notice if you'll be bringing in a big job. By allowing the vendor to plan for your job, you will get better service. Also, you can avoid many last-minute problems by being familiar with your vendor's requirements for submitting work for printing or imaging.

PLANNING MULTISPEAKER PRESENTATIONS

One of the most challenging projects that you may face is the "big meeting," such as an annual stockholders meeting, a scientific conference, or a sales convention. Such meetings involve many people giving presentations over several days. Hundreds, even thousands, of slides may be required.

THE PRODUCTION COORDINATOR

If you are involved in a large project with several speakers and hundreds of slides, a good idea is to choose someone in your organization to act as a production coordinator. The production coordinator is the "Keeper of the Schedule," whose main job is to make sure everything gets done properly and on time, to prod the procrastinators, and to calm the frantic. The coordinator should also act as liaison to any outside vendors. Overall, the coordinator serves to simplify the communication process.

In practice, the production coordinator usually ends up being the same person who does the majority of the graphics design and production. If you are put in this situation, don't despair; just make it a point to delegate as much responsibility as you can to the speakers and anyone else you can recruit to help you out.

THE PRODUCTION CHECKLIST

One way of organizing a complex presentation is to use a production checklist. Create a list of all the separate presentations in the meeting, along with checkboxes for the tasks necessary for completion. Figure 1.2 shows an example of a checklist for a multispeaker presentation.

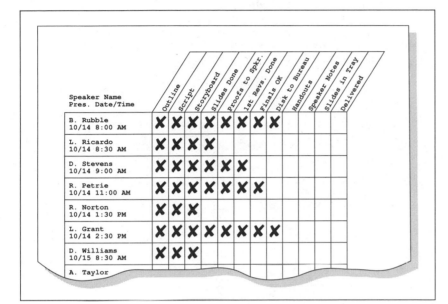

Figure 1.2:

Production checklist

As each script is finished, each group of slides is created, and each slide tray is loaded, check off the appropriate box on the checklist. This way, you can keep track of the various stages of the presentations. You will know who is lagging behind in providing a finished script and which presentations are ready for imaging.

THE REAL WORLD   CUTTING CORNERS

Welcome to the real world, where production schedules fall apart, people procrastinate, and computers crash. Where even the best planning and intentions go awry under the pressure of tight deadlines and personality clashes. Where Murphy's Law is an understatement.

Monday, October 1, 1:00 pm: The place is Hypothetical International. In order to finance expansion into new areas of business outside our already diversified holdings, our management has decided to issue new stock in the company. To ensure a successful stock sale, our Chief Executive Officer (CEO), President, and Chief Financial Officer will be going on the road to talk to financial analysts, stockbrokers, institutional investors, and other interested parties about what a great investment Hypothetical is.

Five people are attending our first production meeting:

George Spelvin, CEO

Alan Smithee, President

Victoria Regina, Chief Financial Officer

Ellen Jackson, Office Services Manager

Jim Gonzalez, Desktop Publishing Specialist

The goals of this first meeting are to get a grasp on the whole project and develop a few guidelines about production scheduling. George, Alan, and Victoria are the speakers. They will prepare the presentation plan and write their speeches with help from their assistants. Ellen will coordinate the project and act as liaison between speakers, in-house production people, and outside vendors. Jim is the artist who will design and create the slides and other presentation materials.

The total presentation will consist of four parts:

Opening remarks by George Spelvin

A general introduction to Hypothetical
International by Alan Smithee

Corporate financial information and details of the
stock offering by Victoria Regina

Closing remarks by George Spelvin

The total meeting time is going to be one hour, with
about 35 to 40 minutes of presentation, plus a
question-and-answer period. All of our speakers have a
pretty good idea of what they want to say, and all of the
speeches will be no more than 15 minutes.

There's not a lot of time for research, but fortunately, most of the information needed to create the
presentations is already in the company's computer.
There will be a few last-minute figures on the stock
offering to be worked out, but the corporate financial
information is ready.

Our preliminary estimate is a total of about 100
slides in the entire presentation. Except for Victoria's
financial data, most of the information will be presented in simple text or graphic slides.

The first presentation is on Monday, October 15 at
Dewey, Cheatham and Howe, a prestigious investment
banking firm. The speakers will be flying to New York
on the previous Sunday afternoon.

Working backward from our speaker's flight time,
the first target date on our schedule will be Friday,
October 12, 5:00 pm. By then, all the speakers should
have their final presentations in hand so that they can
rehearse over the weekend.

The next target date will be Thursday, October 11, 12:00 pm. At that time, we will need to send the final imaging disks to our service bureau and the final hand-out copy to our in-house copy center for copying and binding. By setting a noon deadline, we give both ourselves and the service bureau some slack in case of last-minute changes or errors.

Based on Jim Gonzalez's previous experience, three days should be enough time to produce the slides, so we will set the deadline for slide copy from the speakers on Monday, October 8, 9:00 am. If there is enough to work on before that time, it will be given to Jim as soon as it becomes available. A final revision cycle will be done on Thursday morning, just before the disk goes to the service bureau.

While the speakers are working on the content of their presentations, Jim will be working on the design aspects. We'll set Thursday, October 4 as the date for completion of the design process. The first drafts of the speakers' scripts will also be due on that date.

For their own benefit, the speakers plan a meeting for the end of the day tomorrow (October 2) to go over their respective presentation plans and outlines.

It looks like a good production schedule. We've cut a few corners in the schedule to save time, and we have almost two whole weekends to take up the slack if things go wrong. Unfortunately, there are a few tight spots that will give us trouble later on. And Murphy was an optimist.... Continued in Chapter 2!

SUMMARY

Your first step to a successful presentation is to organize the production process, as follows:

- Create a production schedule working backwards from your meeting date.

- Set deadlines and checkpoints for all important production goals.

- Prioritize your production tasks so no one is delayed by missing information.

- For complex presentations, assign a person to coordinate production tasks and to act as liaison to outside vendors.

- Use a production checklist to keep track of production goals.

chapter 2

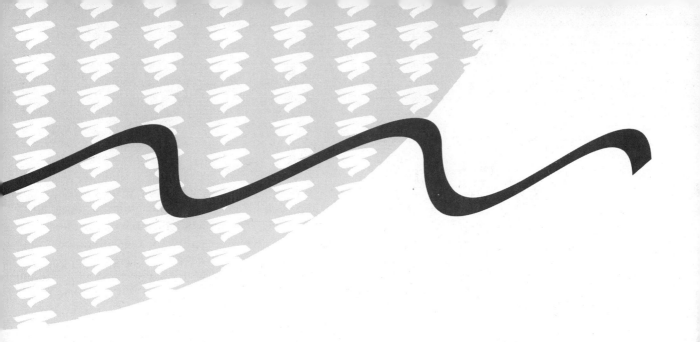

Planning Your Presentation

The first step in creating a presentation is to develop a presentation plan. A presentation plan is not an outline. It is a blueprint that you use to construct your arguments and facts that will lead your audience to the conclusions you desire. You don't have to spend a lot of time on a plan, just enough to have a clear idea of how to structure your presentation.

DEFINING YOUR GOAL AND MESSAGE

Before you begin any work on the presentation, consider what ideas you want the audience to get from it. When the audience members leave the presentation, what do you want them thinking about?

YOUR GOAL

Write one sentence about what it is that you want the audience to **do**. Do you want them to spend their hard-earned cash on your product or service? Do you want them to approve a new, bigger budget? Or do you want them to simply feel better about or more confident in your organization? That one sentence is your *goal*.

YOUR PRIMARY MESSAGE

After you have defined a goal, you need to turn that goal around and make it into a simple, declarative statement, or *message*. Your message should articulate the one main reason why the audience should act in a way that will achieve your goal.

For example, you might want to convey one of these messages:

- Our product is the best.
- A bigger budget will make our organization more efficient and profitable.
- Our company is financially sound.

Everything that goes into your presentation, including the script, text slides, charts, graphs, photographs, and handouts, should convey your message. As you outline and write your speech and design every slide, ask yourself whether the information you're showing helps relay the message.

If you are planning a meeting with several speakers, develop a central, unifying message for the entire presentation. Then the individual speakers should create their own presentation messages to support the overall theme.

For example, the main theme of an education conference might be:

> Computer technology awakens a child's imagination.

Based on this central theme, the speakers' messages might include:

> Multimedia is a tool for art education.
>
> SuperMario morality: Nintendo can teach ethics.

A central theme not only makes the entire presentation flow smoothly, but it also makes the individual presentations more powerful and persuasive because they are supported by the others.

DEVELOPING A TOP-DOWN PRESENTATION PLAN

The "top-down" presentation planning method is structured like a pyramid, as illustrated in Figure 2.1. Your goal is at the top, followed by your message. These top blocks are supported by levels of messages beneath them. This provides the structure for your presentation, which can be easily developed into your final outline, script, and slides.

THE "WHY?" APPROACH

Once you've defined your primary message, your best tool for creating a successful presentation plan is the word *Why*. Put yourself in the position of the audience, and every time you produce a message, ask "Why?". Phrase each new answer with another simple, declarative sentence.

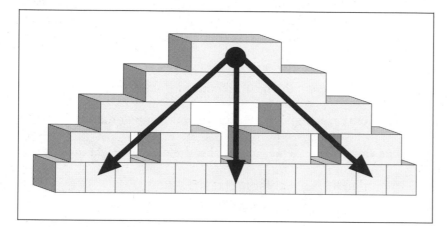

Through this process, you create a solid structure of fact and argument within your presentation.

For example, suppose your primary message is:

Eat your vegetables.

Some of your answers to "Why?" could be:

Vegetables taste great.

Vegetables contribute to good health.

These answers provide the third level of your plan, the supporting elements that contribute to the primary message.

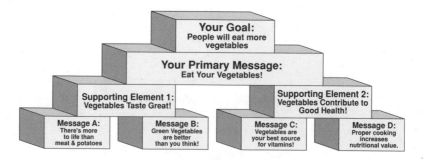

By continually answering "Why?" you will work your way down to the level of detail you need to prepare your outline and script.

When you reach the bottom of your presentation plan pyramid, you should have a series of messages that can serve as entries for your outline and titles for most of your slides. You may also want to use higher level presentation plan items as section heads or other levels of your outline.

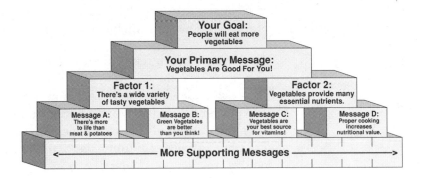

THE SHAPE OF THE PLAN

The presentation plan doesn't have to be symmetrical. A single message can have as many entries under it as you need to make your point.

A presentation plan can't contain everything you need to create a successful presentation. It is only a starting point for creating an outline. For example, a presentation plan has no chronological order. You have to decide the order and pacing of the information to be presented to the audience.

UNDERSTANDING YOUR AUDIENCE

While creating a presentation plan, it's important to keep in mind who is asking the "Why?" question. The level of detail and complexity you need in your presentation is influenced by the make-up of your intended audience.

LEVELS OF INFLUENCE AND FAMILIARITY

The amount of control your audience has over the outcome of your goal will affect the way you select the information to be presented. A presentation to the Board of Directors requesting funding for a new construction project will require a different emphasis than a presentation to the press announcing the same project. At the Board of Directors meeting, the company's benefits will be paramount; at the press conference, the community's benefits will be most important.

The familiarity of the audience with the subject matter will also make a big difference in the way you build your presentation plan. A scientist making a presentation to his peers at a conference will need a high degree of detail and very little background material on the subject. When the same scientist speaks to potential investors for a new biotechnical company, he needs to emphasize the general benefits of his findings and their market potential rather than the technical procedures.

NEED TO KNOW

How much information to include in a presentation depends a lot on how much the audience needs to know. For example, at a stock investor's meeting, the first speaker's presentation might introduce the company in general terms, with just enough detail to familiarize the audience with the company and its history. On the other hand, the financial presentation may have very little general information, but consist almost entirely of the detailed data necessary to explain the new stock issue and its profit potential.

THE AUDIENCE PROFILE

Take the time to work up a short profile of your audience. By knowing who you're talking to, you'll be able to speak to them more clearly and convincingly. Figure 2.2 shows an example of a form you can use to set up an audience profile.

Figure 2.2:

Audience profile form

Audience Profile

Presentation Date and Time: _____

Location: _____

Type of Room: _____

Equipment Available: _____

Equipment Needed: _____

Your Message: _____

Describe Your Audience:

Audience Size: _____

Audience's knowledge of the topic:
    ❑ Very Familiar   ❑ Somewhat Familiar   ❑ Unfamiliar

Audience's expected attitude toward you and your topic:
    ❑ Friendly   ❑ Neutral   ❑ Hostile   ❑ Unknown

How often does your audience attend presentations like this?
    ❑ Often   ❑ Occasionally   ❑ Seldom

How much influence does this audience have over your goals?
    ❑ Much   ❑ Some   ❑ Little   ❑ None

Put Yourself in the Audience:

What level of background information will the audience need?
    ❑ A great deal   ❑ Some   ❑ Very little

What relationship with the audience will be most effective?
    ❑ Casual/Chatty   ❑ Businesslike/Factual   ❑ Aggressive
    ❑ Scholarly   ❑ Evangelical   ❑ Other

If you were a typical audience member (as described above), describe what presentation approach would most likely win YOU over:

_____

_____

THE
REAL
WORLD   FILLING IN THE MISSING PIECES

Wednesday, October 3, 11:00 am: Creating the upper level of the presentation plan for Hypothetical International has been easy. George, Alan, and Victoria have decided that their goal is:

The audience will buy or recommend our new stock issue.

and their primary message for their combined presentations is:

Hypothetical International is an investment in the future.

They have figured out how long the individual presentations should be, and each speaker has developed a main message:

George's opening remarks (5 minutes): The time has come to expand.

Alan's presentation (15 minutes): We have the resources to grow tremendously.

Victoria's presentation (15 minutes): Hypothetical International is a sound investment.

George's closing (5 minutes): You are a part of our future.

Let's take a closer look at Alan's presentation plan. He supports his main message with the three things that prove what a strong organization Hypothetical has: its people, its infrastructure, and its history of success. He then goes on to define seven items that support those three elements, and finally lists supporting information to flesh out his presentation.

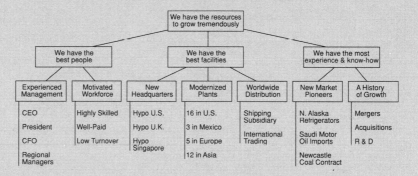

Alan has covered most of the bases, but he has forgotten a crucial part of his speech that will make the overall presentation flow better. Alan decides to add a short segment about general corporate finances, which will lead in to the financial details in Victoria's presentation.

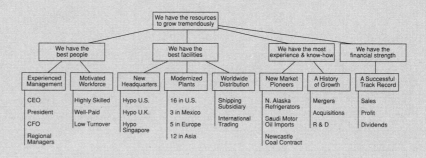

With the addition of his financial segment, Alan's presentation looks like it will contain about 30 slides. We get that total from counting the entries in the bottom row of the presentation plan, and then allowing for a few extra title slides and entries which may have to be split over more than one slide.

SUMMARY

Creating an effective presentation requires careful planning. You can hone your arguments and make a stronger impression on your audience by following these guidelines:

- Define your goal by stating what you want your audience to do.

- Define your main message by articulating why the audience should act toward your goal.

- When creating many presentations for a single meeting, define a theme that ties the different presentations together.

- Continue to ask "Why?" to create more messages that reinforce the main message.

- Tailor your message to the intended audience members. Put yourself in their position when creating your reinforcing messages.

chapter 3

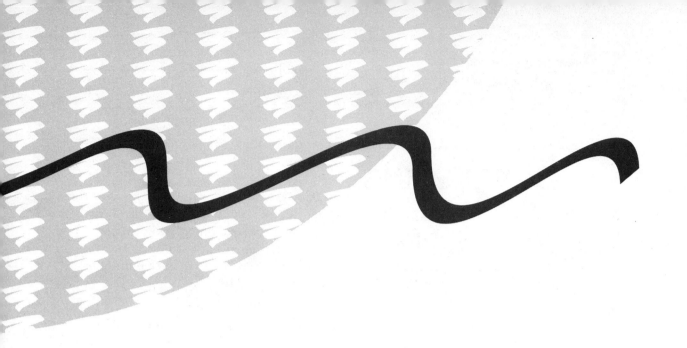

Preparing a
Presentation Outline

Your presentation plan is a hierarchy of messages, which are the things that you want to tell your audience. You construct your outline—the framework for your presentation—from the facts that support your messages.

DEVELOPING AN OUTLINE FROM A PLAN

Making an outline for your presentation is simply a matter of expanding and organizing the messages from your presentation plan. Each message in your plan becomes an entry in your outline. Then continue to develop the outline:

- Add information that supports your messages.

- Determine the relative importance of each message and fact as it relates to your primary message.

- Organize your data so that it tells a story.

OUTLINE ORDERING AND CONTENT

Indent your presentation plan messages based on how far down the "pyramid" they fall. Move your elements around so that there is a logical flow of information. Then start adding your supporting information in deeper levels of the outline.

As shown in the example outline in Figure 3.1, your outline can contain anything that will contribute to developing the overall presentation. For example, an outline could include the following:

- Bulleted list items

- Chart and graph notes (avoid actual figures at this point)

- Speech notes

- Suggestions for illustrations or photographs

PRESENTATION STORYTELLING

After you have a draft of your outline, consider the overall pace and flow of the presentation. You should treat the flow of information in a

Slide Design Seminar

    Designing Professional-Looking Slides and Overheads
Using Desktop Presentation Software

    Good Design Principles Work in All Media:
        Slides
        Overheads
        On-Screen Presentations
        Video

    Elements of Good Design
        Formatting
            Color
            Type
            Graphics

    Formatting a Presentation

    The Golden Rules of Slide Design
        Everything on a slide should:
        Engage the audience's attention
        Provide clear, concise data
        Clarify the speaker's message

    But Most Important:
        Plan Ahead!

    Reflect Your Company's Image
        Type of Business
        Corporate Culture
        Corporate Colors/Logos/Typography
        Other Public Materials
        Individual Speaker Preferences

    Be Consistent
        Develop a Coordinated Color Palette
        Maintain Uniform Type Size/Position/Style
        Keep Illustration Styles Consistent
        Standardize Chart and Graph Formatting
        Watch Out for the Little Things
            Shadows
            Outlines

    Keep It Simple
        Don't overdecorate
        Give your information some breathing room
        Use format graphics to organize the slide frame
        Limit colors/typefaces
        Design for the person in the back row

Figure 3.1:

Sample presentation outline

presentation like the plot of an exciting story. Don't just charge into your facts and figures directly; create a little suspense and anticipation in your audience.

Start your outline with background information, and then zero in on the primary message of your presentation. In any presentation, you should try to create a moment at which the audience puts together all of your information and mentally says "Ah ha! Now I get it!" Once you reach that point, you should briefly summarize your facts again and conclude your speech.

One of the best examples of how to structure any presentation is the format of the PBS television show *Connections* with James Burke. During the course of a program, Mr. Burke takes his audience through a maze of history, sociology, and science spanning hundreds of years, full of events that seem only slightly connected. Then, towards the end of the show, he ties all those events together to explain, for example, how a single event in the 1500s could start a chain that leads to the invention of the atomic bomb in 1945. When he comes to that point in his presentation, you can almost hear the audience go "Aha!" After his message is delivered, he reinforces it with a very quick recap of the chain of events, and then closes with an explanation of how those events affect our lives.

Structure your presentation as a drama to sustain audience interest and enhance the persuasive effect of your message. Let the information build to a conclusion (the main message of your presentation), reinforce the message with a summary, and then close with a strong call for action toward your goal.

In a multispeaker presentation, you can assign parts of the drama to different speakers. Let one speaker give the introduction, one deliver the "Aha!," and another summarize and close.

USING OUTLINING SOFTWARE

Creating an outline can be tedious because you must juggle all your messages and supporting material to devise the best possible presentation. Using outlining, sometimes called idea-processing, software can make the process much easier.

Outlining programs, such as GrandView on the PC or More and Acta on the Macintosh, allow you to arrange your ideas and facts as easily as a word processor allows you to edit your final speech. Some word processing programs, such as Microsoft Word and Lotus Ami Pro, also have built-in outlining capabilities.

Many presentation graphics programs, such as Microsoft PowerPoint and Aldus Persuasion, can import files from word processing and outlining programs, so you don't have to reenter your slide copy from scratch.

USING PRESENTATION GRAPHICS PROGRAMS

A new generation of presentation graphics software has made outline creation an integral part of creating slides. For example, Aldus Persuasion and CA-Cricket Presents have built-in outlining modules that allow you to type in your presentation outline, and then create slides, overhead transparencies, and printed materials directly from your outline entries.

Figure 3.2 shows an example of an outline created in Aldus Persuasion. The program automatically converts the outline material into text and graphics slides. The various icons on the left side of the text represent slide titles and text, and the number of each slide appears in the left margin.

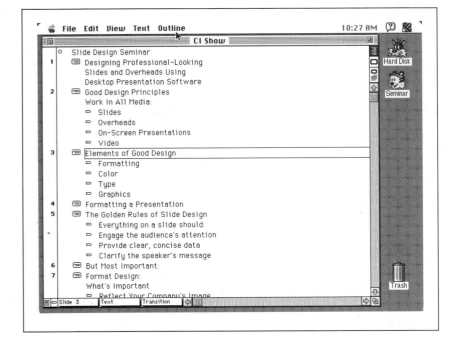

Figure 3.2:

Aldus Persuasion outline

THE
REAL
WORLD   TO THINE OWN SELF BE TRUE

Thursday, October 4, 1;00 pm: ''This is boring!''

George Spelvin looked at the finished outline for his opening remarks and realized that the things he thought he should say and the things he wanted to say were not on the same wavelength.

```
Opening Remarks
    Welcome
    A Changing World Mandates Corporate Change
    U.S. Market Shrinking
        Continuing Domestic Recession
        Reduced Domestic Revenues
        Anticipated Cuts in Defense Spending
    Current World Market is Very Competitive
        Weak U.S. Dollar
        Japanese Protectionism
        Growing EEC Strength
    Hypothetical Built on Highly Competitive Markets
        Electronic Components
        Natural Resources
        International Trading
    A New World Order is a New World Opportunity
        Opening Eastern European Markets
        Vast Natural Resource Reserves
        Soviet-U.S. Joint Ventures
        New Trading Partners
    Uniquely Poised to Expand in Eastern Europe
        Existing Agreements in Hungary, Poland
        Strong Ties to Baltic States
        Experience in New Market Development
            South America
            Middle East
    Expansion is Capital-Hungry
        New Manufacturing Facilities
        Employee Hiring/Training
        Marketing and Legal Costs
    Our New Stock Issue is Seed Money for the Future
        New Capital to Pursue Joint Ventures
        Startup Costs for New Manufacturing
    You Can Be a Part of Our Future
    Our Management Report
        Alan Smithee
            More About Hypothetical International
        Victoria Regina
            Current Financial Condition
            Proposed Stock Offering
```

As the founder and CEO of Hypothetical International, George was responsible for turning a small widget manufacturing firm into a multinational, billion dollar organization. He is a shrewd and successful businessman; but his main strength is as a powerful motivator.

George is a cheerleader. He's a terrific off-the-cuff speaker—infectiously enthusiastic, lively, and articulate. The outline he produced, however, was a sort of laundry list of Hypothetical's plans for the next few years.

The information in the outline was all accurate. It gave a sense of where the company was going, but it wasn't the sort of speech that would get his audience excited about the future of Hypothetical International.

So George tore up his dry, "welcome to our dog and pony show" outline, and wrote nine lines.

Opening Remarks
    Welcome
    A Changing World Mandates Corporate Change
    Hypothetical International Thrives On Change
    The New World Order Is A New World Opportunity
    The Time Has Come to Expand and Grow
    We've Planted the Seeds, Now We Nurture Them
    You and Your Investors Can Be A Part of Our Growth
    Introduce Alan & Victoria

The entries in George's new outline were simple topics about which he could spontaneously improvise a few sentences. Each entry builds upon the previous one, to concentrate more fully on Hypothetical's future.

George's advantage is that he doesn't have to use a lot of facts and figures in his presentation—he has left that to his President and Chief Financial Officer. In his opening presentation, he can do what he does best: excite his audience and get them interested in Hypothetical International.

The main disadvantage of this type of presentation is that there isn't a lot to go on when creating the slides for George's speech.

SUMMARY

A comprehensive outline is the key to a persuasive presentation. Use it as a tool for organizing all of the elements in your presentation. Follow these guidelines when creating your outline:

- Expand your outline with facts, figures, and notes that enhance your message.

- Prioritize and sequence the elements of your presentation.

- Develop the flow of information in your outline so it tells a story.

- Use outlining software or presentation software with a built-in outliner to organize your presentation.

- Whenever possible, import the information from your outline into your presentation graphics software to create your slides.

- Don't be a slave to an overly organized outline. If your personal style is more freewheeling, just include in your outline the topics on which you want to spontaneously expand.

chapter 4

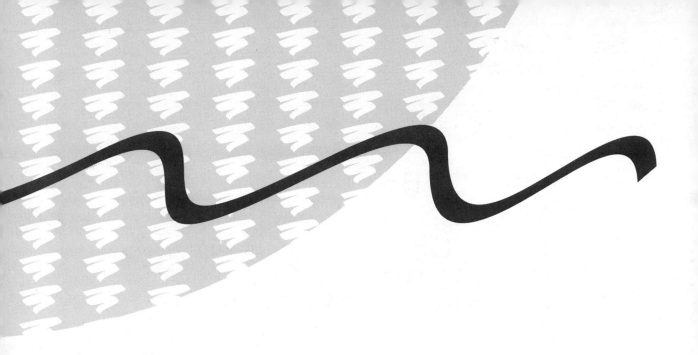

Creating a Script and Storyboard

After you have planned the basic content and structure of your presentation and organized it using an outline, you are ready to develop the two components of the presentation:

■ The *script,* which is what the speaker will say

■ The *storyboard,* which is what the audience will see

DIVIDING THE COMPONENTS OF A PRESENTATION

As illustrated in Figure 4.1, you use your outline to develop your script and storyboard. While you are creating these components of your presentation, keep this basic premise in mind:

Say it with words; show it with pictures.

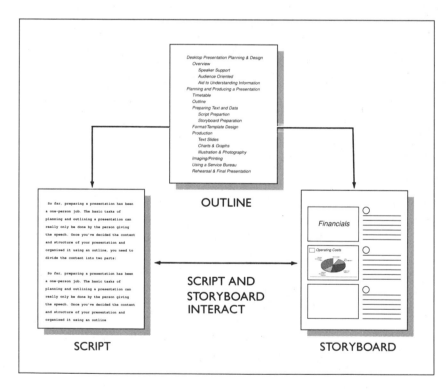

Figure 4.1:

Developing a script and storyboard

An audiovisual presentation is a combination of spoken word, text, numbers, and graphics. The key to success is **speaking** to the audience and **showing** them only elements that support what is being said.

Most audience members can only do one thing at a time. They can listen to the speaker, or they can read the slides and handouts. If you put large amounts of text or data on your slides, the audience members will be forced to spend most of their time reading, not listening.

If you want the people in your audience to spend their time reading, don't waste their time with a speech—print a brochure and mail it. But if you want them to hear what you have to say, don't distract them with excessively complex slides. The slides you create should be an addition to the speech. Do not create slides that compete with your speech for your audience's attention.

Your outline forms the basis of your script and storyboard, but it is just a starting point. While you are writing your speech and creating your storyboard, you will develop new ideas about how to make your points.

Be flexible and adapt your presentation as you create its components. Don't hesitate to change your speech if a graphic enables you to say things in a better way. You may have to reorganize the way you discuss a subject because of the structure of the graphic you are showing. On the other hand, you may find that a graphic you planned to include is unclear or fails to communicate your message. No matter how pretty or dazzling the graphic may be, you should exclude it if it doesn't contribute to the material you are presenting.

PREPARING THE SCRIPT

Your own personal style will dictate how you give your speech. Consider the various styles of politicians, religious leaders, and other experienced public speakers. Each one has a different approach to stating his or her message.

Your goal is to develop an outgoing, dynamic style of public speaking that suits your personality. If you have a lot of experience speaking in public, you probably are comfortable in front of an audience and are used to the sound of your own voice. If you have never spoken in public before, there are a few things you can do in preparing your script to help your presentation succeed. No matter what you have to say, the important thing is to say it in *your* way.

BEGIN BY TALKING INSTEAD OF WRITING

You might think that the way to begin to prepare a script is to write down what you plan to say. In most cases, this is the wrong approach.

People don't talk the way they write. Most of us learned to write in a very formal, academic style which looks good on paper, but is usually stilted and monotonous when read aloud.

Start your script by talking about the topics in your outline. Use a tape recorder to record what you say, and then play it back to get the rhythm and style of the way you talk. Then take the ideas you express verbally and put them down on paper, using pen and paper or your computer. Edit out the repetitions, digressions, the "um's" and the "you know's." What you'll have left is a speech written for the way you speak, not the way you write.

REVIEW AND REVISE

Once you've committed your ideas to paper, don't keep them to yourself. Show your script to people whose speaking abilities you respect and get their input. Have them look for things you missed, faulty logic, grammar, and style. Get your reviewers' opinions on how persuasive the speech is. If they have time, read it aloud for them so they can judge how natural it sounds.

Begin revising your speech by incorporating the suggestions of the people who reviewed it. As you rehearse and create your storyboard, you will need to make other changes to your script. Revising and refining the script is a process that should continue almost to the day of your presentation. However, script changes in the last couple of days should be restricted to minor refinements, since there won't be a lot of time to change your slides.

PRACTICE, PRACTICE, PRACTICE!

Rehearse your speech as much as possible. Starting with your earliest drafts of your script, you should practice speaking aloud to get used to the sound and flow of your words.

A good speaker uses the script on the podium as little more than an outline. In fact, some experienced speakers throw away the script and return to their outline once the speech is well-rehearsed, allowing them to improvise and be more natural.

SCRIPT FORMATTING

The traditional script format is a double-spaced typewritten page. The double spacing allows you to make notes and insert slide-changing cues. As you develop your storyboard, mark your script to indicate where each new slide is to appear, as shown in the example in Figure 4.2.

If you have the resources, there are better ways of formatting a script. With a laser printer that supports scalable fonts, you can print your script in 14-point or even 18-point type with at least 1½ lines of spacing, as illustrated in Figure 4.3. In a darkened room, the larger text will be easier to read, and you will still have plenty of room for notes and cues.

If your presentation graphics program has a function for creating speaker notes, you can print script pages with an image of each slide at the top, as shown in Figure 4.4. This type of script format has several advantages:

- You establish a direct link between your images and speech.
- The speaker doesn't have to look up at the screen to see the slide.
- The speaker can make notes about the graphics directly on the script.
- Each page turn is a reminder to change the slide.

Chapter 12 provides more information about formatting your speaker notes.

/ = SLIDE CUE

/¹ Good afternoon, ladies and gentlemen. Now that John Gordon has briefed us on our fantastic technological growth, it's my turn to tell you whether you made any money /² this year.

Acme Advanced Widgets has a history of steady growth from our first year of operation. In 1980, we started with gross annual sales of $1.5 million./³ By 1985 we had grown to $8.5 million, and our growing computer industry ~~sales~~ boosted sales /⁴ to
MARKET
$26 million in 1990. Increased competition limited our growth in the past few years. We've held our own, though, and sales have increased steadily /⁵ to a 1993 total of $32 million.
EVEN THOUGH
~~While~~ our sales have flattened since 1990, our profit picture remains healthy. /⁶

Our initial startup costs, which had a significant effect on our profit until 1985, have been completely recouped. Our 1987 recapitalization funding has also been recovered, and today Acme finds itself in the enviable /⁷ position of being virtually debt-free.

Our research and development department has made giant strides in developing new widget manufacturing technology which has reduced our manufacturing costs by 65%, made our employees (300% more productive, and increased our overall product margin by 36% /⁸   EMPHASIZE!

The elimination of debt-reconciliation costs, increased manufacturing efficiency and the resulting higher margins has had a remarkable effect on our bottom line. While our sales have flattened, our net profit has climbed sharply. Our initial startup losses are long gone, /⁹ and net profit after taxes was $10.3 million in 1993. /¹⁰

Since 1986, our per-share dividend has risen from 26 cents to $2.51 in 1992.

/ = SLIDE CUE

/ Good afternoon, ladies and gentlemen. Now that John Gordon has briefed us on our fantastic techno- logical growth, it's my turn to tell you whether you made any money / this year.

Acme Advanced Widgets has a history of steady growth from our first year of operation. In 1980, we started with gross annual sales of $1.5 million / By 1985 we had grown to $8.5 million, and our growing computer industry ~~sales~~ boosted / sales to $26 million in 1990.
MARKET
Increased competition limited our growth in the past few years. We've held our own, though, and sales have increased steadily / to a 1993 total of $32 million.
EVEN THOUGH
~~While~~ our sales have flattened since 1990, our profit picture remains healthy /

Our initial startup costs, which had a significant effect on our profit until 1985, have been completely recouped. Our 1987 recapitalization funding has also been recovered, and today Acme finds itself in the enviable position of being virtually / debt-free.

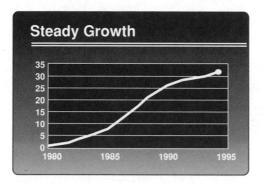

Steady Growth

Acme Advanced Widgets has a history of steady growth from our first year of operation. In 1980, we started with gross annual sales of $1.5 million. By 1985 we had grown to $8.5 million, and our growing computer industry market boosted sales to $26 million in 1990. Increased competition limited our growth in the past few years. We've held our own, though, and sales have increased steadily to a 1993 total of $32 million.

Figure 4.4:

A script page created as speaker notes

CREATING A STORYBOARD

A storyboard is the visual equivalent of a script. It is a collection of small sketches, or *roughs,* which serve as a guide for creating the final slides. You don't have to be a good artist to create a storyboard; simple drawings for charts and graphs, stick figures for people, and handwritten text will do the job.

When other people are designing and creating the slides for your presentation, your storyboard provides the information they need to create your slides. If you are doing it all yourself, developing a storyboard helps you refine your ideas for graphics before you actually create them.

STORYBOARD FORMATTING

The storyboard form is a convenient way of organizing your graphics. As shown in Figure 4.5, a form consists of preprinted slide frames (about 3 by 4½ inches), with space to the side of each frame for notes. You can use your presentation graphics software to create a storyboard master and then photocopy it as needed.

To create your storyboard, you sketch or write the content of your slides in the frame area. Write the figures for charts and graphs in the notes area, or if the chart data is very complex, on the back of the storyboard page or a separate sheet.

If you don't want to go to the trouble of creating a master storyboard page, use 3-by-5-inch or 4-by-6-inch index cards. Sketch the slide graphic on the unruled side, and make your notes on the ruled side. Figure 4.6 shows an example of index card storyboards. An advantage of index card storyboards is that you can easily change the order of the slides by rearranging the cards.

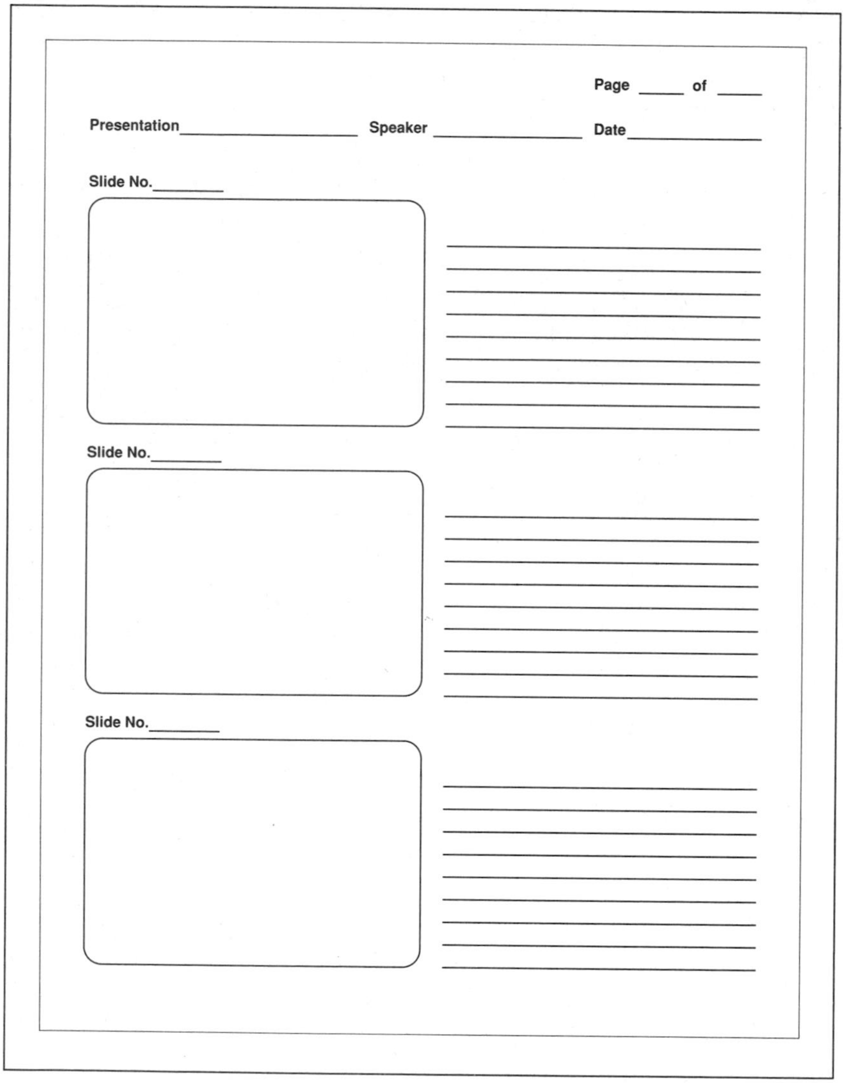

Figure 4.5:

A storyboard form

Page _____ of _____

Presentation_____   Speaker _____   Date_____

Slide No._____

Slide No._____

Slide No._____

Figure 4.6:

Index card storyboards

WORK SMALL

If you use a full sheet of 8½-by-11 inch paper for each slide sketch, you will be tempted to fill it up. The result will be too much information on the slide. What may be readable on a full page will be very cramped on a slide.

When you put the sketch within a small storyboard frame, you will find that too much text is unreadable; complex charts and graphs are difficult to understand; and diagrams and organization charts with many boxes are confusing. Use the limited size of the storyboard frame to help you edit and refine your visuals. Keep in mind that if your text or graphic will not fit in a storyboard frame, it probably is too much to place on a single slide.

GUIDELINES FOR TURNING A SPEECH INTO SLIDES

The slides in your presentation should clarify and highlight specific points in your speech to reinforce the message. Choose the elements in the speech that are most important and design slides to illustrate those elements. The following sections provides some guidelines for developing the contents of your slides.

One Slide: One Message

As you work through your outline and script, remember that each slide you create should have a single message directly related to what is being said. In most cases, each paragraph or two in your script will require at least one slide.

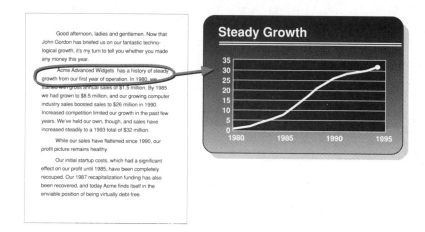

Keep It Simple

To ensure that your slides increase the impact of the words rather than distract from them, design text slides that are short and easy to read and graphic slides that accentuate important points visually.

In your text slides, use short bulleted list items that are to the point. Stick to nouns and verbs and concentrate on the active words in your speech. In your graphic slides, make sure the illustrations, charts, and graphs are clear and concise.

Keep a Steady Pace

The pace of your presentation is an important factor. If you leave one slide on the screen too long, the audience members will become bored. If you change slides too quickly, they will become overwhelmed and tired. A good rule of thumb is to change your slide at least every 45 seconds during your speech.

Don't change slides so quickly that the audience can't read them. Each slide should be on the screen at least three times as long as it takes to read. That way, the audience is reading one-third of the time and listening to the speaker the other two-thirds. Your script should reflect this pace with slide cues that are spaced regularly.

In your script, put the cues slightly before the points that the slides illustrate. This allows for the few seconds it takes for the new slide to appear and for the audience to start reading it.

---

¹ Good afternoon, ladies and gentlemen. Now that John Gordon has briefed us on our fantastic technological growth, it's my turn to tell you whether you made any money this year. ²

Acme Advanced Widgets has a history of steady growth from our first year of operation. In 1980, we started with gross annual sales of $1.5 million. By 1985 ³ we had grown to $8.5 million, and our growing computer industry market boosted sales ⁴ to $26 million in 1990. Increased competition limited our growth in the past few years. We've held our own, though, and sales have increased steadily to ⁵ a 1993 total of $32 million.

While our sales have flattened since 1990, our profit picture remains healthy ⁶

Our initial startup costs, which had a significant effect on our profit until 1985, have been completely recouped. Our 1987 recapitalization funding has also been recovered, and today Acme finds itself in the enviable position of being virtually ⁷ debt-free.

Take Small Steps

Your audience will have a natural tendency to read ahead on a slide while you're talking. You can prevent them from getting ahead by breaking up the information on a slide into smaller parts.

If you have more information on a topic than you can cover comfortably in a single slide, divide it among two or more slides, adding *Continued* in the title to show the connection. Even the Ten Commandments required two tablets.

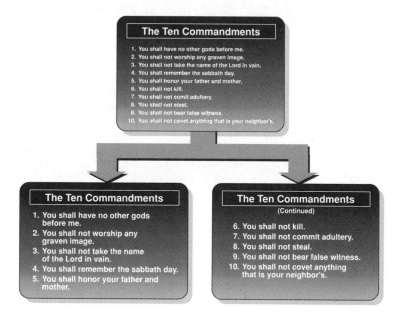

Another way to prevent the audience from reading ahead is to use a *build,* or *reveal,* slide sequence. A build sequence shows the first piece of information in the first slide; the first and second pieces in the second slide; the first, second, and third pieces in the third slide; and so on. You will learn more about creating build slides in Chapters 9 and 10.

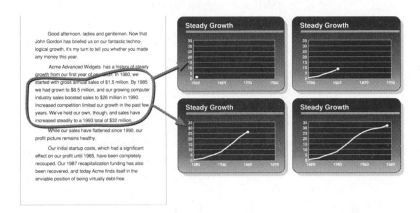

Let Your Pictures Do the Talking

Use graphics wherever possible to present your message. While listening to a speaker, an audience can absorb the content of a graphic much more easily than they can read even a few lines of text.

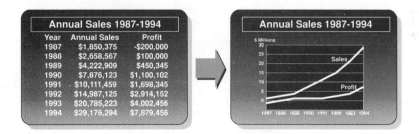

TOO MUCH TO HANDLE

You may find in creating your presentation that no matter how hard you try, there is one slide that defies any editing. It may be a complex chart or a table with too many rows and columns that cannot be reduced. If you are creating slides for someone else, he or she may just insist that 25 lines of copy are the only way the topic can be explained properly.

When you have a chart or table that is too hard to follow in slide form, include a copy of the information in the audience handouts. Then you can use a pointer or some sort of highlighting on the projected slide, and the audience can refer to the handouts for the details.

If you are dealing with someone who insists on overloading the slides, create one of the slides to illustrate the problem. Then have the originator view it from the same distance as the back row of the presentation room. Most people will be more willing to edit the text when they see that the projected slide is unreadable.

THE REAL WORLD   THE BEST LAID PLANS...

Thursday, October 4, 3:00 pm: Alan Smithee just got the bad news. Because of a contract problem with a major parts vendor, Alan must go to Tokyo for four days. His outline is finished and most of his script is done, but he has not had the time to prepare any of his slides in storyboard form. So he hands Ellen Jackson, our Office Services Manager, his notes, his outline, and the first draft of his speech.

''I'll work some more on the speech during the flight, but you'd better see what you can do with what I've got so far. When I get to Tokyo tomorrow, I'll fax you my script revisions, and you can fax me what you've done on the slides.''

Friday, October 5, 9:00 am: Ellen begins to study Alan's outline.

Hypothetical International is poised for tremendous growth
　We have the best people
　　George Spelvin, Founder and CEO
　　Alan Smithee, President
　　Victoria Regina, Chief Financial Officer
　　Regional Vice Presidents
　　　John Bull, Hypothetical Europe
　　　Romaji Kanagawa, Hypothetical Asia/Pacific
　　　Ernesto J. Guevara, Hypothetical Central America
　A Superior Workforce
　　Our Employees are Highly Skilled
　　Pie chart showing distribution of skills
　　We have very low employee turnover
　　Well-Paid
　　Great Benefits
　　Strong Worker Feedback program
　　　　　　　　　　　　　　　ufacturing
　　　　　　　　　　　　　Springfield

She starts to put together a rough storyboard. In the beginning of the outline, Alan gives an introduction to the management of Hypothetical International, so Ellen starts with a title and a few biographical slides.

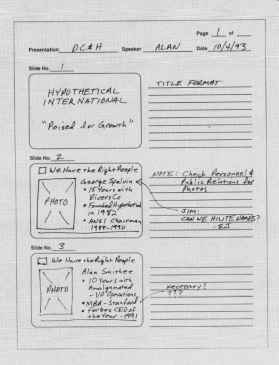

In addition to including the usual biographical information, Ellen includes a photo of each of the officers. She makes a note to check with personnel or public relations to make sure good photos of the three are available.

We're lucky because Alan's presentation is actually quite general in approach. Most of his subject matter is the history and current state of the company—information that Ellen can gather herself. She can safely predict a great deal of the content of his slides just by the outline entries.

Because of good preliminary preparation by Alan, a major disaster has been avoided. If Alan hadn't finished an outline and a rough draft of his script, nothing would have been done until he returned from Japan on Tuesday, leaving only a few days to create his entire presentation.

Alan's absence during this stage of the production process affects our production schedule. Because Ellen is choosing the material for Alan's slides, we can assume that there will be more than the usual number of changes and revisions. We need to anticipate a more complicated and extensive revision cycle.

We can avoid a lot of changes to the actual computer artwork by delaying production of Alan's slides and concentrating on George and Victoria's presentations first. By putting off Alan's presentation to the end of the slide-creation period, we give him more time to look over Ellen's storyboards and revise them to fit his needs.

We can avoid a lot of changes to the actual computer artwork by delaying production of Alan's slides and concentrating on George and Victoria's presentations first. By putting off Alan's presentation to the end of the slide-creation period, we give him more time to look over Ellen's storyboards and revise them to fit his needs.

SUMMARY

Your script and storyboard represent the two components of a presentation: your speech and your slides. Here are some guidelines for developing them:

- Using your outline as a guide, divide your presentation into words (your script) and pictures (your storyboards).

- Don't let your slides substitute for the speech. Deliver your message in your speech and reinforce it with your slides.

- Your script should reflect the way you talk, not the way you write.

- Have another person review your script. Don't hesitate to make revisions.

- Practice your speech as much as possible.

- Use a storyboard sheet or index cards to sketch your roughs.

- Make your storyboards readable, but not fancy. Remember, they're just rough sketches for your final slides.

- Tie the message of each slide to a single, specific message in your script.

- Don't overload your slides with too much text or complicated graphics. If necessary, divide the information between two or more slides.

- Maintain a steady pace of slides that gives the audience time to read your slides without becoming bored.

part 2

Producing Your Presentation

chapter 5

Organizing Presentation Production

Efficient management of the presentation production process will improve your chances for success. This chapter describes how to avoid crises by organizing the production of the slides. It offers suggestions for streamlining the production process and eliminating confusion and bottlenecks.

STARTING SMALL

Recently, a large advertising firm bought a Macintosh system and software for creating in-house slide presentations. But before the computer was barely warm, management decided to do a very important product-introduction show with more than 200 slides. The outcome was almost a foregone conclusion. The production staff—without any experience in using the new software or in handling a large presentation—was overwhelmed.

As the meeting date got closer and closer, there were massive color changes, revisions, additions, and deletions to the presentation. In the process, the 200 slides were sent to the service bureau three separate times for imaging on a rush basis. By the time the presenters took the stage, nobody was happy with the final product, and the slides actually cost more than if they had been produced by an outside vendor.

You can't learn everything about producing an effective presentation from a book. Hands-on experience is the best teacher. So before you dive into a big show, try your hand at creating a small, 10 to 20 slide presentation. Go through the whole process from scheduling to final slide output and learn by doing.

Practically speaking, everybody's first desktop presentation experience is a trial by fire. Creating a presentation is a complex process which few people get right the first time. If your first attempt is not successful, don't give up. With experience, you will soon develop a method of presentation planning and design that is right for you and your organization.

PLANNING YOUR PRESENTATION DESIGN

The overall design of a presentation provides a context for the information you include in it, but the design itself also conveys information. The colors you choose, the typefaces you use, and the layout of the graphics in a presentation say a lot about who you are and what you represent. It's important that your design be appropriate for your speaker, your company, and your message.

Once the presentation's design is established, you create the actual slides by applying the rules and guidelines you have set for the design. Since many of your design and layout decisions are made beforehand, the actual slide-production process will go smoothly and quickly.

CREATE A CONSISTENT DESIGN

The first task in creating the slides for a presentation is to create a format to serve as a backdrop and style guide for the slides. Take the time to develop styles for the entire presentation, not just your background and title. If you are including charts and graphs in your show, plan how they will be treated (colors, two-dimensional or three-dimensional, with or without grids, and so on). Devise treatments for photo inserts and other illustrations in the presentation. There will always be slides that don't fit your predetermined formats, but you will save a lot of time in the final production process by deciding in advance how the most common slide types will be designed.

Create examples using your software, and then save them to disk. When you need to create a slide that is similar to one of your examples, open the file and make the necessary changes. Then save it as a new file, without overwriting your original. The original file examples are your *templates,* or the patterns for your actual slides.

Some presentation programs, such as Aldus Persuasion and Harvard Graphics 3.0, supply predefined format masters and templates, as illustrated in Figure 5.1. You can modify these templates or design your own templates for different types of slides. To create your slides, you simply enter the actual text or data. Using a standard format for the presentation allows you to maintain consistency and shorten your production time.

IMAGE SAMPLE SLIDES

Changes in the basic format of a presentation after all the slides are completed can be difficult and time-consuming. To avoid last-minute format

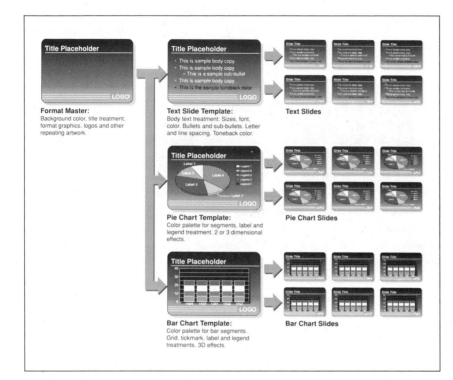

revisions, make sure that everyone involved has a chance to review and approve the design before proceeding with actual slide production.

To get a true representation of what your final presentation will look like, have a few samples imaged as slides or overhead transparencies before deciding on your final design. Depending on your computer and software, what looks good on your screen may be totally unacceptable when imaged on film. Try to include all of the fonts and colors used in your design in the samples.

Another advantage of processing sample slides is that it gives the service bureau an idea of what to expect when you are ready for final slide production. The service bureau will be able to spot potential problems with your files, such as missing fonts, file format incompatibilities, tight framing, or graphics and text overlapping slide margins.

When you get your imaged format samples back, have all the people who are involved in the presentation take a look at them. If they are satisfied, have them approve the design as formally as necessary. If the design is not satisfactory, you can revise it without a large investment of time and money.

When the presentation is a team effort, the design and approval process should take place at the same time as the speakers are preparing their outlines and scripts. By working in parallel, the design process can be finished just about the time the speakers are ready to submit storyboards containing the content of their slides. If you are working alone, don't put off getting your samples imaged; last-minute problems are harder to solve when you're on your own.

ORGANIZING SLIDE TYPES AND REVISIONS

As you learned in Part 1 of this book, organization is the key to streamlining the creation of a presentation. By organizing the order in which slides are created, you can speed up the production process, as well as help maintain consistency. By organizing your revision schedule, you can group changes into a single session.

GROUPING YOUR SLIDES BY TYPE

After spending valuable time planning the most effective order for your thoughts and arguments, it may seem counterproductive to reorder them when it comes time to produce your slides. But you will be able to create slides more efficiently if you create all the text slides at the same time, then all the charts, then all tables, and so on. By grouping your slide production by type, you can develop a "fast track," which will enable you to make design decisions more quickly and maintain design consistency among similar slides.

If you are using DOS-based programs, such as Applause II and Lotus Freelance Graphics, which save each slide as a separate graphics file, it doesn't matter which slide you create first. Simply sort your storyboard by slide type before beginning. If you are using a Microsoft Windows or Macintosh presentation graphics package, such as Microsoft Power-Point or Aldus Persuasion, you will probably want all your slides in the same presentation file. In this case, create each different type of slide and then use the program's slide-sorting features to arrange the slides in the final presentation order before saving the file.

ORGANIZING YOUR REVISION CYCLES

Change is inevitable. No matter how many times a presentation is reviewed, revised, and rewritten before the slides are created, changes will still be required throughout the production process.

A guaranteed way to lose your sanity is to attempt to keep up with small, piecemeal revisions to a presentation while you're still in the process of creating new slides. A constant flow of small changes is distracting and will often lead to other errors.

To eliminate piecemeal changes, set aside a block of time near the end of your production schedule devoted to corrections and revisions. Delay making changes until your scheduled time. The result will be fewer overall revisions, because a speaker will often change the wording or the figures in his slides several times before the final version. If you postpone making corrections until the end of the review process, you will avoid the intermediate revisions and go directly to the final round of changes to the slides.

DEALING WITH MISTAKES

The easiest way to avoid last-minute panic attacks is to remember that the slides and handouts you are preparing are only an enhancement to the speech. With careful proofing, any major errors in your slides will be caught in the course of review and revisions.

The simpler and more direct the information in your slide, the less likely it is an error will go undetected before final imaging. However, it's not the end of the world if there is a typographical error on a slide. Minor errors are often overlooked when projected. The only "unforgivable" sin is spelling a person's or company's name incorrectly.

If some small errors sneak through the proofing process, you can usually handle them with some well-chosen words during the course of the presentation. You can correct an incorrect figure in a chart or table verbally. A humorous remark can often relieve any embarrassment caused by an error in a slide. If you mention it first, the audience will be on your side.

Slides with errors that are seriously misleading or unacceptable should be eliminated from the presentation. It's better to talk without slide support than to have your slides contradict what you're saying.

THE
REAL
WORLD   LAST-MINUTE MADNESS

Thursday, October 11, 10:00 am: The article in the *Wall Street Journal* shocked the members of the presentation team. Billie Bob Boone, the infamous corporate takeover specialist, had purchased five percent of Hypothetical International's stock. A hurried series of phone calls and faxes from Hypothetical's management confirmed the stock purchase, but no one could discover from Boone's office whether further purchases were planned. Though very suspicious of Boone's plans, George and Alan, under advice from their investment bankers, decide to go through with the new stock issue.

11:00 am: Billie Bob Boone's stock purchase has caused a lot of commotion among the stockbrokers and analysts. To head off any wild rumors, Hypothetical has its Public Relations department issue a press release about Boone's purchase, and George decides to rewrite the second speech of his presentation to address this issue and engage in a little damage control. In addition, Victoria will have to revise a slide that shows the distribution of Hypothetical stock.

Most of George's original speech is a summary of the stock offering and a bit of salesmanship. He decides that none of it will have to be discarded. However, he needs to add a short section about the Billie Bob Boone stock purchase and how it will affect Hypothetical.

Victoria's revision is routine; a simple change in a pie chart reflecting the distribution of stock.

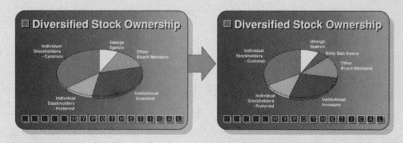

ORIGINAL SLIDE   REVISED SLIDE

12:30 pm: Jim Gonzalez has been working furiously to finish the last revisions on the rest of the presentation slides, and he will fit in Victoria's pie chart revision. According to the production schedule, diskettes were due by noon today at the service bureau for imaging. Jim and Ellen decide to send the first three presentations to the service bureau and warn the service bureau staff that a fourth presentation will be sent tomorrow for rush processing.

2:00 pm: To put the best possible light on the situation, George decides to downplay the potential effects. He is going to emphasize the fact that Boone's purchase is quite small compared with the combined resources of the current board. He will also point out that Hypothetical has none of the problems associated with most of Boone's takeover targets. He prepares a quick outline, and it appears there will be about eight new slides in the final presentation.

It will take a while to track down some of the figures he needs. George sets the Research department (his secretary, Ruth) to work, and then starts working on his speech and some rough sketches for his slides.

5:00 pm: Unfortunately, some figures for the new slides are still unavailable. But to get things rolling, George sits down with Jim and Ellen to go over the last few slides in the presentation. Jim will create the slides this evening, leaving empty places for the missing information. When the information is available in the morning, Jim will just plug in the missing figures.

7:15 pm: Jim prints proof copies of George's additional slides (minus a few figures) and leaves them on the chairman's desk for approval.

Friday, October 12, 10:00 am: With the financial data he needs finally available, George marks up the proofs of his new slides, filling in the gaps. He sends the copies to Jim, who makes the final changes, prints new proofs, and has them approved by George.

11:30 am: A diskette containing George's final presentation, ready for imaging, is sent by messenger to the service bureau. Ellen alerts the service bureau that the final disk is on the way and that they would like the final slides back by 5:00 pm.

1:00 pm: The slides for the first three presentations arrive from the service bureau. Ellen and Jim, using storyboards as a guide, place the slides in trays for projection and deliver them to George, Alan, and Victoria. The speakers review their slides in a conference room and begin rehearsing their speeches.

5:00 pm: The final slides arrive from the service bureau. Due to the last-minute changes, there isn't a final outline or storyboard for George's second presentation. Ellen delivers the slides to George with an empty slide tray so he can put them in order for his speech.

SUMMARY

Creating effective presentation graphics is a skill learned through experience and practice. Here are some guidelines for avoiding disaster:

- Do some small slide projects before tackling a major presentation.

- Don't design just a pretty background. Develop a comprehensive design that anticipates many of the types of slides in your presentation.

- Save design examples to disk and use them as templates to create your final slides.

- Use computerized templates (sometimes called style sheets or masters) if your presentation software offers them.

- Have format samples imaged and approved before proceeding with final slide production.

- Organize your production by slide type.

- Avoid piecemeal revisions to slides; try to schedule changes so they can be done all at once.

- Don't panic. Small errors in your slides will often be overlooked by the audience, or they can be corrected verbally by the speaker.

- Have a strategy prepared for dealing with last-minute changes.

chapter 6

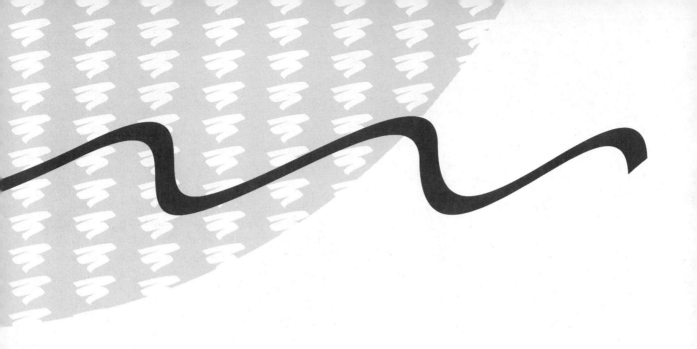

Format Design: Slide Frame Layout

A consistent format used throughout a presentation allows the audience to forget the "environment" and focus on the information in the slides. Designing any presentation format involves manipulating three main elements: slide frame layout, color, and typography. This chapter focuses on slide frame layout, which is the arrangement of recurring elements that serve as the framework for your information. Slide frame elements include backgrounds, logos, titles, and other decorative items.

Your first consideration in the format of your presentation is how it will be produced. There are three different types of media used for most presentations: 35mm slides, overhead transparencies, and computer screen shows. Before you design your slide frame layout, you must decide which medium you will use to present your message.

CHOOSING YOUR MEDIUM

Each presentation medium displays images in a different way. The most pleasing arrangement of the elements on your slides depends on the shape and size of the projected images, as well as the quality of their reproduction. If you haven't decided which medium to use, weigh their advantages and disadvantages, and then select the one that best suits your needs.

35MM SLIDES

The most popular medium for presentations is 35mm slides. A 35mm slide consists of a short piece of color transparency film (Kodak's Ektachrome is most common) mounted in a 2-inch-square cardboard or plastic frame. The actual image on the film measures 24mm by 36mm (approximately 1 inch by 1½ inches), although the slide mount opening will usually be smaller, cropping the image slightly.

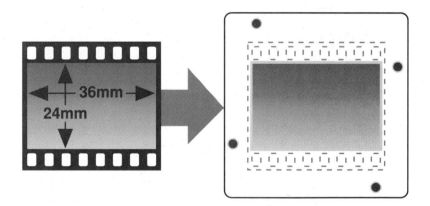

Advantages and Disadvantages of 35mm Slides

35mm slides are small, inexpensive, and easy to project. Because slides are imaged on high-quality color film, the colors are rich and the images have a depth and realism which can't be matched by other presentation media.

Their small size makes slides more manageable and portable than overhead transparencies. When kept in their trays, they are easy to handle and relatively safe from most mishaps. A case containing a slide projector and a tray of up to 140 slides can easily fit under an airplane seat, and the only other things you need to give a simple presentation are an electrical outlet and a blank wall.

However, there are some disadvantages to 35mm slides:

- Most slide projection setups require at least a partially darkened room for maximum readability.

- A speaker can't write on or directly affect a projected slide for emphasis (except for the limited use of a pointer).

- Because of the imaging and processing requirements of slides, last-minute changes (less than 4 hours) can be impossible.

Formatting Considerations for 35mm Slides

The 35mm slide frame has a unique shape that sets it apart from other presentation media. The 2:3 ratio (height:width) appears wider when projected than overhead transparencies and video images. You need to design your layout to match the wider slide frame. If you don't create your slides in the proper ratio, you will usually end up with partially filled slides, wasting valuable space, as illustrated in Figure 6.1.

When you start up your desktop presentation program, check the page setup to make sure that your page or frame size is set to 35mm slide. Many desktop presentation programs' default page setup is for overhead transparencies, which are narrower and higher than 35mm slides, so checking your page setup is important. If your presentation program doesn't automatically format for 35mm slides, create a custom page size in the standard slide shape. The actual size isn't important; it can be 6 by 9 inches, 7 by 10.5 inches, or any other dimensions with a 2:3 ratio.

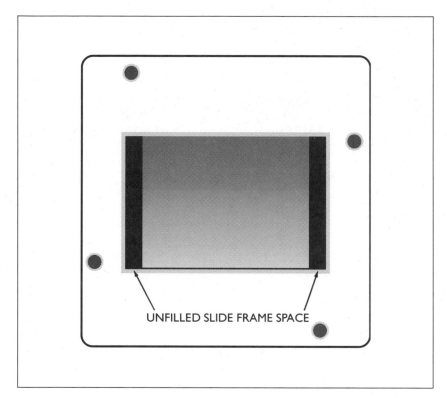

Figure 6.1:

Improper ratio results in partially filled slide

UNFILLED SLIDE FRAME SPACE

OVERHEAD TRANSPARENCIES

Overhead transparencies are often the choice for small presentations that involve a lot of interaction between the speaker and the audience. An overhead transparency is an 8-by-10-inch or 8½-by-11-inch piece of film, usually mounted in a 10-by-12-inch cardboard or plastic frame. The actual opening in the overhead frame is 7½ by 9½ inches.

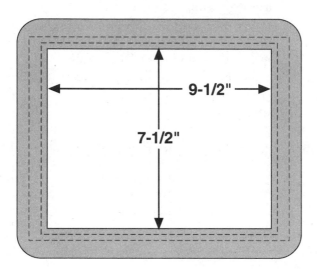

Advantages and Disadvantages of Transparencies

The transparencies (also called vugraphs or foils) used with an overhead projector are large enough to be written on directly. The speaker can emphasize a point on a prepared transparency or improvise graphics "on the fly" on blank transparencies.

Overhead transparencies can be made using many different types of printers. Your choices range from creating inexpensive black-and-white transparencies on a laser printer, to producing high-quality, full-color transparencies on a dye-sublimation printer or through photographic processing. This wide range of output choices makes overhead transparencies affordable for any budget.

However, the size of the transparencies and projection equipment make them more difficult to manage than 35mm slides. Overhead projectors are bulky and heavy compared with slide projectors—not the sort of thing a business traveler wants to lug around an airport. The overhead transparencies themselves are also quite large and more easily damaged by scratches, dust, and fingerprints. Depending on the process used to create the transparency, a replacement may be necessary each time a speaker writes on it. As with slides, it is often difficult to revise overhead transparencies at the last minute.

Formatting Considerations for Transparencies

An overhead transparency is less rectangular than a 35mm slide, so you should make sure the page setup for your presentation program is set accordingly. If you are using a program that doesn't directly format for overhead transparencies, choose a custom page size of 7½ by 9½ inches.

A common notion is that because it is so much larger than a 35mm slide, you can put more information on an overhead transparency. The fact is that the projected image from an overhead transparency is no larger than the image from a slide. Therefore, you shouldn't put any more copy or graphics on a transparency than you would place on a 35mm slide.

Pocket Overheads

Some service bureaus have recently started offering imaging services for *pocket overheads,* which are 4-by-5-inch overhead transparencies. Pocket overheads are shown with a special projector that is smaller and lighter than a standard overhead projector.

The media and equipment are more portable and easier to handle than the standard size versions, and the 4-by-5-inch projectable area is large enough to write on. Unfortunately, the projectors for pocket overheads are still quite expensive, and there are only a few service bureaus offering this imaging product.

Pocket overheads have the same formatting requirements as regular overhead transparencies.

SCREEN SHOWS

The computer screen is an entirely new medium for the presenter. A computer screen show can come in several forms:

- Direct projection or display: The signal that would normally go to your computer screen is diverted to a video projection unit or large video monitor. The slides in your presentation are then displayed using your presentation program or a screen show utility.

- Overhead flat-panel display: This device is a special display screen attached to the video output of your computer, which is placed on the projection stage of an overhead projector. The flat-panel display projects the computer's screen image as if it were an overhead transparency. Like direct displays, flat-panel displays are controlled using presentation software. When run with a laptop computer, this type of slide show is convenient and portable.

- Prerecorded videotape or videodisc: Your presentation is recorded to tape or disk, often with a sound track added. This type of presentation is not common for business meetings, but it is frequently used in self-running point-of-purchase displays and trade show exhibits. In a videodisc presentation, you can access individual frames anywhere in the show in random order. This allows you to jump to particular images in response to audience questions.

Figure 6.2 illustrates the various types of screen shows.

Advantages and Disadvantages of Screen Shows

Computer screen shows are ideal for small- to medium-sized meetings. They offer many advantages over 35mm slides and overhead transparencies, including the flexibility for last-minute revisions, random access to any visual, and even options for animation and other special effects.

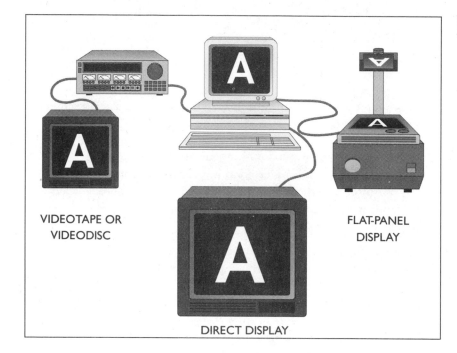

Screen show options

VIDEOTAPE OR
VIDEODISC

FLAT-PANEL
DISPLAY

DIRECT DISPLAY

Many corporate conference rooms now have equipment for computer and video projection.

The price to be paid for these benefits is low resolution, jagged text and graphics, and expensive, bulky projection equipment. If you are considering using prerecorded video, you should be aware that it is more difficult and expensive to revise and update than any other presentation medium.

Formatting Considerations for Slide Shows

The success of a computer screen show depends on the computer and video equipment used for the presentation. The equipment that will be used to display your show is usually different from the system you are using to create it. Before you begin creating a screen show, make sure you know how it will be displayed so that you can set up the presentation accordingly. We will cover some of the technical aspects of screen shows in Chapter 13.

The basic shape of all screen show frames is the same as your computer screen and essentially the same as an overhead transparency (approximately 4:5 ratio). The layout is similar to the transparency format, but the low resolution of the computer screen will force you to be more conservative in the amount of text you put in each frame. Small text will be very jagged and hard to read when projected on even the best video equipment.

If your presentation is going to videotape or to a projection video system, you should allow extra background space around all your text and graphics. Keeping your copy in the "video safe area" will prevent any of the image from being cut off.

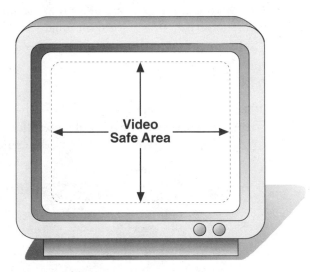

The color, sharpness, and intensity of a flat-panel display will vary significantly from the display of a standard computer monitor. Before finalizing your designs, test your output on the display you will use for the presentation.

CREATING A PRESENTATION FORMAT

Your overall presentation format starts with the elements shared by most slides: titles, backgrounds, and decorative elements. Then you can proceed to expand the design by devising treatments for specific slide types throughout the presentation. The following sections provide some guidelines for designing the format for the common elements of your presentation. The layout and design of specific slide types are covered in Chapters 9, 10, and 11.

DIRECT THE AUDIENCE'S ATTENTION

Like the other components of your presentation, the format of your slides should help convey your message. You need to place your message in a strong position where it will be read.

Use Natural Patterns

When a slide is projected on the screen, the eyes of the audience members follow a pattern. The normal pattern for a plain area with no text is a zigzag across the screen, starting in the center.

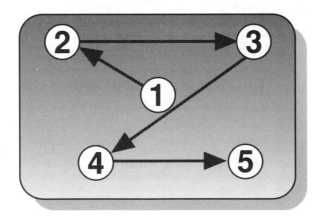

Since people look there first, you might think that the best place to put your message is in the center of the slide. But this only works if your entire presentation consists of single-sentence titles. Centering doesn't leave much room for the supporting information most messages require.

Rather than trying to squeeze your title into the middle of the slide, place it at the top or top left of the frame. Then there will be ample room for the supporting information that follows. This placement takes advantage of the natural reading pattern of top left to right. Your audience will feel more comfortable and receptive when you present the information in a familiar manner.

Emphasize Important Areas

You can help the audience members understand your slides by designing a format that emphasizes areas that require their special attention. Use the format to ensure that the audience focuses on the points you want to make.

One way to draw attention to an item is to place it prominently—at the center of the top of the frame. Other ways to emphasize areas of a slide are with color, size, and graphics:

- Color: Using bright, contrasting colors will always attract attention. You don't have to be outrageous, just different enough to distinguish the item from the rest of the slide.

- Size: The biggest thing on a slide will demand attention. Text that is larger or bolder than that around it will always be read first. Any part of a graphic that is larger and more dominating will have a greater effect on the audience.

- Graphics: Text associated with a graphic will stand out compared with plain text. For example, placing your title in a box or adjacent to some sort of decorative graphic will attract attention to it.

Figure 6.3 illustrates the four main ways to emphasize items on a slide and direct your audience's attention.

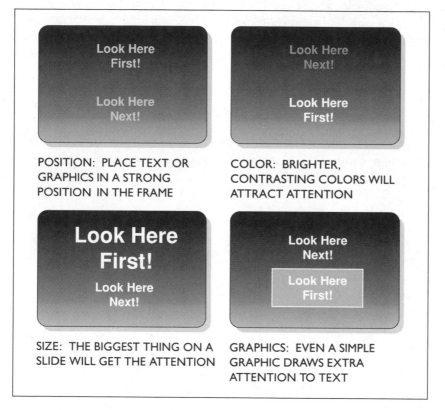

Figure 6.3:

Directing attention to slide elements

BALANCE GRAPHIC ELEMENTS

An empty slide frame is a blank canvas on which you arrange the components of your slide. Any graphic element on a slide has "weight," which draws attention to it. Too much weight in one part of the slide frame will cause the slide to appear unbalanced.

When designing a presentation format, you must juggle these graphic weights to create a balanced, stable framework for your message. The two largest pieces you will need to balance are the title for each slide and an area for the main content. Logos, rules, and other graphic devices serve as "trim weights" to help balance the relationship between the title and the content.

Your slide content (text, charts, and pictures) usually can be treated as a single unit, so you can think of your content weight as a single large box in the frame. Content placed in a slide without a title needs to be centered to look properly balanced.

The title is another single unit on the slide. You should balance its weight with that of the content block.

If you center the content block and then add a title above it, the slide will not be balanced. Your format will be top-heavy, with too much emphasis on the top of the frame.

Move the content block down a bit on the slide to maintain the balance. The content block has more weight than the title, so it doesn't have to move down very far to balance the slide. A small change in position, brightness, or size in a heavy element can be more effective than a large change in a smaller element.

Another way to balance the title and content blocks is to add a logo or other graphic. Placing a logo graphic at the bottom of the slide balances the weight of the title and allows you to keep the content block in the center.

Keep in mind that color can add and subtract weight from a graphic element. For example, if the type in the logo is much thicker than the type in the title, you can adjust the balance by making the logo a darker color than the title. This reduces the weight of the logo so that it is closer to that of the brighter title.

USE SPACE WISELY

Regardless of your presentation medium, there is only a limited amount of space to hold the message on each slide. You will need to create a format that uses the available space to the best advantage.

For readability, the text and graphics should be as large as possible in the frame. However, placing graphic elements too close to the edge of the frame will cause your slides to look overcrowded. Also, artwork near the frame borders is often cropped by the slide mount. The final cropping may not match the frame indicated in your presentation graphics program.

On the other hand, don't waste the space in your slides by leaving a wide margin around your content. Desktop publishers who are fond of white space in their designs for print should resist the temptation to go for that "elegant" look in presentations. You sacrifice readability of your type and graphics when you frame your slides loosely. An empty frame with small type in the center will just strain the eyesight of the people in your audience.

To achieve a reasonable balance of sensible margins and readability, create a margin on all four sides of your slide frame that is at least 5 percent of the total width of the frame. For example, if your slide frame size is 10 inches wide by 6⅔ inches high, any graphics or text that the audience must see clearly should be placed at least ½ inch away from the edge of the frame. Figure 6.4 shows the 5 percent margin versus too tight or loose framing. You can ignore the margin when formatting backgrounds, rules, photos, or other graphics that you intend to run off the edge of the slide (called a *bleed*).

Figure 6.4:

Formatting the space on a slide

Use as much of the space within your margins as possible for the title and content blocks of your slides. As illustrated in Figure 6.4, placing your information in a small area in the center wastes valuable space. Use the full slide area for all your content, not just text. Charts and graphs should be expanded to fill the area (unless changing the graph would distort your data). Photos and illustrations should be prominent so that they are effective.

SLIDE TITLE TREATMENT

The main message of your slides should be in the slide title. So to make sure your audience gets the message, your title needs to be prominent, easy to read, and consistently positioned from slide to slide.

Normal slide titles should be positioned in the strongest possible position in the frame, usually the upper left or upper center. The text justification should match the title position: center-aligned text for centered titles, flush-left text for upper-left titles.

Use a larger type size or a different type style to highlight the title. A good rule-of-thumb is to make your title size approximately 25 to 50 percent larger than your body copy. For example, if your body copy is in 24-point type, use 36-point type for your title. A bolder typeface will also make the title appear larger, even if you're using the same size for title and body text. Color is another way to highlight the title (see Chapter 7 for details on using color).

36 Point Title
- 24 Point Body Copy
- 24 Point Body Copy
- 24 Point Body Copy
- 24 Point Body Copy

Bold 24 Point Title
- 24 Point Body Copy
- 24 Point Body Copy
- 24 Point Body Copy
- 24 Point Body Copy

A plain title floating at the top of the slide may seem a bit lonely and insignificant, especially if it is only one or two words. There are several ways that you can enhance the impact of the title and help it stand out from the rest of the slide content:

■ A graphic rule will divide the slide frame into distinct title and content areas, helping to give equal status to short and long titles.

■ A box or some other type of frame strengthens short titles. However, a box treatment is often inappropriate for long titles, because the bulk of the box can overpower the actual content of the slide.

■ A distinctive graphic can help anchor and enhance a title by drawing attention to it. Use simple graphics, such as geometric shapes, that do not compete with the title.

Figure 6.5 illustrates each of these treatments for titles. When deciding how to format your titles, consider their average length. If you have any titles that are likely to carry over into two lines of text, make sure your title design will look as good with two lines as it does with one.

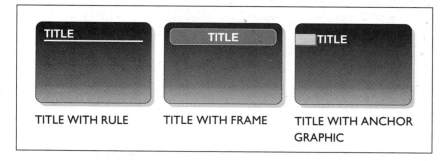

Figure 6.5:

Formatting the title

FIXED-FORMAT GRAPHICS

A consistently placed graphic can contribute to the balance and organization of your slide frames. The most common fixed graphic element in slides is a rule associated with the slide title. You can also add other rules, borders, shadow boxes, logos, and other decorative elements to create attractive, distinctive slides.

Format Rules and Borders

Format rules are additional lines placed within the slide frame. They are usually used at the bottom of the frame to help balance the weight of a title with its accompanying rule. Format rules help the audience focus on the contents of the frame.

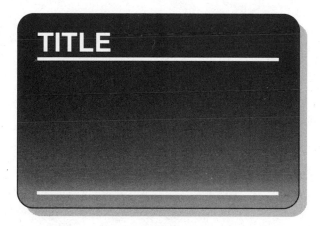

Frame borders are thin lines that surround all or part of the slide frame. Full-frame borders, which surround the entire slide area, can become inconsistent in the final slide-mounting process. Most slide-mounting systems allow the film to shift slightly in the slide mount. This shift will cause the area between the border and the slide-mount opening to vary slightly in width, especially from left to right. The only way to eliminate this shift is to place your slides in special pin-registered slide mounts, which use the sprocket holes in the film to align the frame precisely in the mount opening.

Drop Shadow Boxes

A drop shadow box is a more sophisticated version of a border. It consists of a box to hold the content of your slide and a simulated shadow that gives the appearance of depth.

Some presentation software packages include a selection of drop shadow boxes that you can place on slides. You can create a drop shadow box by placing a box, copying it, offsetting the copy slightly, and setting the copy behind the original.

When choosing shadow colors, try to make the shadow look as natural as possible. Imagine that there is a bright light shining above your background. On dark backgrounds, use a darker version of the background color or black for the shadow. If the shadow is lighter than the original box, it will draw attention away from the top box. On overhead transparencies with light backgrounds, the shadow should be a slightly darker version of the background color.

Corporate Logos

Corporate logos are often included as part of the basic presentation format. Usually, placing the company logo on every slide is overdoing it. No matter how much you love it, by the hundredth slide, your audience may actually be tired of looking at the thing. Use your logo sparingly, perhaps only on the main title slide for your presentation and then on just a few others.

If you do need your corporate logo on every slide, keep it small and unobtrusive. Don't compete with what you have to say on a slide just to tell your audience who you are. Include your logo either alone or as part of some other decorative graphic on the slide. Here are some ideas for logo treatment:

- Use a logo in the lower-right corner of the frame to help balance an upper-left title.

- Create a decorative graphic that incorporates your logo. Making your logo part of a larger graphic de-emphasizes it and makes it less intrusive.

- "Watermark" your logo in a color very close to that of your background. It will still be present on every slide, but unobtrusively as part of the background.

Figure 6.6 illustrates these types of logo treatments.

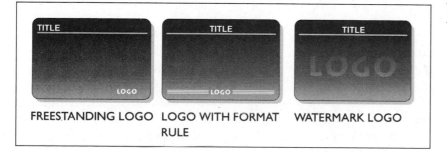

Figure 6.6:

Logo treatments

Other Decorative Graphics

You can add to the appearance of your presentation with almost any sort of decorative scheme, but beware of getting carried away. If your format becomes too cluttered with graphic ''gingerbread,'' your design will begin to compete with the content, and your message will become unclear.

Avoid placing graphics in the central areas of your format, where most of your information will go. Keep your backgrounds simple and uncluttered. Remember, in presentation graphics, the message is the medium.

CREATING MASTER SLIDES OR TEMPLATES

Once you've determined positions and design for your title, logo, and any other decorative elements in your presentation design, the remaining area of your slide frame is left for your text, charts, graphics, and photos. To maintain consistency and style, create a sample of each type of slide to serve as a model for the slides in your presentation. Your model slides are called masters or templates.

You will need to create from two to ten format samples depending on the size and complexity of your presentation. Create formats for only the slide types that are repeated throughout your presentation. If you have a single pie chart, for example, it isn't worthwhile to set up a master and then have to do it all over again to create the actual slide.

If you have several slides throughout your presentation which defy categorization, create a generic slide format consisting of just a title and background. Use this generic format for those one-of-a-kind slides.

How you go about creating your master slides or templates depends a great deal on your software. Many presentation graphics programs (such as Ashton-Tate's Applause II and Aldus Persuasion) support some form of templates that allow you to predesign and then quickly format your text and charts. Most drawing and illustration programs require you to create individual sample files and save them on disk.

TEXT SLIDE TEMPLATES

Set up templates for two basic sizes of text:

- A template for text slides with one or two lines of larger text
- A template for slides with seven to eight lines of smaller type

If you have special text slides, such as those with quotations, block text, or tables, create a template for each type.

For your templates, define the colors for your text and bullets and choose type styles and sizes. Keep in mind that your templates are not the place for worst-case scenarios. They should represent typical slides. For example, do not select a text size based on the slide with the most text, or your presentation might have many slides with only one or two lines floating in white space. If you have one or two "megatext" slides, don't create templates for them; create them from scratch later.

CHART AND GRAPH TEMPLATES

Like text slides, chart and graph slides should have a consistent format throughout the presentation. Set up templates for each type of chart and graph that is used several times in the presentation.

Your templates will establish the formatting for chart and graph elements:

- Decide whether your charts will be flat or have some depth (two-dimensional or three-dimensional).
- Select a series of colors to be used for lines, bars, columns, and pie slices.
- Choose grid, scale, and tick mark conventions.
- Decide how and where data labels will be used.

Before you create any diagrams, organization charts, or flow charts, give some thought to how they will fit into your content area. For example, if you need to create a flow chart of a process, format it to fit in a horizontal area, as illustrated in Figure 6.7. If you place a standard vertical flow chart on a slide, it will be too small to read. See Chapter 10 for details on designing charts and graphs.

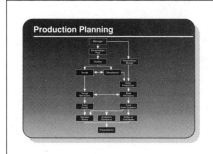
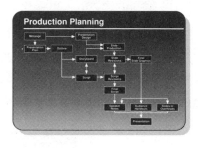

Figure 6.7:

Format a flow chart horizontally

ILLUSTRATION AND PHOTO TEMPLATES

You probably will not have to do much work preparing templates for illustrations. Most drawings have their own shape and scale. Usually, you will just drop them into the center of your content area.

If you are using a series of photo inserts, plan how they will be treated. Decisions about drop shadows, rules, and other design elements associated with photos should be made in advance. Chapter 11 provides details about including illustrations and photos in presentations.

PREFORMATTED TEMPLATES

Many presentation graphics programs come with preformatted templates, which are designed to allow the user to create attractive presentations without having to do a lot of formatting. You can use the templates as they are or modify them to suit your needs. They are a valuable resource when you are in a hurry, as well as a good tool for learning how to design slides. Review the templates that come with your presentation program to get ideas for your own designs.

The main problem with using the templates that come with your software is that everyone else who bought the program has the same ones. If a package comes with 12 preformatted designs and 100,000 copies of it are sold, more than 8000 people are using the same slide design. If they all show up at the same conference, there will be a lot of sleepy audiences, no matter how good that one design is. If you must use a preformatted template straight from the box, try to at least add a company logo to the design to personalize it.

BREAKING THE RULES

Ralph Waldo Emerson said: "A foolish consistency is the hobgoblin of small minds." Even the most attractive and efficient format cannot solve every design problem you encounter when creating your slides. Formatting a problem slide may require that you break your own rules.

The best example of breaking the rules is to get rid of a few, as shown in Figure 6.8. If your design has format rules at the bottom of the frame and they get in the way of a large, important graphic that can't be reduced, eliminate the bottom rules on that slide.

RULE AND LOGO CAUSE PRODUCTION SCHEDULE TO BE TOO SMALL

REMOVING RULE AND LOGO ALLOWS LARGER, MORE LEGIBLE CHART

Figure 6.8:

Breaking the rules

Here are some other instances where you may have to bend your own rules:

- Special text colors in tables
- Photos with unusual shapes or cropping
- Scientific charts and graphs that require specially shaped grids
- Special effects and graphics that look better when they bleed off the frame margins

Remember that what you are doing is an *exception,* and that even these exceptions should retain most of your original design. Don't just stray from your design in an attempt to relieve monotony. A good presentation will have enough variety from text, charts, and illustrations to maintain audience interest. Don't break your rules unless you have a good graphic reason to do so.

THE REAL WORLD   INSTANT DESIGN, OR HOW I LEARNED TO STOP WORRYING AND LOVE AUTOTEMPLATES

Tuesday, October 2, 10:00 am: Jim Gonzalez sits down at his computer and starts to think about the sort of design he wants to use for the presentations to be given by George, Alan, and Victoria.

2:00 pm: Four hours and a half-eaten sandwich later, Jim is still trying to figure out what to do for a basic slide design, so he decides to modify one that came with his presentation package.

It is an attractive format, although the purple background has to go. Jim changes the background to a neutral gray and the graduated fill from top/bottom to left/right, and then rearranges some of the format graphics. He decides to keep the row of boxes on the bottom and use them as a graphic device to display the company name (George insists!). He deletes the top row of boxes, which he considers a little too flashy, and uses a single box as an anchor graphic for a flush-left title. He also eliminates the decorative box under the

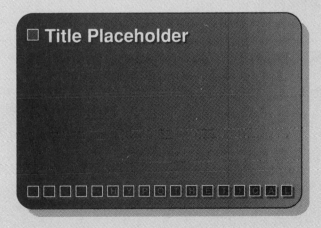

original title because it uses up too much space (Victoria needs room for her financial charts). He now has the beginnings of a distinctive presentation design.

With the basic design established, it's easy to create the format samples. Jim prepares a few text treatments, two charts, and a photo insert, and the samples are ready to go to the service bureau for imaging.

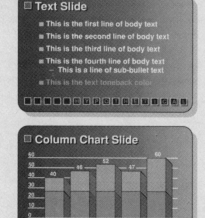

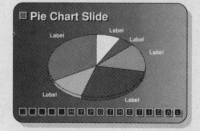

SUMMARY

The first part of creating an effective, exciting design for your presentation is to arrange the basic elements that are common to all of your slides. The arrangement of repeated elements, such as titles, backgrounds, and rules, forms the slide frame layout. In formatting the slide frame layout, use the following design guidelines:

- Choose the appropriate medium for your presentation (35mm slides, overhead transparencies, or screen show) and make sure your presentation program page setup matches that medium.

- Use natural reading patterns, color, size, and graphics to direct the audience's attention to the important parts of your slides.

- Balance the graphic elements on your slides to serve as a stable framework for your message.

- Create a series of format samples to define your graphic decisions for as many slides as possible in your presentation.

- Allow a 5 percent margin on all sides of the frame to prevent cropping and overcrowding. Then use the full amount of frame space for your text and graphics.

- Use rules, frames, or anchor graphics when designing your title treatment. If necessary, allow for two lines of title text in your design.

- Use corporate logos judiciously. If you must use a logo on every slide, treat it as part of the overall design. Don't overemphasize it at the expense of your message.

- Don't be afraid to break your own rules when the slide design calls for it.

- When using preformatted autotemplates, try to customize them to suit your own personality.

chapter 7

Format Design: Using Color

Color is an extremely effective tool for presentation graphics. Unlike printing color pages, which is often prohibitively costly, producing a color presentation is relatively inexpensive. Because of the way slides are imaged in a film recorder, the processing cost for a slide with two colors is exactly the same as that for a slide with two thousand colors. This makes it possible to use a far wider range of colors than is available for printed graphics.

This chapter provides the information you need to design a color presentation. It explains the mechanics of color and how you can achieve the effects you want by using it properly.

TAKING ADVANTAGE OF COLOR

The primary purpose of color in a presentation is to create an attractive environment for your message. Studies show that a color presentation is more memorable and effective.

The use of color can contribute to your presentation in several ways:

- Color choices can influence the mood and receptiveness of your audience.

- In a darkened room, audience attention can wander; color provides the visual variety necessary to maintain audience interest.

- Color can focus audience attention on a particular point in an individual slide.

- Color can be used to enhance meaning and clarify information.

- A presentation color palette establishes a consistent environment for your information.

Many computer programs allow you to select from a palette of millions of colors. But when asked to name as many colors as possible, most people cannot come up with more than a couple dozen. The gap between what colors the average person can name and the millions he or she can actually see is the gray area (no pun intended!) where taste and personal style influence the way we use and talk about color.

Keep in mind that color is very subjective; no two people perceive a color in the same way. Even the words we use to describe colors are very indefinite; one man's violet is another man's purple; what you may call turquoise someone else may call cyan.

Many people have very strong opinions about particular colors. If you are designing a presentation for others, try to get an idea of their likes and dislikes and allow for their preferences in your design. If a speaker particularly dislikes a color, use it sparingly or not at all. If he or she has favorite colors that would work well in a presentation, use them.

Different cultures ascribe distinct values to colors. For example, in Islamic countries, green has very strong religious connotations and should be used carefully. If your presentation is to be given overseas, check with local consulates or embassies for guidance about color customs.

DEFINING COLOR

You don't have to know how color works to appreciate a painting or to choose a color for the kitchen walls. But in order to produce a color design, you need a basic understanding of color, as well as tools to describe and manipulate it. The tools used to define and work with color are called *color models*. The types of color models you may encounter while working with presentation graphics software are described in the following sections and illustrated at the end of the chapter.

RGB COLOR MODELS

The color model most commonly used in presentation graphics is RGB (Red, Green, Blue). The color monitor on your computer uses red, green, and blue phosphors to create the colors on your screen. A color film recorder uses red, green, and blue filters to expose the 35mm film that goes into your slides. (See Film Recorders at the end of this chapter.)

The RGB model is based on the mixture of colored light. (See RGB Color at the end of this chapter.) It is often called *additive color* because colors are formed by combining lights. When the three primary colors (red, green, and blue) are projected together as beams of light on a white background, the beams mix to create a white light. Where any two of these colors overlap, a secondary color is created. For example, where the red and green lights overlap, yellow is created. By varying the brightness of the red, green, and blue, you can create millions of different colors.

Each secondary color is the *complementary* color of one of the primary colors, and vice versa. The three complementary pairs are red-cyan, green-magenta, and blue-yellow. If you project a mixture of a primary color and its complementary color on a white background, the resulting color is white.

CMY COLOR MODELS

The CMY (Cyan, Magenta, Yellow) color model is used mostly in printing. The CMY colors are the complementary, or secondary, colors in the RGB color model. Cyan, magenta, and yellow are the process colors used in four-color printing (the fourth color is black). (See CMY Color at the end of this chapter.)

The CMY color model is based on the mixture of pigments viewed under white light. It is often called *subtractive* color because the pigments absorb some of the colors from the white light, and the ones they reflect result in the color you see. For example, the reason a splash of paint looks yellow under white light is that the paint absorbs the blue portion of the white light and reflects the red and green portions, which your eye perceives as yellow (as with the RGB color model).

When you mix any two CMY colors together, you get a primary RGB color. If you mix all three CMY colors, the resulting color is black.

HSB COLOR MODELS

Creating colors with the RGB or CMY color model can be difficult because you must mix the right amount of primary or secondary colors. Another approach is to use HSB (Hue, Saturation, Brightness) color models, which contain a specific number of colors. You can create other colors by manipulating the intensity of the colors in the model.

The HSB model (also called HSL for Hue, Saturation, Lightness, or HSV for Hue, Saturation, Value) defines primary colors, or *hues,* throughout the spectrum in the form of a wheel. The wheel starts with red and then travels in a circle through orange, yellow, green, cyan, blue, violet, and magenta, ending back at red. The number of primary hues can vary from a few to thousands. For example, the Apple Color Picker on the Macintosh supports up to 65,536 hues. (See HSB Color at the end of this chapter.)

Lighter versions of the primary hues, called *tints*, are created by decreasing the *saturation* of color by adding white. Maximum saturation is the pure hue; minimum saturation is white.

Darker versions of the primary hues, called *shades,* are created by decreasing the *brightness* by adding black. Maximum brightness is the pure hue; minimum brightness is black.

Mixed colors, called *tones,* are created by adjusting both the brightness and saturation of a hue. This is equivalent to adding various levels of gray to the primary hue.

SPECIALIZED COLOR MODELS

There are several other color models available to computer users, most of them designed for matching screen output to printed output. The most common model of this type is Pantone Matching System, which is supported by many drawing and illustration programs. (See Pantone Color at the end of this chapter.)

The Pantone system uses a palette of several hundred colors optimized for both video display and printing inks. Any color-matching system is imperfect because of the wide variety of monitors and the way users adjust them. But the Pantone system, like most others, includes printed reference materials which show what the final printed colors will look like. Since Pantone colors were developed originally for printing inks, they don't always translate well to the RGB output used for 35mm color slides or other color film output.

USING COLOR EFFECTS

Scientific studies have shown that specific colors have predictable effects on our emotions and attitudes. But we really don't need studies to point out the influence of color. Our language is full of phrases that reveal our emotional relationship to color:

- Sadness: "I'm feeling blue."
- Anger: "She's seeing red."
- Desire: "He's green with envy."

You can exploit the power of color in your presentations by understanding how colors affect your audience. The following sections describe color contrast, haloing effects, and the differences between warm, cool, and neutral colors. These color effects are also illustrated at the end of this chapter.

FORMAT, HIGHLIGHT, AND TEXT COLORS

The color choices in a slide can be broken down into three main areas: format, highlight, and text.

Format colors are those used in the basic design of your presentation. These include the background colors and any colors used for recurring items, such as graphics and logos. When you are creating 35mm slides, your format colors will usually be the darkest colors on your palette; on overhead transparencies, they will be a combination of dark and light colors, depending on your format design.

Highlight colors are the colors you add to your palette for illustrations, chart and graph elements, text bullets, and other graphic objects which have meaning and content. These colors should fall in the midrange of brightness—bright enough to stand out from the background, but dark enough to support white or lightly colored text. Similar highlight colors are used for 35mm slides and overhead transparencies.

Text colors include your basic text color, headline and subhead colors, toneback text colors for reveal series (see Chapter 9), and special colors for highlighting body text. In 35mm slides, these colors should be the lightest in your palette so they will stand out against your format and highlight colors. On overhead transparencies with clear or light backgrounds, these will be your darkest colors.

COLOR CONTRAST

Color contrast is the relative difference between two adjacent colors. The difference may be in hue, as in red and green; it may be in saturation, as in light pink and primary red; or it may be in brightness, as in brick red and primary red. The difference may also be a combination of both, as in yellow and dark blue.

Contrast is defined in terms of foreground and background objects. In presentation design, your text and graphics are the foreground objects that rest on the slide background color.

High contrast is essential to readability and clarity in slide design, so it's important to select highlight colors for text and graphics that contrast strongly with the background. The best way to provide contrast is through a combination of brightness and hue.

For example, on identical blue backgrounds, a yellow letter will be easier to read than a red letter or even a light blue letter. The light blue letter may be brighter than the background, but its similarity in hue diminishes its contrast. The red letter may be extremely different in hue, but its lack of brightness makes it difficult to read. The yellow letter contrasts in both hue and brightness, increasing the contrast and improving readability. (See Color Contrast at the end of this chapter.)

HALOING EFFECTS

When two objects with high color contrast (such as red and cyan) touch each other on a slide, you may see a thin white line where they touch. This effect is called *haloing*. (See Haloing at the end of this chapter.)

The electron beam used to expose the film in a film recorder is slightly fuzzy. Each line of the film recorder slightly overlaps the next to create a smooth color field. However, when two complementary colors touch each other, the slight overlap of the beam causes the colors to mix, creating a white edge. This effect varies greatly depending on the quality of the film recorder, which means that haloing is more likely to occur with inexpensive desktop film recorders.

You can eliminate most haloing in slides by including a thin black border around complementary-colored objects, or by giving the text a drop shadow (see Chapter 8). The black line will interrupt the overlap in the film recorder, lessening the halo effect.

WARM, COOL, AND NEUTRAL COLORS

Color can be divided into three main categories: warm, cool, and neutral. As you might expect, the warm colors are the colors of fire: reds, oranges, and yellows. The cool colors are those of water and air: greens, blues, and violets. The only truly neutral colors are white, black, and grays. However, for design purposes, subdued versions of warm and cool colors, such as browns, tans, and slate blues, also serve as neutral colors since they usually have a lot of gray in them. (See Color Categories at the end of this chapter.)

Warm colors, such as reds, oranges, and yellows, are the attention-getters in a presentation design. Slides with a preponderance of warm colors stimulate the audience and cause feelings of heat and energy. However, warm, bright backgrounds are much too flashy for slides; the intensity of the colors will tire the audience. Dark reds and oranges can be used in backgrounds, but carefully, since it is difficult to find cool, contrasting colors that work well with them for foreground objects.

Cool colors, such as blue and green, have a more relaxing effect on an audience than warm colors. In general, slides with mostly cool colors make an audience more receptive and passive. Dark, cool colors are ideal for backgrounds because they contrast well with warm color highlights, forcing the audience to pay attention to your content rather than the background. You also can use brighter cool colors, which would be overwhelmed by a warm background, as highlights.

True neutral colors—black, white, and gray—act as a blank slate for the highlight colors you use with them. Without an addition of some color (either with a logo or format graphics), neutral backgrounds can be very boring. You also can use "warm neutral" colors, such as brown and tan, or "cool neutral" colors, such as blue gray, to avoid the bland gray look. Neutral tones are the perfect background for a full range of highlight colors, both warm and cool.

In your presentation, you can use various combinations of warm, cool, and neutral colors to influence your audience. The background, because of its large area, will have a more profound effect on the general mood of an audience than the highlight colors used with it:

- Warm backgrounds are generally suitable for presentations that are intended to excite and stimulate the audience, such as sales and marketing meetings.

- Cool backgrounds are best suited to presentations that require the audience to be relaxed and receptive to information, such as business and scientific presentations.

- Neutral backgrounds (especially gray) serve as a backdrop for the other colors you choose, so your highlight colors will have more effect on the audience.

As shown in Figure 7.1, you can control the audience response to your presentation by various combinations of background and highlight colors.

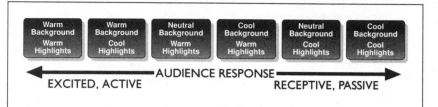

Figure 7.1:

Audience response to warm, cool, and neutral colors

ENHANCING YOUR MESSAGE WITH COLOR

In a presentation, anything that helps your audience concentrate on the speaker and the slides is a plus. Color is one of your strongest tools for guiding an audience. The following sections describe some techniques for using color to enhance your message.

USE COLOR TO INCREASE LEGIBILITY

As you create your presentation, you are viewing it on your computer screen from 2 feet away. The audience may be up to 100 feet from the screen, and they need all the help they can get to see your information clearly. Strong contrast between your text and background colors will increase the readability of your slides.

Unless you are deliberately trying to create a watermark effect (where an object is subdued so that it appears as part of the background), use enough contrast to create a visible edge where any object touches the background. Without proper color contrast, objects will appear weak and out of focus.

USE COLOR TO MAINTAIN AUDIENCE ATTENTION

A darkened room, a big lunch, and a monotonous speaker can all add up to a comatose audience. To keep your audience awake, use occasional splashes of color throughout your presentation. Color can provide the visual stimulation your audience needs to remain alert and interested.

Here are some ways you can use color to add variety to a presentation:

- If you have several slides that consist of a single line of text, place that text in a colored box.
- Use color charts and graphs wherever possible.
- Add a color graphic or photograph to illustrate your point.

The techniques for adding visual interest are illustrated in Figure 7.2.

 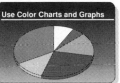 

Figure 7.2:

Using color to add variety

USE COLOR TO EMPHASIZE OR DE-EMPHASIZE POINTS

During a presentation, you may want to call attention to a line of text or part of a graph. When you use color as a pointer, your audience will have no trouble distinguishing the special elements from the rest of the text or graph. You can also use color to draw attention away from certain information. Large, low-contrast elements will seem less important than smaller, brighter ones.

Here are some ways to use color to highlight elements:

- Instead of underlining important words within a text block, put them in a bright, contrasting color.
- Put the most important element of a chart or graph in a bright color to direct the audience's attention to it.

■   In a graph, use darker colors for data that is unfavorable to your message to diminish its impact.

Figure 7.3 illustrates the methods for directing attention with color.

USE COLOR TO LINK
RELATED PRESENTATION ELEMENTS

Color can link elements that are used repeatedly throughout a presentation. For example, if your speech contains references to different departments in your organization, select a "signature" color for each department and use it in charts and graphs throughout the presentation whenever that department name appears. The audience members will identify the color with the department, and it will be easier for them to read and understand the charts and graphs.

You can also assign unique highlight or format colors to different sections of a long presentation to distinguish them without sacrificing a consistent appearance. For example, if you have several speakers, use the same slide layout for the entire presentation, but give each speaker a unique color palette.

For a large presentation, you can combine color linking techniques to define a strong, overall color strategy. The color strategy for a presentation with six speakers from different departments might be as follows:

Speaker/ Department	Background Color	Format Color
S. Shelberg Operations	Dark blue	Violet
D. Morgan Research & Development	Dark violet	Magenta

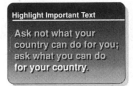 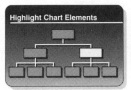 

Figure 7.3:

Highlighting specific elements

Speaker/ Department	Background Color	Format Color
M. Nilsson Personnel	Dark rose	Gold
J. Flannery Marketing	Dark red	Orange
J. Forsayeth Finance	Dark teal	Yellow
J. Schoonover Sales	Dark orange	Tan

The color scheme could be expanded to include colors for the company's eight geographical divisions:

Division	Highlight Color
Northeast	Light blue
South	Yellow-orange
Midwest	Light green
Mountain States	Tan
West	Orange
Canada	Red
Europe	Violet
Pacific Rim	Magenta

USE COLOR MOTION TO EXPLAIN PROCESSES

Graphics that depict a complicated process or series of events can be confusing. You can help the audience understand what you are illustrating by guiding them through a graphic or text sequence with *moving highlights.*

In a moving highlight, the entire graphic or text is visible at all times. As the speaker talks about individual elements, that element is highlighted and the rest of the sequence is toned back (made darker than the highlighted text), usually with a lighter shade of the background color. Figure 7.4 illustrates a moving highlight on an organization chart. See Chapter 9 for details on creating moving highlight series.

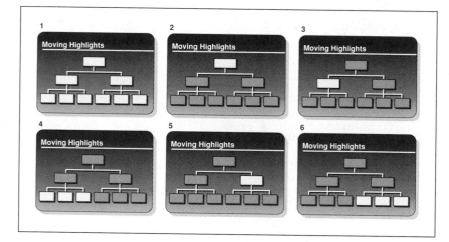

Figure 7.4:

Moving highlights in an organization chart

This effect can be applied to any type of slide: text, charts, and diagrams. As an introduction to the overall process, begin with a slide in which all the elements are highlighted. Then you can proceed to use moving highlights to describe the process in detail.

USE GRADIENT FILLS FOR DEPTH AND REALISM

You can add drama to a presentation by using a gradient fill for your background. A background with a gradient fill is shaded from a light color to a dark color or black. The shading gives a feeling of depth to the slide frame. It will also enhance contrast between your background and foreground elements since much of the background will be in dark shades.

As illustrated in Figure 7.5, there are a variety of gradient fill types. When choosing a gradient fill, make sure it fits the style and mood of your presentation as much as your other colors. The most traditional is a top-bottom gradient with the brightest part at the bottom of the frame. Other types, such as left-right or diagonal, are a little more stylish. Element-weighted, title-weighted, and radial fills are the flashiest, and should be used with care.

Choose a background gradient and stick with it throughout a presentation. Changing the gradient of a slide can be even more jarring than

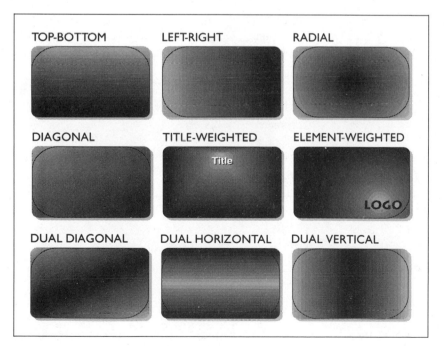

Figure 7.5:

Gradient fills for backgrounds

changing the background color. The change in gradient appears as motion in the background, which can be very distracting.

Because gradient fills can significantly increase the time it takes to image your slides, you should use them cautiously. Generally, top-bottom gradient fills take the least time to image, followed by left-right and diagonal, and then radial, which take the most time. If you plan to use a left-right, diagonal, or radial gradient fill for your slide background, have your service bureau pay close attention to imaging times when you send in your test samples. If your slides take significantly longer than average to image, make sure to allot extra time for slide imaging in your production schedule.

CHOOSING COLORS TO SUIT YOUR OUTPUT

A large consideration in your choice of colors for your presentation is the method you will use to show them to the audience. Overhead transparencies generally have light backgrounds; 35mm slides have dark backgrounds. Colors that work well on 35mm slides can sometimes appear washed out on transparencies. In a presentation to be transferred to video tape, use of the wrong colors can cause problems.

The following sections provide tips on selecting colors for the various types of presentation media. Sample color schemes for 35mm and overhead transparency presentations are presented at the end of the chapter.

35MM SLIDES

Because they are normally projected in darkened rooms, the following color scheme provides maximum readability for 35mm slides:

■   Dark backgrounds. Light backgrounds should be avoided in slides because they are very prone to dust and dirt. A small dust particle can be enlarged 4000 percent or more when a slide is projected.

- White or pastel text.
- Medium hues and tones, dark enough to contrast with your text colors, for graphic elements and charts.
- Bright, intense highlight colors.

Gradient backgrounds are especially effective on 35mm slides. Cool backgrounds are the most versatile, since they allow you to use the widest range of highlight and text colors. They also make audiences more relaxed and receptive. Warm backgrounds are more exciting for the audience, but they can be overbearing if they are too bright. It is also difficult to pick cool highlight colors that work well unless the backgrounds are quite dark. Neutral backgrounds (especially grays) can be boring unless you perk them up with some exciting highlight colors. Use cool and warm grays to avoid the "plain gray" look.

OVERHEAD TRANSPARENCIES

Room lights can wash out the intense colors of 35mm slides, which is why they are usually projected in darkened rooms. If a lighted room is required, overhead transparencies are much more readable. An effective color scheme for an overhead transparency presentation includes the following:

- Light or clear background
- Black or very dark text
- Primary, secondary, and other bright, intense colors for graphic elements and charts

The dithering on many color printers makes it difficult to use subtle tints and shades on overhead transparencies. The semitransparent inks used in most color printers are not as rich on transparency film as they are on paper. Pastels and mixed tones will often have heavy dithering patterns.

Dithering patterns are an effect of the dots which create the colors in four-color printing. When an area is pastel or gray, the printer must use very small dots of cyan, magenta, and yellow to create it. These smaller dots are visible when projected on a screen. Primary colors are created by larger dots that blend together and appear more like a solid color.

If you are having photo-quality overhead transparencies made using a dye-sublimation printer or through a photographic process such as Cibachrome, you can use the same colors as you would for 35mm slides. But remember, your room will have to be darkened as if you were projecting slides.

VIDEO AND SCREEN SHOWS

Generally, the guidelines for using color in 35mm slides can also be applied to computer screen shows:

- Dark backgrounds for maximum contrast.

- White, light gray, or pastel text. Avoid haloing by limiting hue contrast with background colors.

- Medium hues and tones for graphic elements and charts. But avoid primary colors.

If your presentation is to be transferred to video tape or otherwise converted to broadcast-standard video (as for a video projection system), you should avoid large areas of pure primary and secondary colors (red, green, blue, yellow, cyan, and magenta). These primary colors will overload the video screen, causing an effect called *blooming,* in which the areas of color will appear fuzzy and too bright. If your video tape has a sound track, these colors can create so much excess video signal that they interfere with the sound track on the tape, causing an audible hum.

Haloing is also common in video projection. In fact, it can even appear as a vibrating effect, called *video crawl.*

MATCHING SCREEN COLORS TO FINAL OUTPUT

Because of the translation and conversion necessary to transfer your color choices from the computer program to the final output, what you see on the monitor may not be what you see in your finished presentation. Color film has a much wider range of color and contrast than is available with even the most expensive video boards and monitors.

A good 256-color monitor (such as the Macintosh RGB monitor or a high-quality VGA screen) will give a reasonable representation of your final film output. If you are going to be working with photos digitized on a scanner, you may need a system that supports millions of colors, and a larger, high-resolution screen. But no matter what hardware you use, what you see on the screen is merely an approximation of your final output. Do not base your color selections on how the colors appear on your screen.

The only way to be sure of what the colors will look like on the final output is to image color samples. Create sample slides similar to the ones shown at the end of this chapter. A single sample could include the entire slide background with format graphics, sample text formatting, and a graphic such as a pie chart to show the main highlight colors you intend to use. Check the color samples before finalizing your slide format design.

Even if you are giving a screen show, the colors on your monitor might look different on the one you will be using for the presentation. The quality and mechanical condition of the monitor and projection equipment affect the appearance of colors. Test your color selections for a screen show or video on the final projection equipment whenever possible.

THE
REAL
WORLD   VARIATIONS ON A COLOR SCHEME

Thursday, October 4, 1:00 pm: Jim Gonzalez presses the slide-advance button on the projector, and his first sample slide fills the screen of Hypothetical's executive conference room.

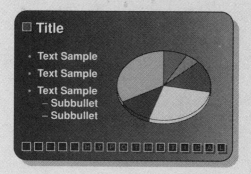

The format is one he adapted from a predesigned template in his software package. He changed it to include some company colors: red boxes with gold borders on a blue-to-black gradient background, white title and text, and a series of bright colors for graphics.

The first comment is from George. "Good work, Jim. This looks better than the last show we had done by Slides R Us."

Victoria approves as well: "A very pretty design."

"It's too bad Alan's in Japan. I'd like to hear his opinion. What do you think of that background?" says George.

"It seems a little...bright." replies Ellen. "You know, Acme Worldwide uses the same colors in their logo."

"These are the colors from our logo," says Jim. "But now that I look at them on the screen, they do seem too much like circus colors. I did a couple of variations. Here's number one."

Jim changes the slide. The second format is the same layout, but with a gradient red-to-black background and a gold title.

"Ouch! Jim, if the Board and I ever expand the company into show business, this will be perfect. What else have you got?"

"One more." Jim is starting to worry about having to start over. He changes the slide. The final format uses a gray background instead of the red, with a white title.

"That's beautiful, Jim," says Victoria.

"That's more like it. Except the title looks too plain." George comments.

"Why don't I use the gold title on this background? That will put a little more color in the slides. I'm afraid the gray background by itself may be too boring," says Jim.

"Fine. Let's go with this design, except with a gold title. Will you do another test, Jim?"

"If that's the only change, I don't think so. We can see in the boxes what the gold will look like on the gray.

I'll change the templates I have now, and start working on some more."

Ellen asks Jim to do something special: "Jim, could you print a copy of this sample and mark all the colors on it? I'll fax a copy to Alan in Japan so he can see what's happening."

"Sure, Ellen. I'll have it on your desk this afternoon."

George ends the meeting: "Thanks, everyone. I think we're on track."

"And so far, on schedule!" says Ellen.

SUMMARY

Color is a powerful tool for presenting your message clearly and forcefully. Here are some guidelines for using color:

- Allow for personal and cultural preferences when selecting colors for a presentation.

- Color models such as RGB and HSB allow you to describe and control color through your computer.

- Warm, cool, and neutral colors have different psychological effects on the audience. Use these differences to enhance and clarify your message.

- Color contrast is essential to readability. Choose background and highlight colors for maximum contrast, but beware of haloing and dithering effects.

- Use color to hold your audience's attention and guide them through a presentation.

- Control the flow of information to the audience by using color to emphasize and de-emphasize presentation elements.

- Link related presentation elements by assigning signature colors to frequently used topics, divisions, departments, and so on.

- Use moving highlights to help explain complex processes and time-related events.

- Never commit to a new presentation design without reviewing and approving sample color 35mm slides, overhead transparencies, and video projections.

- If you are designing slides for someone else, create a few variations as backup in case your first choice isn't acceptable.

chapter 8

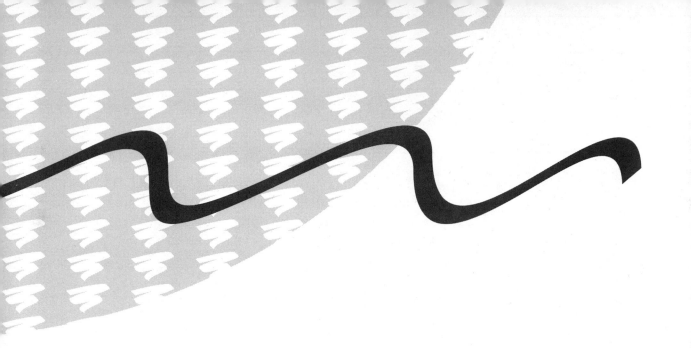

Format Design:
Typography and Type Styles

The typefaces you use throughout your presentation are an important element of your format design. With literally thousands of typefaces available, choosing one or two for your presentation can be a challenge.

Good typography is essential to a presentation. Since an audience usually has only a few seconds to read what is up on the screen, the typefaces must provide clear, readable text. Type, like color, can also set a mood.

An understanding of typography will help you choose the most effective type for your presentation. This chapter begins with descriptions of typefaces and fonts, and then provides practical suggestions for choosing and formatting type in your presentations.

UNDERSTANDING TYPEFACES

A typeface or type style is an alphabet designed for use in mechanical (or electronic) printing processes. There are literally thousands of typefaces from which to choose.

ANATOMY OF A TYPEFACE

The style used to draw letters defines the typeface. Lowercase letters consist of three main parts:

- The body, or *x-height,* spans the largest area or body portion of the letter. The bottom of the x-height lies on the baseline.

- The *ascender* is the part of the letter extending above the x-height.

- The *descender* is the part of the letter extending below the baseline.

Figure 8.1 illustrates parts of a typeface: the x-height, ascender, and descender and their relationship to the baseline.

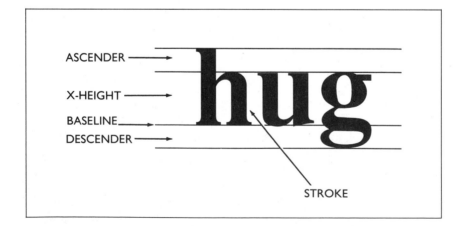

Figure 8.1:

Parts of a typeface

Strokes are the actual lines forming the letters. Depending on the typeface, strokes can vary greatly in width or thickness.

TYPE CHARACTERISTICS

Typefaces have several distinguishing characteristics. The three main differences between type styles are whether they are Roman or Italic, whether they are Serif or Sans Serif, and the width and thickness of their strokes (called *stroke weights*).

Roman versus Italic

Letters carved into the stones of ancient Roman ruins inspired early typeface design. Named *Roman* after their origin, these letters are drawn with strong, regular, vertical and horizontal strokes. They serve as the basis for most typefaces used today.

One printer in Venice, Aldus Manutius, developed a very compact, slanted typeface based on the handwriting style of the time. This innovation allowed him to print smaller, more portable books. This style developed in Italy became known as *Italic* throughout the rest of Europe. Today, his name and portrait are recognized as the trademark for a certain popular desktop-publishing software firm.

Serif versus Sans Serif

The Roman stonecutters made a small twist with their chisels to prevent chipping at the end of a stroke. This twist resulted in a small wedge-shaped extension, called a *serif*. Serif typefaces mimic this stroke.

SERIFS

Later type styles omit the serifs. They are called *Sans Serif* (*sans* is French for without). *Oblique* refers to the slanted (Italic) versions of Sans Serif typefaces. Figure 8.2 shows Serif and Sans Serif typefaces.

Stroke Weights

The difficulty of developing molds for typesetting confined early type designers to using even, regular stroke thicknesses when designing type styles. As technology improved, it became easier to produce type styles with exaggerated differences between the thicknesses of various strokes. Stroke weight is another characteristic that defines a type style.

Uniform Stroke Weight
Exaggerated Stroke Weight

SERIF
Times Roman   *Times Italic*
SANS SERIF
Helvetica Roman   *Helvetica Oblique*

Figure 8.2:

Serif and Italic; Sans Serif and Oblique

TYPE FAMILIES

Typefaces are grouped into *type families* based on their characteristics. The main families are Oldstyle Serif, Modern Serif, Sans Serif, Transitional, and Decorative. Note that the dividing line between categories is fuzzy, and some styles fall between them.

Oldstyle Serif Typefaces

The original Roman alphabet provides the pattern for the design of Oldstyle Serif typefaces. The master for these letters is the inscription

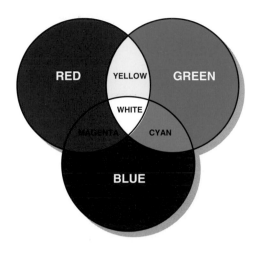

COLOR MODELS

RGB Color (*Additive*): Created by combining red, green, and blue (*primary* RGB colors) light to make white. Where the primary colors overlap, *complementary* colors (cyan, magenta, yellow) are created.

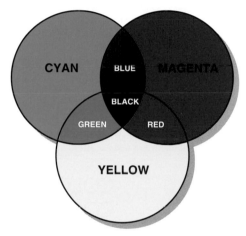

CMY Color (Subtractive): Created by mixing pigments that subtract primary RGB colors from white light and reflect the rest. Combining any two CMY colors creates a primary RGB color.

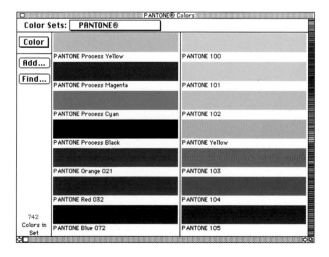

Pantone Matching System: A collection of several hundred colors chosen for printed output. Pantone and similar systems do not always convert well to the RGB output used in film recorders.

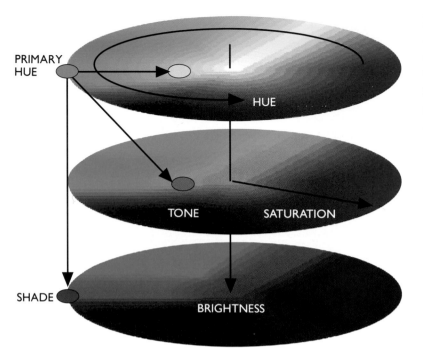

HSB Color (*Hue, Saturation, Brightness*): A model based on a wheel of a fixed number of colors called *hues*. Hues are modified by adjusting the *saturation* (color intensity) and the *brightness*.

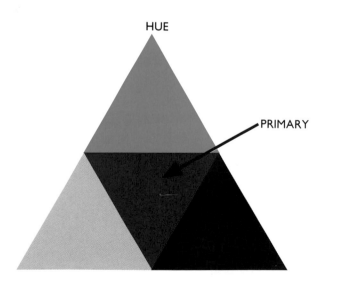

COLOR CONTRAST

Identifying Contrast: The primary red triangle shows contrast with green (hue), pink (saturation), and brick red (brightness).

Enhancing Contrast: The yellow type is more readable because it contrasts in both brightness and hue, not just brightness (light blue) or hue (red).

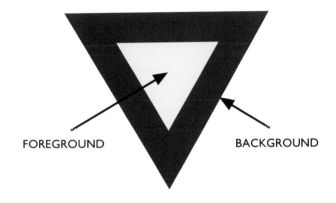

FOREGROUND BACKGROUND

Foreground and Background: The yellow triangle is the foreground color on a background of blue. The blue triangle and the callouts are also foreground colors against the white background of this page.

WARM COOL

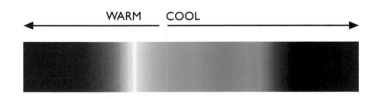

COLOR CATEGORIES

Warm and Cool: The spectrum is based on the emotional effects of color.

NEUTRAL GRAY

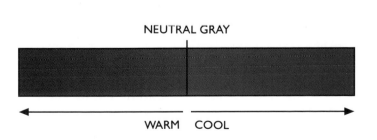

WARM COOL

Neutral: Neutral gray is a starting point for the range of cool and warm neutral colors.

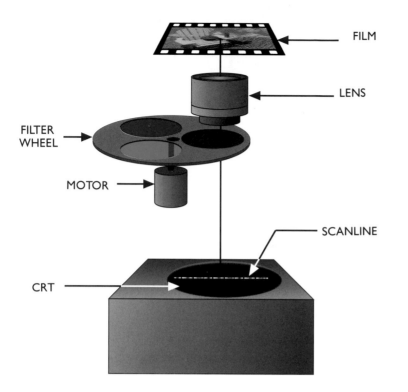

FILM

LENS

FILTER
WHEEL

MOTOR

SCANLINE

CRT

COLOR
AND FILM
RECORDERS

Film Recorders: A film recorder converts data from the computer to gray-scale scan lines, which are photographed through red, green, and blue filters. The film image is built up one color and one line at a time, with up to 8000 individual pixels per line. See Chapter 12 for more information about film recorders.

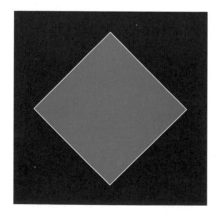

Haloing: A slight white line that appears where adjacent complementary colors (such as red and cyan) meet. Changing colors or adding a black border can minimize haloing.

COLOR FORMAT SAMPLES

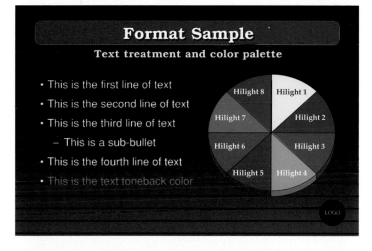

Warm Background 1: A traditional design, with the upper-left title balanced by a lower-right logo. The dark red gradient provides a dramatic setting for bright format rules and white copy.

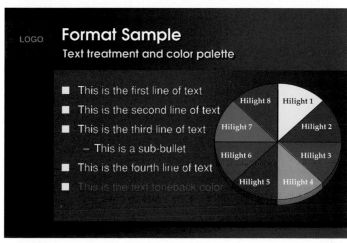

Warm Background 2: The orange-rust background is broken up with dark pinstripes, which add texture. The intense background requires white and yellow text. The toneback color is a light orange. Highlights are primary colors.

Warm Background 3: This dramatic use of gradients is subdued by the deep rose color, which is warm without being overwhelming. The rose color also supports cool highlight colors better than most other warm colors.

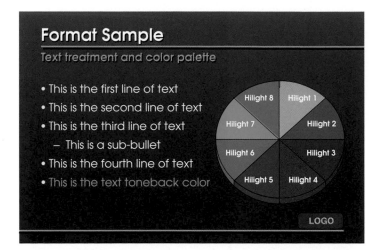

Cool Background 1: A traditional combination of a blue gradient background with a warm (yellow-orange) rule. The highlights are well distributed throughout the palette. Since cool backgrounds are more passive, they take a wider variety of highlight colors.

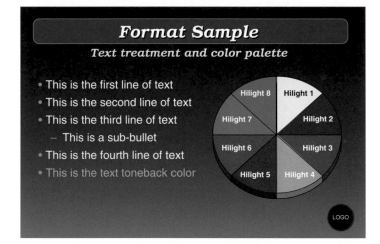

Cool Background 2: Pure green backgrounds tend to look too intense and can upset an audience. But teal, with its hint of blue, is usually more acceptable. The same pinstripe design gives texture to the background.

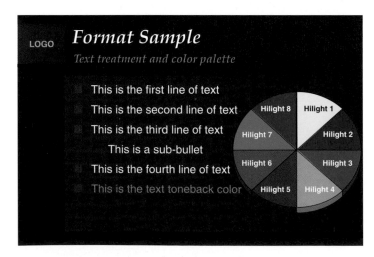

Cool Background 3: Combinations of dark blues, purples, and roses give a rich, elegant look. Use primary colors for highlights to make your graphics stand out.

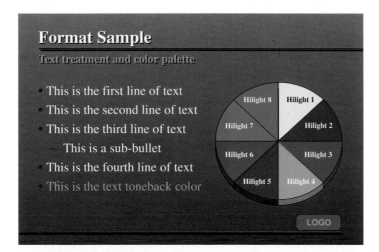

Neutral Background 1: The neutral gray background gives this design a chameleon-like quality. The red rules add warmth, but the cool cyan subhead is readable. Changing the rule or text color will affect the entire look of this format.

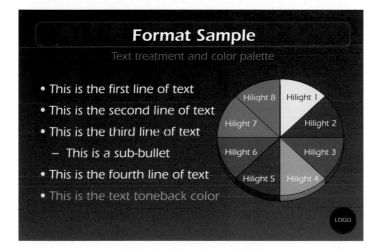

Neutral Background 2: The slight magenta cast to the gray on the background makes this format warmer, and the rose-colored title bar complements the background. The light blue subhead adds variety, and the yellow bullets are attention-getting.

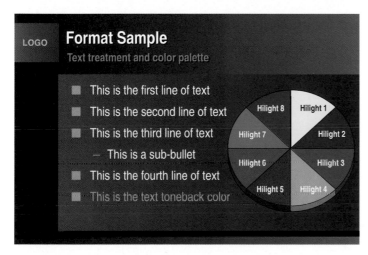

Neutral Background 3: A slate blue background gives a cool, neutral effect to this format; gold highlights add warmth. The square bullets echo the graphic in the upper-left corner.

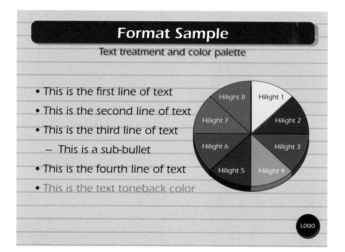

Vugraph Background 1: Use solid colors rather than gradients for vugraphs. The title and subtitle provide decorative color to the format. The body copy is black for readability.

Vugraph Background 2: A variation on the pinstripe theme, with the same elements as its slide version. The pinstripes are slightly darker than the background. Graphic elements add color. The title text is white, since it is placed on a dark background.

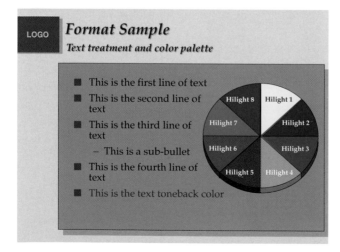

Vugraph Background 3: Large areas of colors can be effective (but make samples to check the ouput). The color of the drop shadow is a darker shade of the background. The toneback text color is also darker than the box color, although lighter than the regular black text.

engraved on the Trajan column in Rome. The beauty of the letters comes from the casual balance of the stroke weights and serifs. A characteristic of Oldstyle Serif is that the capital letters (especially the J's) fall below the baseline, into the descender area. Figure 8.3 shows several Oldstyle Serif typefaces.

Janson Roman Caslon 3 Roman Bernhard Modern Roman	**Figure 8.3:** *Oldstyle Serif typefaces*

Because of the low x-height of Oldstyle serif faces, they are not easy enough to read to be used as body copy for projected presentations. However, you can use them for titles to add an elegant and traditional note to your presentation.

Modern Serif Typefaces

First developed in the late 1700s, Modern Serif typefaces are more draftsman-like than Oldstyle, and they have exaggerated differences in their stroke weights. Designed for use in mass publications, they're the staple of English-language publishing. Newspaper publishers developed typefaces such as Times Roman to satisfy their need for easy-to-read type. Figure 8.4 illustrates some Modern Serif faces.

The orderly, symmetrical quality of their letters make Modern Serif typefaces an appropriate choice for presentation materials. They're easy to read in both body text and titles, and they tend to give a conservative, solid look to your presentation.

New Baskerville Roman

Goudy Roman

Palatino Bold

Figure 8.4:

Modern Serif typefaces

Sans Serif Typefaces

Sans Serif typefaces are characterized by somewhat uniform stroke weights and a lack of serifs. They started appearing in the mid-nineteenth century, mainly as large headline and display text.

The early Sans Serif designs were a big departure from the traditional typefaces used in publications of the time, and they were often referred to as "grotesque." The designs improved, and people became more accustomed to them. Today, the use of Sans Serif typefaces is widespread. The Helvetica typeface, designed in the early 1950s by Swiss type designer Adrian Frutiger, is the most popular of the Sans Serif faces. Figure 8.5 shows three Sans Serif typefaces.

Avant Garde Roman

Futura Book Roman

Eurostile Roman

Figure 8.5:

Sans Serif typefaces

The clean lines and easy readability of Sans Serif typefaces make them very suitable for presentations. They give a presentation a modern, progressive look. A good rule-of-thumb is When in doubt, use Helvetica.

Transitional Typefaces

Transitional typefaces have characteristics of both the Serif and Sans Serif categories. Optima is Sans Serif, but its combination of thick and thin strokes give it the look of a Serif face. The Lubalin Graph typeface has serifs, but the uniform stroke weights of the lines make it look more like a Sans Serif face. Examples of Transitional typefaces are shown in Figure 8.6.

Optima Roman
Lubalin Graph
Serif Gothic

Figure 8.6:

Transitional typefaces

The suitability of Transitional typefaces for presentations depends on how readable they are and if they reflect the image you want to project to your audience.

Decorative and Display Typefaces

Decorative and Display typefaces include special designs, ranging from fancy wedding invitation scripts to weird psychedelic poster letters. Some of these faces can be useful for emphasis or special effects. Figure 8.7 shows some Decorative and Display faces.

Figure 8.7:

Decorative typefaces

LITHOS

Fette Fraktur

University Roman

The acceptability of Decorative faces is subject to the trends of fad and fashion. Use them carefully, and avoid them in corporate presentation designs that have to remain fashionable for years.

UNDERSTANDING FONTS

In traditional typesetting, a *font* is a set of molded metal letters belonging to a particular typeface in a specific size. Each variation of a typeface—smaller or larger, Roman or Italic—is a separate font. Some typefaces have further variations, such as narrower and wider or condensed and expanded versions of the basic typeface. However, all the variations are influenced by the design characteristics of the original typeface.

TYPEFACES VERSUS FONTS

In desktop publishing, the definitions of font and typeface have blurred. The new typesetters can generate letters in any point size electronically, thus eliminating the original size definition of *font*. Today, *font* and *typeface* usually refer to the actual type style or the printer font containing the encoded electronic information to generate characters for your printer.

Further contributing to the melding of the two terms is the influence of the Macintosh Font menu and its method of handling type. In the Macintosh menu, *style* refers to whether a typeface is bold, italic, or underlined. This system has also been adopted by Windows-based presentation programs.

FONT CHARACTERISTICS

Fonts are mainly distinguished by their size and weight. Most of the terms used to describe fonts are derived from older printing methods.

Uppercase and Lowercase

When setting type by hand, a printer selected letters from two large, stacked wooden cases containing all the pieces of available type, each different letter in a separate small bin. The upper case held all the capital letters; the lower case held all the small letters. This terminology is still used today.

Type Size

Type size is measured in *points* (a point is about $1/72$ inch). In cold and hot type printing systems, the height of the metal slug holding the molded letter determines the point size of a font. For many computer fonts, the point size is the combined height of the ascender, x-height, and descender.

POINT SIZE

The type size of a computer font, as well as the actual appearance of the font, will vary among type manufacturers. For example, Adobe's 26-point Garamond differs greatly from Bitstream's 26-point Garamond in letter height and design. Both companies based their designs on the original hot type font, but the resulting computer fonts reflect the styles of the artists who created them. Figure 8.8 shows four examples of 26-point Garamond Bold from different type manufacturers.

Type Weight

Another characteristic that distinguishes a font is its weight, which is based on the thickness of the lines and total density of the characters. The description of the font weight varies depending on the type style. Some typefaces have only one or two weights (regular and bold); others have six or more. Figure 8.9 illustrates the various weights in the ITC Eras font family.

Type Width

A regular font also can be redrawn to be narrower or wider than normal. Condensed or compressed fonts have a narrower look. Extended or expanded fonts are wider.

Adobe Garamond Bold
ITC Garamond Bold
Garamond Three Bold
Stempel Garamond Bold

Figure 8.8:

26-point Garamond Bold comparison

ITC Eras Light   **ITC Eras Demi**
ITC Eras Book   **ITC Eras Bold**
ITC Eras Medium   **ITC Eras Ultra**

Figure 8.9:

Type weights in the ITC Eras family

FONT FAMILIES

All the different variations of an original font design make up a *font family*. Some font families have only a few variations. Other families, such as Helvetica or Univers, have dozens. Figure 8.10 shows the fonts in the Futura family.

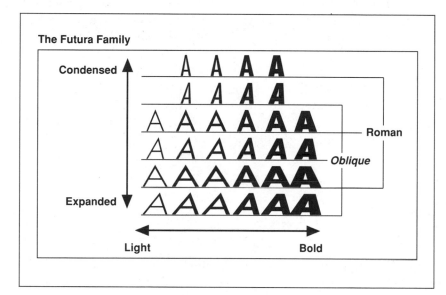

The Futura Family

Condensed

Roman

Oblique

Expanded

Light   Bold

Figure 8.10:

The Futura family

USING COMPUTER FONTS

Computer fonts come in two types: screen fonts and outline fonts. *Screen fonts* are used to display a representation of your final work on your computer monitor. *Outline,* or *printer, fonts* are used by laser printers, typesetters, and film recorders to produce your final output. Both types of fonts contribute to creating a WYSIWYG (What You See Is What You Get) display on your computer.

SCREEN FONTS

Screen fonts provide the What You See part of WYSIWYG. You might think screen fonts are important only when you are producing a screen show. However, the representation of fonts on your screen affects any type of presentation. Accurate screen fonts are essential to knowing what your final output will look like. If your screen fonts are not representative of your output, what looks great on your computer screen may be very disappointing in your 35mm slides or overhead transparencies.

Screen fonts are stored in your computer's memory as *bit-maps*, which are collections of dots (*pixels*) displayed on your computer's monitor. Each point size of a screen font is stored as a series of pictures for the individual characters. Screen fonts can take up a lot of space, both on disk and in your computer's memory.

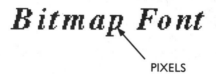

PIXELS

Bit-maps show an approximation of the final output to paper or film. If you select a point size that is the same as one supported by a screen font on your computer, it will usually be close to your final output. However, if you choose a type size that isn't supported, you can run into some serious differences between your WYSIWYG screen representation and your final results.

Having accurate screen fonts in all the sizes you're using in a presentation increases your productivity and saves trips to a laser printer or service bureau to test your designs. Some desktop presentation programs handle screen fonts well; others have displays that have very little to do with what your final output will look like. Generally, Windows 3.0 (and later) and Macintosh programs are far superior in their font capabilities than DOS-based programs.

OUTLINE FONTS

Outline fonts are the What You Get part of WYSIWYG. They are actually small programs that provide a geometric description of the shape of every letter in a font. The description consists of a series of control points and handles, which define the angles and curves of each character, as illustrated in Figure 8.11.

Figure 8.11:

Outline font

HANDLE   CONTROL POINT

Because the shape of each character is defined by geometry, not by the placement of pixels, outline fonts are *resolution independent*. Outline fonts take advantage of the maximum sharpness and resolution of your output device. A laser printer will print outline fonts at 300 dots per inch (dpi). A typesetter will print them at up to 2540 dpi. A high-resolution film recorder will reproduce the same fonts at up to 8000 dpi.

The most common type of screen/printer font combination is a Post-Script font. Each PostScript font (IBM or Macintosh) comes with an outline font file and a screen font file. The screen font consists of several standard sizes of bit-maps (usually 10, 12, 14, 18, and 24 points) for screen display, and the outline font contains the program for describing the characters to a printer.

ADOBE TYPE MANAGER AND OTHER SCREEN FONT MANAGERS

Specialized programs such as Adobe Type Manager (ATM) can produce bit-map screen fonts on the fly directly from the outline printer fonts, as illustrated in Figure 8.12. This method allows you to see any size type in a more accurate display on your monitor. Some programs (such as CorelDRAW!) have this capability built in and use their own proprietary font system.

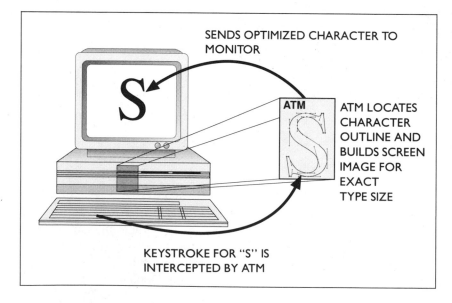

Figure 8.12:

How an ATM font works

USING FONTS WITH A SERVICE BUREAU

Because many presentation programs have different ways of handling fonts, it's important to check with your film recorder or printer manufacturer or with your service bureau to find out about font compatibility. Programs such as CorelDRAW! and early versions of Harvard Graphics have their own font systems, which may or may not be supported by your service bureau.

Many service bureaus require customers using PostScript fonts to send their printer and screen fonts along with their presentation files. No matter what type style you choose, always prepare a test file when creating your presentation format design to see if the fonts you have selected can be reproduced in your final output.

CHOOSING TYPEFACES

Your typeface choices will directly affect the look and readability of your presentation. Most presentation programs come with a small assortment of fonts that are suitable for slide design. For example, Microsoft PowerPoint and Aldus Persuasion come with Helvetica and Times Roman, which both work well in presentations. On the other hand, CorelDRAW! comes with more than 150 fonts, some of which are definitely not suited to slide design.

Select a typeface for your slides that is attractive and readable when projected on a 10-foot-high screen. Avoid gimmicky or overly ornate fonts that draw attention to themselves. Remember, the purpose of your text is to convey information to the audience, not to impress them with incredible typefaces.

Don't pick a typeface that's hard to read from a distance. Tall, narrow typefaces and typefaces with exaggerated serifs are particularly difficult to read from across a room.

Mixing typefaces within a presentation—one for titles and one for body copy—is common. However, putting too many typefaces in a presentation will make it look disorganized and slapped together. Because it is essential to keep a consistent look throughout your presentation, a good rule-of-thumb is to limit the number of typefaces to two. For example, you can use an attractive serif face for your title and a readable sans serif face for your body copy.

Figure 8.13 shows examples of legible typeface combinations that work well in 35mm slide and overhead transparency presentations. The following sections describe some of the considerations involved in making your typeface selections.

Title: **Friz Quadrata Bold** Text: Janson Text Roman	Title: **Bodoni Black** Text: Times Roman	Title: **News Gothic Bold** Text: Times Roman
Title: **Futura Heavy** Text: Helvetica	Title: **Eurostile Demi** Text: Optima Roman	Title: **Serif Gothic Bold** Text: Futura Book
Title: **Optima Bold** Text: Helvetica	Title: **Avant Garde Bold** Text: Helvetica	Title: **Futura Con. X-Bold** Text: Bernhard Modern Bold

Figure 8.13:

Presentation typefaces

TYPE AND THE CORPORATE IMAGE

The typefaces you choose for a presentation have a distinct influence on how your audience perceives you and the organization you represent. Different type styles can be aggressive or relaxed, casual or formal.

Oldstyle Serif faces, such as Caslon, convey a feeling of tradition and history.

The quick brown fox jumped over the lazy dog.

Modern Serif faces, such as Times Roman, are clearer and more readable on slides than Oldstyle, yet they retain the same feeling of tradition and stability.

The quick brown fox jumped over the lazy dog.

Sans Serif faces, such as Avant Garde, can imply a dynamic, future-oriented outlook.

The quick brown fox jumped over the lazy dog.

Using an inappropriate font can ruin even the best presentation. For example, a Decorative typeface, such as Fraktur, can make even the most serious subject matter seem trivial.

𝕿𝖍𝖊 𝖖𝖚𝖎𝖈𝖐 𝖇𝖗𝖔𝖜𝖓 𝖋𝖔𝖝 𝖏𝖚𝖒𝖕𝖊𝖉 𝖔𝖛𝖊𝖗 𝖙𝖍𝖊 𝖑𝖆𝖟𝖞 𝖉𝖔𝖌.

When choosing a typeface for your presentation, think about the sort of impression you want to make on your audience. Select fonts that reflect the image you want the audience to perceive.

TYPE AS FASHION

Typefaces have always been subject to fads and fashions. Graphic designers quickly pick up on innovative, new typefaces, and suddenly those typefaces are everywhere. But when a newer, more distinctive typeface appears, the older face gets placed in the history books.

Consider the effect of fashion on typefaces and how it relates to your presentation. If the presentation you are designing will be given repeatedly, it must stand the test of time. Choose typefaces whose appeal will be enduring. If the presentation is a unique event for a really with-it corporation, the latest trendy typefaces, which might seem dated after a while, might be good choices.

TYPE FOR EMPHASIS

Don't underestimate the power of typeface to surprise and delight your audience. A fancy or unusual typeface, used sparingly, can put that extra spark in your presentation.

As shown in Figure 8.14, a single word or phrase in a jazzy typeface can make a point more emphatically than the same words in a regular presentation type style.

READABILITY: THE BOTTOM LINE

The most important consideration in your selection of typefaces is how easy and clear to read they are. The true test for readability is to put yourself in the place of a viewer sitting in the back row of your audience. If you can read everything clearly from that distance and angle, you've succeeded.

Different projection environments can affect the ability of your audience to read your slides. Slides designed to be projected for a large audience in an auditorium need to be much simpler and easier to read than those meant for a small audience in a conference room.

Figure 8.14:

Using unusual type for emphasis

The readability of your slides is also governed by how much text you put on them. See Chapter 9 for guidelines for judging how much text is too much.

CHOOSING TYPE SIZES

Different presentation programs, particularly DOS-based applications, have distinct ways of designating type sizes. Depending on the page size used in your program, a type size large enough for body copy in one presentation may be too large for the title in another. Because of these variations, the following suggestions are in terms of relative, rather than exact, type sizes.

TITLE TEXT SIZE

Generally, you should pick a large type size for your title. Set the longest anticipated title in your presentation in a size that fills the available space you've allowed for your title area. If your title typeface seems small or crowded, you may need to edit some of your titles to make them shorter. If the text looks enormous on the slide, make it smaller. The title should be clear and easy to read, without overwhelming the other elements of the slide.

BODY COPY SIZE

In most cases, your body copy, subtitles, and subheads should be set at least one standard type size smaller than the title. For example, if your titles are in 36-point type, you should set your body copy in 30- or 24-point type.

There are special cases that may not allow you to follow this guideline. If you have more words in your title than in your body copy, you might want to make the body text a larger size than the title. If you have a large amount of copy that just can't be cut or split between slides, smaller type sizes will have to do.

Keep in mind that if your final output is a screen show or video, you will have to use larger type. The low resolution of the video screen causes small text to fill in and become unreadable.

SIZE OF OTHER ELEMENTS

Other items in your slides, such as footnotes, should be about half the size of your body copy. Try to avoid footnotes if possible. They're seldom readable and almost never read. Information so insignificant that it needs to be a footnote is usually not worth putting in a slide at all.

If legal considerations require a footnote or attribution in your slide, make it very small and don't worry about whether the audience can read it or not. Your legal obligation is filled as long as the information is on the slide.

MIXED TYPE SIZES WITHIN A PRESENTATION

If you must make a drastic point size change from one type size to another, do it in increments or steps. For example, if your body copy size is commonly 18 points and you have one slide that must have 36-point body copy, build up and down from it as follows:

- Preceding slides with 18-point body copy
- Slide with 24-point body copy
- Slide with 36-point body copy
- Slide with 24-point body copy
- Following slides with 18-point body copy

This incremental approach gradually introduces the audience members' eyes to larger text, avoiding the shock of going directly from 18-point text to 36-point text. Often, the audience won't even be aware of the type size differences between one slide and another. However, if you want to create a dramatic effect, you can do so with drastic type size changes.

CAPITALIZING WORDS

Another typography consideration is when to capitalize words. The capitalization in your text will affect its readability. There are several capitalization styles:

- All Caps: As a rule, avoid text in all uppercase letters, or *all caps*. Most typefaces are much harder to read in all caps than in uppercase and lowercase letters. People read words by recognizing their shape as well as by consciously seeing the actual letters. Words in all caps lose their shapes.

- Headline Caps: Traditionally, slide titles and bulleted copy use initial, or headline, caps. *Headline caps* refers to the capitalization of all words in a title or heading except internal conjunctions, prepositions, and articles. Avoid using periods after copy set in headline caps, and try to avoid setting full sentences this way.

- Sentence Caps: For body copy, if the text reads as a complete sentence with subject, verb, and object, use *sentence caps*. A period after a bulleted item set in sentence caps is optional.

Figure 8.15 shows the capitalization styles.

THIS IS ALL CAPS
This Is Headline Caps
This is sentence caps

Figure 8.15:

Capitalization styles

You can use either sentence caps or headline caps for bulleted text or other lists. Usually, shorter bulleted items look better in headline caps than longer items. If your bulleted items aren't complete sentences, use headline caps and don't put periods at the ends of the items.

Again, the most important consideration is consistency. Try not to change your capitalization rules from slide to slide, and never mix capitalization styles within a slide.

EMPHASIZING TYPE

You may want to emphasize certain text within your slides. There are several methods of making particular words or phrases stand out in a mass of text:

- Bold type: The most common way of emphasizing type is to change the type style to a boldface. Be aware that using a lot of boldface in a slide can be very tiring on an audience because it appears to make the text brighter as well as bolder, thus overemphasizing it.

- Italic type: Another typical way to add emphasis is by changing to an italic type style. Usually, an italic emphasis is better than a boldface one because it highlights the text without making it appear brighter.

- Underlining: Avoid highlighting text in a slide by underlining it. Underlined text can be quite difficult to read from a distance. Also, in some presentation programs, it's difficult to accurately align an underline beneath its text.

- Color: Often overlooked, color is the best way to highlight text in a slide. It's just as easy to change the color of text as it is to change its type style. The best colors to use for highlighting text are yellow and very light blue. Both stand out, even from white text. If you need to highlight a word in colored text (as in a title), use white; the contrast will be more than adequate to make your point.

Your audience members will pay greater attention to the words you emphasize with a different style or color, and they will remember them easily. But be careful not to get carried away. Excessive use of type emphasis will dilute the effect and make your text look too busy and cluttered.

LETTERSPACING AND KERNING

Some illustration and page-layout programs provide controls for the spacing and kerning of characters in a text block. *Letterspacing*, or *tracking*, refers to the average space between characters in a line of type. Tight letterspacing will place more characters in a given line length than loose letterspacing.

Kerning refers to the adjustment in the spacing of pairs of letters. When two characters such as *A* and *V* are set next to each other, their normal spacing will cause a gap between them, which can be unattractive. Tightening the kerning of the letters forces them closer together, eliminating the gap.

Most presentation graphic packages don't give the user much control over letterspacing and kerning. Normal letter spacing is usually fine for slide work.

If you are working with a program that does give you control, such as CorelDRAW! or PageMaker, remember text to be read from a distance needs wider spacing than normal text. Text spaced tightly will tend to clump together and be very difficult to read from the back of the presentation room. The only place you should consider using kerning is in titles, where the large type size will sometimes create unsightly letterspacing.

ALIGNING TEXT

Text alignment refers to the placement of the text within the slide frame. There are four ways of aligning text:

- Left alignment: Text aligned along the left margin of a text block is *left aligned*. This is the most common way of aligning titles, body copy, and bulleted text. Bulleted text on slides should always be left aligned so that the bullets will line up.

- Right alignment: Text aligned along the right margin of a text block is *right aligned*. This alignment can be used for columns of numbers, so that the decimal points and numbers line up.

- Center alignment: Text centered on a line is *center aligned*. Use this alignment for titles and subtitles. You also can use center alignment for the occasional block of copy that acts as a statement or quotation. Do not center bulleted text because the bullets will not be aligned, and they will look out of place.

- Justification: Text evenly aligned along the left and right borders of a text block is *justified*. Justification gives a distinctly blocky look to sentences and paragraphs. Avoid this alignment in slide design because the large text size, coupled with relatively short line lengths, will result in irregular and unwanted spaces between letters and words. Hyphenation can eliminate some of this unsightly space, but too many hyphenated words in a block of text make it difficult to read.

Figure 8.16 illustrates the four kinds of text alignment.

USING SPECIAL TYPE EFFECTS

Some presentation graphics programs provide several special type effects that can enhance your slides. But use special effects sparingly. Too many special effects will make your slides look more complex than they actually are.

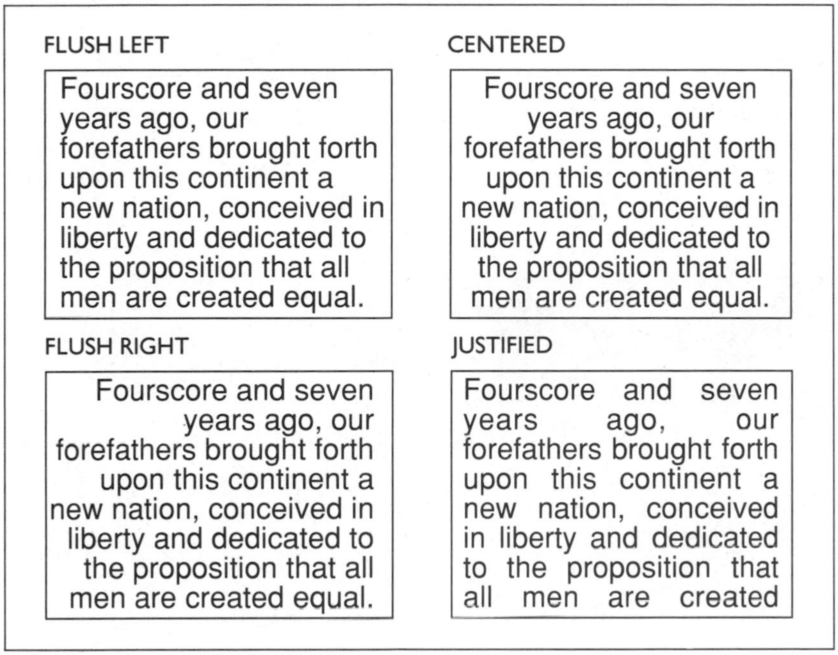

FLUSH LEFT

Fourscore and seven years ago, our forefathers brought forth upon this continent a new nation, conceived in liberty and dedicated to the proposition that all men are created equal.

CENTERED

Fourscore and seven years ago, our forefathers brought forth upon this continent a new nation, conceived in liberty and dedicated to the proposition that all men are created equal.

FLUSH RIGHT

Fourscore and seven years ago, our forefathers brought forth upon this continent a new nation, conceived in liberty and dedicated to the proposition that all men are created equal.

JUSTIFIED

Fourscore and seven years ago, our forefathers brought forth upon this continent a new nation, conceived in liberty and dedicated to the proposition that all men are created

Figure 8.16:

Text alignment

DROP SHADOWS

The most common type effect used in slides is the drop shadow. A drop shadow gives the illusion that there is a bright light illuminating the slide area.

When you are placing drop shadows, remember to keep all the shadows in the same direction. If some are down and left and others are down and right, the audience will sense something wrong with your slides, even though they may not know exactly what it is.

BOTTOM RIGHT

Drop Shadow

BOTTOM LEFT

Drop Shadow

TYPE ZOOMS

Type zooms on a few words provide a very dramatic effect. This effect can make your text look as if it's popping right out of the screen.

Use type zooms only for very special occasions. They can become tiring and irritating when overdone.

THE
REAL
WORLD   THE CASE OF THE MISSING FONT

Wednesday, October 3, 4:00 pm: Jim takes a call from Larry Thomas at Slides R Us, Hypothetical's imaging service bureau. Since Jim's samples are due back at the end of the day, a phone call this late does not bode well.

"Hello, Larry. Why do I have a feeling this is bad news?" inquires Jim.

"You're learning fast, Jim. What fonts did you use on this job?"

"Everything's in Helvetica...Ooops."

"Right the first time. Your Hypothetical text at the bottom must be in a different font. It came out as Courier on the slides, and all the letter spacing is messed up."

"You're right, Larry. The logo is in Serif Gothic Light. That's our corporate font."

Larry laughs and says "No problem. How soon do you really need these slides?"

"I have a meeting with the bigshots after lunch tomorrow," replies Jim.

"OK, here's what we'll do." Larry pauses a moment. "I checked our font support list and we do have that font. I'll reshoot the slides tonight and have them on our first processing run. I can have the slides to you by ten o'clock tomorrow morning."

"If you have the font, how come it didn't come out the first time?" Jim asks.

"You didn't list it when you sent in your order. We have over six hundred fonts available to our customers. We can't keep them all on line at once, so we only load the fonts needed for each job we shoot. Make sure you always tell us every typeface you use in a job, and this won't happen again."

"Thanks, Larry. Other than the font problem, how do they look?"

"Very nice work, Jim. I like the red background, but I'll bet your bigshots go for the blue. Do you want me to send the bad samples over now?"

"No. It's not worth a delivery charge. Just send them with the reshoots. Thanks for your help. Bye."

"Thanks, Jim. Bye."

SUMMARY

Depending on your software, there are thousands of typefaces available for creating presentations. While you are selecting the right ones for your presentation, keep the following tips in mind:

■   The most important criterion for selecting any presentation type-face is readability.

- Screen and outline fonts combine to give you optimum readability, both on your screen and on your slide.

- Check to see which fonts are supported by your service bureau or output device. Process test slides before finalizing your type choices.

- Choose the typeface to match your message: serif faces for tradition and stability, sans serif faces for a modern, progressive look, and display and decorative faces for special effects.

- Avoid trendy, fashionable fonts for presentation designs that have to last. When in doubt, you can't go wrong with Helvetica or Times fonts.

- Don't use more than two typefaces on a slide. Avoid the "ransom note" look.

- Avoid using all capital letters in your slides; stick to headline or sentence caps.

- Always align bullet list items flush left.

- Avoid using full justification on text blocks in slides. The large type size and relatively short line length will create too many gaps in justified text.

chapter 9

Creating Text Slides

In an average presentation, more than 75 percent of the slides are text slides. Avoid the temptation to depend too much on text slides. A presentation made up entirely of them will be boring. Always mix illustrations, charts, and graphs in with your text slides to relieve the visual monotony.

Several types of text slides are useful for presentations. No one kind should be used exclusively; including different types of text slides adds interest and variety to your presentation. This chapter provides guidelines for creating text slides and specific layout suggestions for the various types.

UNDERSTANDING THE PARTS OF A TEXT SLIDE

Although there are several different types of text slides, they all share some common features. Text slides might include a title, subtitle, subheads, bulleted text, sub-bulleted text, and standard paragraphs. Figure 9.1 shows typical text slide elements.

THE TITLE

The title states the basic message of the slide. It should be the largest text on the slide, drawing the viewer's eye from the center of the frame and reinforcing the message. You can also draw attention to your title by using a different typeface or color than other text on the slide, or by framing it with

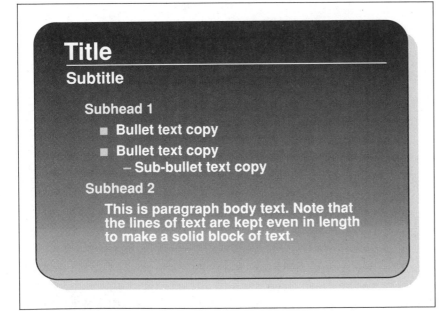

Figure 9.1:

Components of a text slide

a line (as in Figure 9.1) or box. See Chapter 8 for more information about title typefaces; see Chapter 7 for details on using color.

The positioning of the title, which should be consistent throughout the presentation, is dictated by your format design. As described in Chapter 6, the most common positions for a slide title are in the upper-left corner or centered in the upper quarter of the frame.

The length of your titles will affect the appearance of your slides. If a title is too long, it obscures the basic message with excess information.

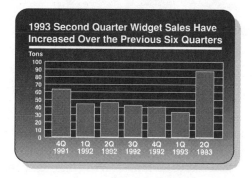

However, if you trim a title too much, it says nothing to the audience, and leaves your information open to misinterpretation.

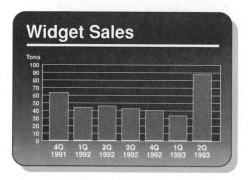

As in newspapers, some people read only the headlines; so make sure your headline tells the most important part of the story. Use simple, declarative statements for your title.

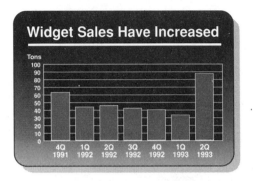

THE SUBTITLE

If you need to expand on the title information, use a subtitle. The subtitle modifies or adds to the title. It should be set in a smaller text size than the title so that it is subordinate to the title. Be consistent in the placement of your subtitle, keeping it in a fixed position relative to the title.

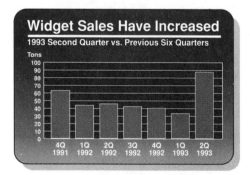

Use a subtitle to divide information into digestible chunks. With a subtitle, you can communicate a definitive message without sacrificing accuracy.

THE SUBHEAD

Some text slides need subheads to clarify the body text. Using a subhead allows you to categorize and divide sections of body copy. A subhead differs from a subtitle in that it modifies the body text rather than the title.

Since subheads are associated with body text, their placement depends on the positioning of the body text within the slide frame. Here are some methods that you can use, by themselves or in combination, to make the subhead stand out from the rest of the body text:

- Using a different font
- Changing the weight of the font (usually bolder)
- Changing the text color
- Indenting the body copy

Don't make the subhead text a larger point size than the body copy or you will overemphasize it. Also, avoid using underlines to highlight subheads or any other body copy. As explained in Chapter 8, many film recorders don't support underlining, and it makes text difficult to read.

THE BODY COPY

The body copy is the core of the text slide. After reading the message of the slide in the title, the audience looks to the body copy for details. This is where you make your point. Body text size should be somewhat smaller than your title or subtitle, but don't make it too small. Remember, if it's important enough to go on the slide, it should be readable.

Generally, body copy should be centered in the area below the title, as shown in Figure 9.2. The visual center of a slide is slightly higher than

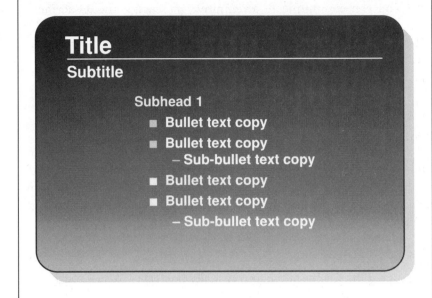

the physical center. This means that if you put the body copy in the exact center of the frame, the slide may look bottom-heavy. If this happens, move the body copy up a bit to balance the overall look of the slide. It's much better to have your copy slightly higher in the frame than lower. In Figure 9.2, the centered body copy is closer to the title bar than to the bottom of the frame, which is correct body copy positioning.

AVOIDING TEXT OVERLOAD

The most important thing to remember while creating your text slides is that you have only a limited amount of space available. If you try to put too much text on a slide, your audience members will spend all their time reading. Very few people can read and listen simultaneously; so while they're reading, they're not listening. Keep the text on your slides simple so that your audience can focus on the content of the speech.

There are no strict rules about how much text is too much, but you can check whether the amount of text is readable. If you are working on a standard 13- or 14-inch computer monitor, view each slide in full-screen size (or as close as possible), sitting 6 to 7 feet away from the monitor.

If your program has a screen show utility, use it to preview your presentation for legibility. If you can clearly read the text on your screen, it will project well in an average meeting room, on a standard 40-inch projection screen. If you have to squint to read it, zoom in, or otherwise increase the size of the text on the screen, try to reduce the information on the slide. You can split the information between two slides or design another way of showing the information.

DESIGNING TITLE SLIDES

Every presentation should have a title slide that introduces the speaker and states the topic of the presentation. Showing a title slide allows the audience to get settled and prepare themselves for the speaker. The title slide can be projected while the speaker is being introduced. If you're giving a solo presentation and running the slides from the podium, show the title slide and then shuffle your papers for a few seconds to allow the audience to get comfortable before introducing yourself.

TITLE SLIDE LAYOUT

The design of a title slide should be kept very simple. Allow one-third to one-half the slide area for the presentation title. Place it in the upper portion of the frame. Use the remainder of the frame for the speaker's name, position, and any other necessary information. Figure 9.3 illustrates an effective layout for a title slide.

Your title slide should reflect the overall appearance of the presentation, but it doesn't have to be in the same design as your regular text slides. Title text size can (and probably should) be larger. However, you should

use colors and type styles that are consistent with those in the presentation to avoid an abrupt transition from the title slide to the remaining slides.

Title slides may also include company logos, conference graphics, meeting names, dates, and similar information, but keep the other elements subordinate to the title. The point of your title slide is to introduce the topic and the speaker; everything else should be secondary. The exception is if your presentation introduces your organization or company to a new audience, in which case, you can make the corporate logo more prominent by placing it above the title, as shown in Figure 9.4.

Figure 9.5 shows a typical title slide. Notice that the title is emphasized by the box that encloses it. A smaller version of this box around the title can be repeated in the regular text slides. The title slide identifies the specific areas the speaker will be addressing: Widget Division Annual Sales. The line immediately beneath the title tells the audience who the speaker is and his relationship to the company: The Divisional Sales Manager.

Figure 9.4:

Placing a logo above the title

Figure 9.5:

Sample title slide

Finally, there's a conference identification: 1993 Sales and Planning Conference. The audience members probably already know what conference they are attending, but it's a traditional touch to keep this information on title slides, especially when there are several different speakers at a conference.

SECTION TITLE SLIDES

In long presentations, consider breaking up the flow of informational slides with section title slides. These provide signposts to let the audience members know where they are in the presentation. For example, suppose you are creating a presentation of 60 to 70 slides with the following agenda:

■ Division Sales and Marketing Philosophy

■ 1992 Sales Results

■ 1993 Marketing Plans

■ 1993 Sales Forecast

In such a thorough presentation, it would be easy for the audience to lose its bearings in a flurry of numbers and statistics. When you add section title slides for each agenda item, the audience will be less likely to confuse 1992 sales results with 1993 sales predictions.

One way to create section title slides is to list all the topics in order in a moving highlight series, as illustrated in Figure 9.6. Place each slide with a highlighted topic in front of the appropriate section of the presentation. Moving highlights are described in more detail later in the chapter.

As with title slides, section title text should be larger than body copy text, and the colors and general layout should be consistent with the rest of the presentation. Figure 9.7 shows an example of a section title slide for the same presentation as the title slide shown in Figure 9.5. To maintain consistency, the section title is enclosed in a box similar to the one in the main title slide, and the typeface and colors on the slide are the same as those used on the title slide.

Figure 9.6:

Moving highlight series for section title slides

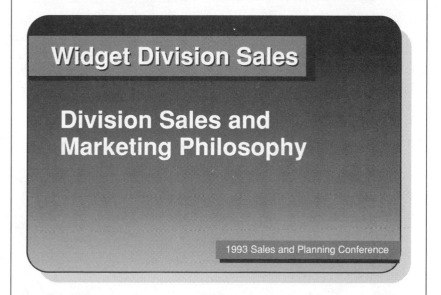

Figure 9.7:

Sample section title slide

In a particularly long presentation, you can add some variety by giving each section a different color scheme. This technique is practical only if you have at least a dozen slides in each section; fewer will give a disjointed impression to your show. When you use different colors for sections, a section title slide is essential. Without a slide to announce the change, the audience members may not detect a new agenda item immediately, and they will think your slides changed color for no particular reason. See Chapter 7 for more information about choosing color schemes.

HANDLING SINGLE TEXT BLOCK SLIDES

Some of your text slides may contain a single text block with a direct statement or quotation. Usually, the text block should be centered under the title.

In this sort of slide, you should try to limit the total amount of copy to a single paragraph with no more than two or three sentences. If you need to, edit the copy. One way to shorten a long quotation is to break it up into its most important points, using an ellipsis (...) to represent the missing parts. Leave in just the parts that make the point, as in the following example:

> "If...the motion of the earth were circular, it would be violent ...and could not be eternal, since...nothing violent is eternal ...It follows, therefore, that the earth is not moved with a circular motion."
>
> *St. Thomas Aquinas*

If you wish to attribute the quotation to its author, the standard position for the author's name is in the lower-right area beneath the quotation. Set it apart from the other text by using italics, smaller type, color, or any combination of these styles.

> **Our Philosophy**
>
> **"To make the best possible widget at the best possible price and to provide the best possible service."**
>
> *– S. Whiplash, President*

CREATING BULLETED TEXT SLIDES

The most effective tool for emphasizing specific points in a speech is the bulleted text slide. In this type of slide, each important point in a speech (or each single sentence) is set off by a preceding small mark or bullet. The bulleted format visually reinforces the main elements of a speech, which helps the audience remember supporting facts more readily.

> **The Finest Products**
>
> - The Original Red Widget
> - SX2000 Frictionless Widget
> - Battlemax GI Widget
> - WidgetWorld Action Toys
> - EduWidget for Preschool

Limit your bulleted items to no more than seven lines of copy, with ten to twelve words per line. If you need more than seven lines, divide the items among two or more slides. An effective text slide provides clear, concise information. Don't clutter up your copy with meaningless phrases and puffery. As Sgt. Joe Friday says on *Dragnet:* "Just the facts, ma'am!"

Although bulleted text slides work well in presentations, you don't want to show a procession of endless lists of bulleted text, with no variety. Make sure you mix in other types of slides to avoid "Listitis."

BULLET MARKS

As great as the temptation may be to use fancy bullet marks, remember that their only purpose is to help the audience identify individual points on the slide. For that purpose, a simple dot or dash will be enough.

If you want something a little different from the standard round dot for your bullets, use another basic geometric shape: square, triangle, diamond, or a simple arrow. Check marks may also be suitable. Avoid bullets that look like ancient Viking runes, wrought-iron fence posts, or pointing fingers. They'll look fine for the first few slides, but the audience will soon tire of them. Figure 9.8 shows some symbols that work well as bullet marks.

Use a different type of bullet mark for each sublevel of your outline. This will help the audience understand a sub-bullet is part of the main point, not another main point. For example, if you're using a large round dot for your main bullet points, use a long dash or a small square for your sub-bullets.

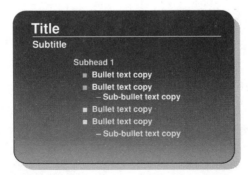

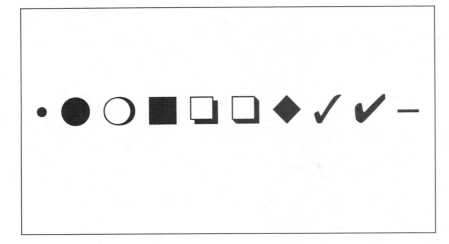

LINE SPACING IN BULLETED TEXT SLIDES

When setting up a bulleted text slide, you should add extra space after each bulleted item to help the audience keep your points separate. Usually, an extra half line is plenty to separate bulleted items. If you have sub-bullets, the spacing between the main point and the sub-bullet points should be *less* than between main points, so that the sub-bullet points are visually tied to the main point. Figure 9.9 illustrates the recommended line spacing for bulleted text slides.

If you find the line spacing you've chosen is just a little too much for the text you've entered, and the last line of copy is too close to the bottom of the slide, reduce your line spacing a bit. Reducing the line spacing is a much better solution than decreasing the text size. The audience members may notice things are a bit more cramped, but they won't care as long as everything is readable.

Some desktop presentation programs do not support half lines between bulleted items. If you are using one of these programs, you will have to set your main bulleted text in double spacing and the sub-bullets in single spacing.

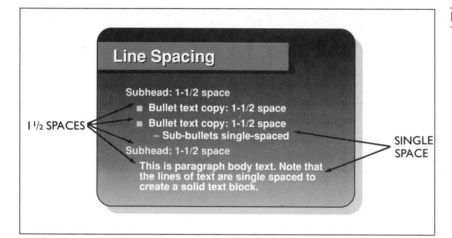

Figure 9.9:

Recommended line spacing

BALANCING THE COPY BLOCK

The copy on a text slide should form a clean, well-balanced block. For example, if you are creating a bulleted text slide with one long item and several other shorter items, the longer item should be split on two lines so that its right margin does not extend too far past the other items. Figure 9.10 illustrates how a long bulleted item can be divided.

You also should watch out for *orphans*, which are single words at the end of a paragraph or bulleted item left on a line of their own. Adjust the

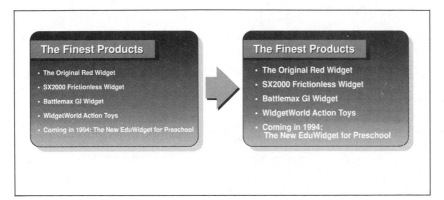

Figure 9.10:

Balancing a long bulleted item

margin of your text block to force extra words into the short line, as illustrated in Figure 9.11.

Because of all the variables involved in their design, you cannot rely on your desktop presentation program to automatically generate perfect text slides. You should check every slide for balanced copy blocks and orphans.

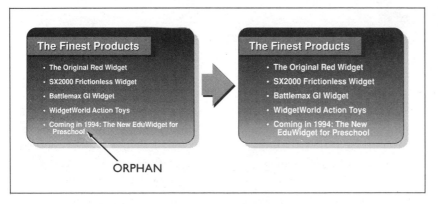

Figure 9.11:

Eliminating orphans

CREATING TEXT BUILD AND REVEAL SLIDES

When playing poker, a cardinal rule is not to tip your hand—don't let your opponent see your cards. The same rule applies when giving a speech: avoid letting the audience know in advance what's in the speech. It is only natural for an audience to read all the material on a slide at once. You can prevent the audience from getting ahead of the speaker and make sure they listen to what is being said by using build, reveal, and moving highlight slides.

BUILD SERIES SLIDES

A *build series* consists of bulleted text slides that each reveals one item at a time to the audience. By controlling the amount of information the audience gets at a single time, you can focus attention on the topic at hand, prevent the audience from getting ahead of the speaker, and provide extra visual interest to what may be an ordinary text slide. Here are some situations in which you should use text build slides:

■ When you must spend a long time (1½ or more minutes) on a single slide

■ When you want to keep an audience in suspense

■ When you need to give a step-by-step description of a process or series of events

Create the slide exactly as if you were doing a regular (nonbuild) text slide. Position and balance the copy. Then make duplicates of the original and delete individual bulleted items from the bottom up. Figure 9.12 shows an example of a text slide build series.

Don't reposition the copy either vertically or horizontally; keep the top line in the same place. When you project the slides, new lines should appear

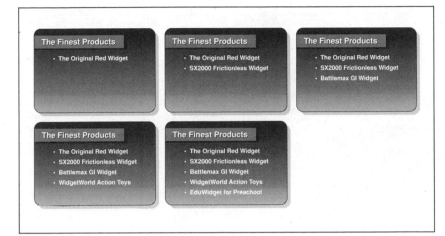

below the text already in the frame. If you move the items, it will look as if your text is jumping around in the frame as you change from one slide to the next. The blank space below the visible items also creates anticipation in the viewers for what's coming next and makes subsequent points more effective by fulfilling their curiosity.

Some desktop presentation programs, such as Aldus Persuasion, allow you to set up build slides automatically by assigning lines of text to different layers. The program will generate the extra images necessary to create the build.

TONEBACK REVEAL SLIDES

A variation on the standard build series is the *toneback reveal series*. Create toneback reveal slides in the same way you set up a standard build, except when you reveal a new item, dim the previous items (bullets and text) by changing their color, as shown in Figure 9.13. This technique allows the speaker to focus the audience's attention even more directly on the current point.

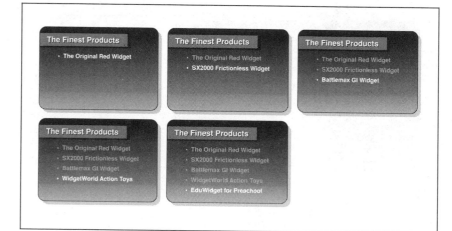

Figure 9.13:

Toneback reveal series

For slides with dark backgrounds, choose a lighter tint of the background color to tone back the previous items. On a black or dark gray background, tone back your bulleted items to medium or light gray. On a dark blue background, use a light to medium blue for toned back items. Make the revealed item white or yellow so that it stands out.

For overhead transparencies, the toneback color should be a darker shade of your light background color. Use black or your normal text color for revealed items.

MOVING HIGHLIGHT SLIDES

A simple variation on the toneback reveal series is the *moving highlight series*. All the items are always visible, but the current point is highlighted with a brighter color and the rest are toned back. Figure 9.14 shows an example of a moving highlight series.

STEPBACK REVEAL SLIDES

A *stepback reveal series* is useful for explaining complex information without confusing the audience. A stepback reveal series works like a standard or toneback reveal series, except each main point may have several sub-bullets

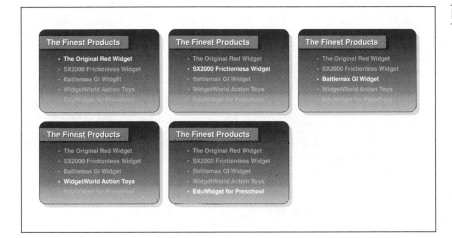

Figure 9.14:

Moving highlight series

beneath it. Each new main point and its sub-bullets are revealed, and the previous main points, without their sub-bullets, are toned back, as illustrated in Figure 9.15. This type of reveal series allows the speaker to address details. Because the previous main points remain visible, the audience is reminded of what came before and won't get lost along the way.

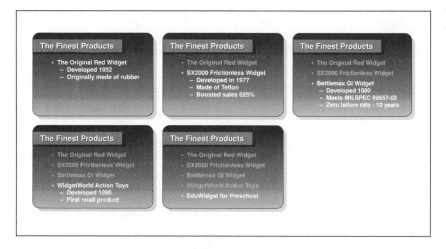

Figure 9.15:

Stepback reveal series

A stepback reveal series is difficult to plan because you must determine the type size and layout of the slide on a worst-case basis. You have to allow for the maximum number of lines taken up by a series of sub-bullets as well as the main points.

In the example in Figure 9.15, the third main point has three sub-bullets, creating a total of six items on the slide (two toned back main points, the current main point, and three sub-bullets). The next (fourth) main point in the series has two sub-bullets, also for a total of six items on the slide. The last point has no sub-bullets. The fourth main point, which has an extra half line of space, is the worst case. The text size, line spacing, and other layout settings are based on the fourth slide. This ensures that the text does not jump around in the frame as each new item is revealed.

Use stepback reveal series when it is important for the audience to see levels of information. However, if it's possible, you should divide the information into separate slides instead of relying on a stepback reveal series.

CREATING TABULAR TEXT SLIDES

Tabular text slides offer a way of visually arranging text to clarify relationships. They are useful for presenting complex information that requires a visible structure. Figure 9.16 shows an example of a tabular text slide.

TABLE LAYOUT

You might think that the tabular framework can hold more text than a regular text slides, but this is not true. Tabular text slides should follow the same design rules as any other text slide. Limit the text to seven lines per slide, *including* column heads. Try not to use more than six columns. If you have a condensed typeface, such as Helvetica Narrow, you can

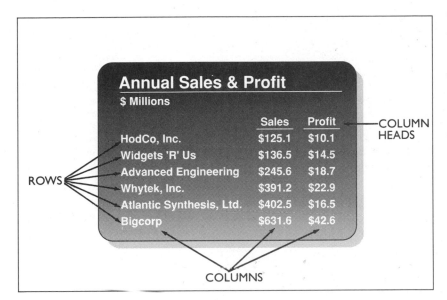

use it to make narrower columns, but remember that condensed type-faces are harder to read at a distance.

The columns should be far enough apart to separate them and prevent text from running together, but too much space between columns makes it difficult for the eye to track from one column to another. A good rule-of-thumb is for the space between columns to be at least the width of two numbers, but no more than half the width of the narrowest column. Figure 9.17 shows proper and improper column spacing.

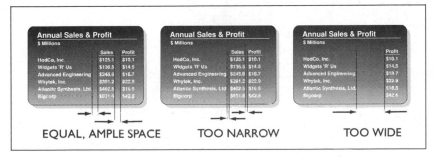

Figure 9.17:

Column spacing

TABLES WITH GRIDS

One way of helping your audience read a table is to enclose the text in a grid. The grid lines make it easier for the audience to line up columns and rows, especially in large table. Figure 9.18 shows an example of a table with a grid.

Keep your grid lines unobtrusive; they are just guides and shouldn't compete with the content. You could tone back the grid with color, as in a toneback reveal series, which will make the table easier to read.

Use grids in tables only when they are a real aid to understanding. A simple two-column table will look cluttered if you surround it with superfluous lines.

Figure 9.18:

Table with a grid

Annual Sales & Profit
$ Millions

	Sales	Profit
HodCo, Inc.	$125.1	$10.1
Widgets 'R' Us	$136.5	$14.5
Advanced Engineering	$245.6	$18.7
Whytek, Inc.	$391.2	$22.9
Atlantic Synthesis, Ltd.	$402.5	$16.5
Bigcorp	$631.6	$42.6

USING CHARTS INSTEAD OF TABLES

Tabular text slides are usually too complex to be read at a glance. Most tabular data is better understood when presented in the form of a chart or graph. Charts and graphs are easier to read and understand quickly, as well as easier to remember once the presentation is over. Figure 9.19 shows a bar chart created from the data in the table in Figure 9.18.

Whenever you feel the need to include a table in a presentation, try creating a chart or graph (or series of them) to take its place. You will often find that the graphic representation communicates your message more effectively.

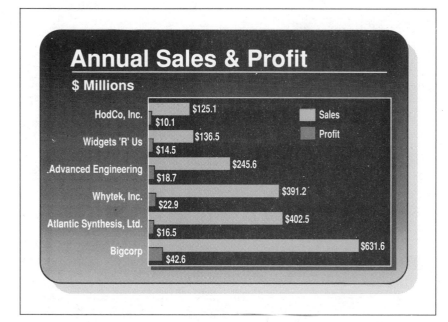

Figure 9.19:

Bar chart slide created from table slide data

THE REAL WORLD   THE SEVEN-POINT TEXT SOLUTION

Wednesday, October 10, 10:00 am: Alan Smithee was very busy on the trip home from Japan. He spent the trip refining and adding to his presentation, and when he arrived at the office this morning, he sent his additions down to the Art Department. Jim has just received Alan's additional slides.

Jim immediately makes a trip up to the fourteenth floor. Alan has done a good job of roughing out the slides he wants to accompany his speech, but one tabular text chart is much too cluttered.

"Alan, I've been going over the new stuff, and everything looks great except this chart," says Jim as he places the rough draft on the desk.

COMPETITIVE COMPARISON

	Strengths	Weaknesses	Annual Sales
Acme Corporation	• Strong Cash Flow Position • Stable Management	• Older Technology • Poor R&D Effort	$90,000,000 (-5% vs. 1988)
Consolidated Industries, Inc.	• New, Innovative Product Line • Strong R&D	• Inexperienced Management • Poor Marketing	$50,000,000 (+15% vs. 1988)
Diversified Products, Inc.	• Young, Aggressive Management • Talented MarketingTeam	• Heavily Leveraged • Dependent on 3rd Party Technology	$20,000,000 (+6% vs. 1988)
Unitech, Ltd.	• Strong Europe Market Base • Very Strong R&D/Product Lines	• London HQ = Long Lines of Command • No U.S. Market Experience	$10,000,000 (+250% vs.1988)

"I know, it's complicated, but I really do need to cover all this information. I've cut it as much as I can."

"When this is projected, the text is going to be much too small for most people in the auditorium to read. We could include a handout in the information packet to help them follow along."

"I'd rather not have paper copies of our competitive analysis floating around after the meeting." says Alan. "I don't want Consolidated to find out our opinion of their management—it might be just the thing to make them work harder. And we don't want our competition working harder! What other options are there?"

"Well, looking at your speech, I can see that you're probably going to spend almost two minutes covering this information. If you leave it this way, the stockholders will have read everything you want to tell them by the time you finish with the Acme Corporation. Why don't we break this down into several slides?"

"What do you have in mind?"

Jim pulls out a storyboard pad and sketches a rough drawing.

Competitive Analysis
Acme Corporation
- **Strengths**
  - Strong Cash Flow
  - Stable Management
- **Weaknesses**
  - Older Technology
  - Poor R&D Effort
- **Annual Sales**
  - $90,000,000 (-5% vs. 1991)

"Let's make individual slides for each competitor. We can lay it out like this...."

Alan stops him. "That's terrific, except I want to show the relative sales of the four companies, and I will spend some time talking about how those sales figures compare to ours."

Jim stops to think for a second. "Why don't you try combining all of your scattered comments about annual sales into a single paragraph or two, and I'll give you a bar chart, like this, to show the comparison."

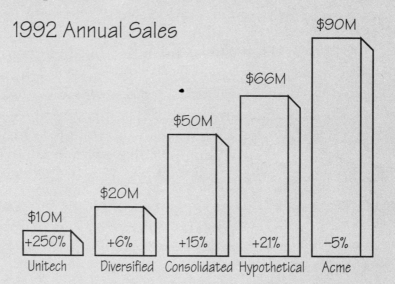

"That's fine, Jim. I'll talk about strengths and weaknesses first, then switch to sales figures. You can even leave the annual sales figures out of the actual text slides. I'll talk about them on the bar chart."

"OK Alan, I'll have proof copies of all the slides to you by this afternoon. Thanks."

SUMMARY

Text slides are the backbone of any presentation. Since your text slides have so much influence on the look of your show, it's crucial that they are well-designed. Here are the guidelines for creating attractive, readable text slides:

- Step back from your monitor to judge the readability of slides. The view 6 or 7 feet away from a standard monitor will give you an accurate idea of what the slides will look like when projected.

- Use title and section title slides to divide your presentation and introduce new topics.

- Make your message the slide title. Keep it short and to the point.

- Use a subtitle when more information is necessary to clarify your message.

- The body copy is the information that supports your message. Use subheads where necessary to organize your text.

- Don't overload your slides with too much text. A good rule of thumb is no more than seven lines of copy and ten to twelve words per line. Split large amounts of text into multiple slides.

- Use simple bullet marks for bulleted text slides.

- Create a balanced copy block with lines of even length. Avoid long lines and orphans.

- Use build, reveal, and moving highlight series to control the flow of information and increase audience interest and suspense.

- Limit your tables to seven rows of text (including column heads) and six columns of data. Use charts and graphs instead of tables whenever possible.

chapter 10

Charts and Graphs:
Visualizing Data

It has been said that the average person doesn't truly understand any number larger than twenty: the highest number that can be counted on fingers and toes. Although this boundary of comprehensibility is debatable, it is true that the large numbers used in business presentations are often beyond the easy comprehension of the average person. Financial and statistical information can be difficult to understand when presented as text. Long rows and columns of figures are often more confusing than enlightening.

Charts and graphs make abstract figures more understandable by providing visual cues to the values and relationships expressed in the numbers. Whenever you need to present any form of numerical data to an audience, you should consider using a chart. Information presented in chart form is clearer and more memorable than text.

There are a variety of chart types that are suitable for presentations. The type you select should be appropriate for your message and the structure of the data. Different messages and data are better suited to certain types of charts and graphs. To help you choose the right chart for your message, this chapter includes a guide to the main types of charts used in general business presentations, with descriptions of variations and enhancements. But before describing the specific types of charts, we will review the concepts and elements that are common to the layout of most charts.

CREATING MESSAGE-DRIVEN CHARTS AND GRAPHS

When you are creating charts, the one message per slide guideline is expanded to one message and one chart per slide. The one message per slide concept is particularly important when you are creating charts and graphs for your slides. A chart that tries to say or do too much will inevitably confuse and mislead the audience. And, although you may have to make exceptions to the one chart per slide rule, you should exhaust all your single-chart options before deciding to use multiple charts on a slide.

The most effective chart slides, like other slides, are those that are *message-driven*. Each chart slide must have a single, well-defined message to present to the audience. From that message, you develop a chart that contains only the data necessary to support the message.

For example, a slide with the message Midwestern Division Sales Volume is Rising could have a bar or line chart showing the rise in sales volume for the Midwest region. Any other information, such as sales for other regions, is unnecessary and should be left out. On the other hand, if the message of the chart is Midwestern Sales Volume Is Growing Faster than Eastern Division Sales Volume, the information about the other region would be appropriate. Figure 10.1 shows how charts can give a clear picture of the message.

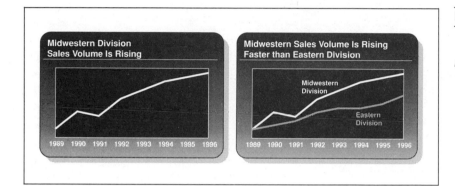

Figure 10.1:

Sales volume charts are message-driven

Always make sure that the title of any chart slide clearly describes the message of the chart. The audience members may draw their own conclusions from your graphics unless you tell them what they are supposed to see. The combination of the title and the graphics in the chart will make your message much more memorable.

IDENTIFYING THE GRAPHIC ELEMENTS

All charts are visual representations of numerical data. If you can't measure something, you can't chart it. The numerical data is represented on the chart by a graphic item, such as a rectangle in a column or bar chart, a portion of a circle in a pie chart, or a line in a line chart. Each graphic item in a chart represents two pieces of information:

- The name of a measurable item (called a category), which is identified on the chart by a *label*

- A quantity associated with the item (called a data point), which is plotted on the chart as a *value*

The graphics in a chart are created on a plotting area which defines the boundaries of the chart and provides a framework for customizing the look of your charts. There are two basic types of plotting areas: rectangular and circular. The circular plotting area is mainly used for pie charts. All of the other chart types described in this chapter use a rectangular plotting area.

LAYING OUT RECTANGULAR PLOTTING AREAS

The design and layout of any chart has more to do with the way you choose to display its details than with the graphics you use to represent your data. Develop a standard layout for a rectangular plotting area and use it as a guide for all your rectangular charts. For example, once you have set up a basic layout for a column chart, you can use it as a model for the other charts with a rectangular plotting area: bar, line, area, scatter, pictograph, and so on.

As shown in Figure 10.2, a rectangular plotting area includes four basic elements:

- The *chart frame*, which defines the boundaries of the plotting area
- The *scale*, which serves as a ruler for the audience to measure the relative size or position of the plotted values
- The *baseline*, which is the zero point on the scale
- The *labels*, which name the items being plotted
- The *grid or tick marks*, which mark increments of the scale

These elements can be set up in a variety of layouts, as described in the following sections.

RECTANGULAR CHART FRAMES

The basic chart frame consists of a box that defines the area in which your data will be plotted, the size of your chart, and its placement in the

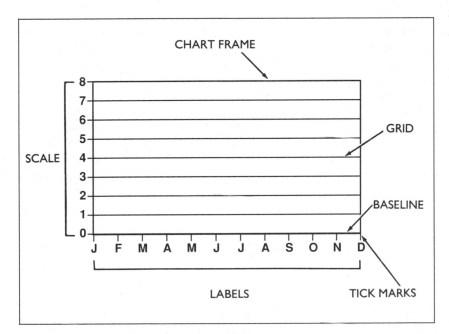

Figure 10.2:

Basic elements of a rectangular plotting area

slide frame. You can lay out this box in several ways:

- A *full frame* is a filled or unfilled box that surrounds the plotting area. For presentation purposes, this is the best all-around choice. It will support many different chart types and is easily adaptable to a wide variety of scaling and grid options. Filling a full chart frame with a dark or black background provides the greatest amount of contrast for your data.

- A *half frame* is unfilled and defines only the left and bottom portions of the frame. This traditional framing has an old-fashioned look to it. A half frame is useful for most kinds of charts that need a scale but not an accurate grid. This type of frame is not recommended for scatter charts, which require a full grid to be readable.

- A *baseline-only frame* is a single line at the bottom edge of the frame. Because just labels are shown, this type of frame should be used with only column, bar, area, and pictograph charts that originate at the baseline and include visible data values. Scatter and line charts need more visual connection between the baseline and the graphics representing the data. By using baseline-only frames with simple bar and column charts, you can avoid cluttering up your presentation with unnecessary graphics.

■ A chart with *no frame* is enclosed in an invisible box. The guidelines for showing a chart without a frame are similar to those for using a baseline-only frame. It is particularly important that you omit the frame *only* when your chart graphics originate at the baseline, since the frame's baseline must be implied by the position of your graphics.

The four types of rectangular chart frames are illustrated in Figure 10.3.

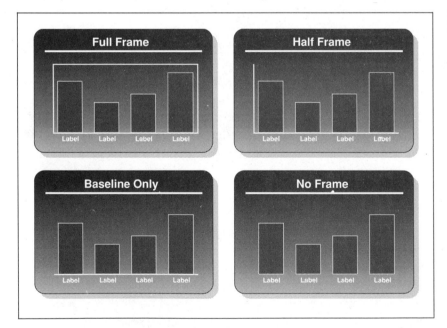

Figure 10.3:

Rectangular chart frames

RECTANGULAR CHART SCALES

The values in a chart are plotted against a *grid* or *scale*, which allows the viewer to measure the relative size or position of the data. The basic grid for most charts consists of an *x-axis* and a *y-axis*. The x-axis extends from left to right; the y-axis extends from bottom to top.

Your chart scale should be located along the y-axis for column, line, and area charts. Bar charts use a scale along the x-axis. Pictograph and combination charts can use either axis, depending on your data. Scatter charts require a scale along both axes. Figure 10.4 illustrates chart scale locations.

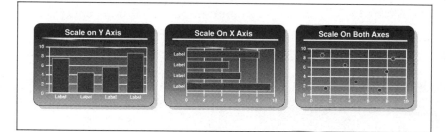

Figure 10.4:

Scales on x, y and both axes

Most presentation graphics, charting, and spreadsheet programs will automatically select the proper scale for the chart type you choose and allow you to customize it as necessary. You may have to adjust the automatic scales created by software designed to produce printed output. The following sections provide guidelines for setting up a chart scale that will be readable and enhance the message of your chart.

Keep Scale Increments Evenly Spaced

The spacing and values of your scale should be evenly distributed visually and numerically to give a true picture of the data you are presenting. The values of your scale do not have to be in increments of fives or tens, however. Any set of evenly spaced values can be used to create a valid scale. For example, a scale of zero to sixty can be designed in six different ways, using from four to twelve even steps:

0   20   40   60

0   15   30   45   60

0   12   24   36   48   60

0   10   20   30   40   50   60

0   6   12   18   24   30   36   42   48   54   60

0   5   10   15   20   25   30   35   40   45   50   55   60

You might want to use special scale increments, especially when you are creating charts that require two separate scales. For example, if you wanted to compare annual sales in dollars to annual shipments in tons, the chart may need separate scales to clarify your message. Figure 10.5

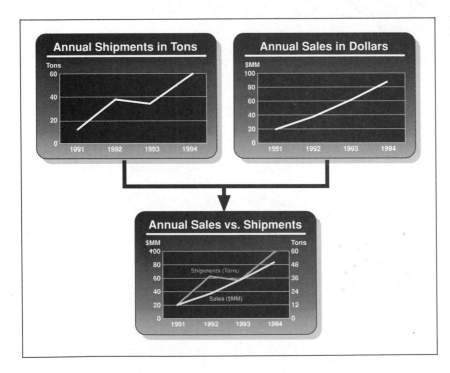

Figure 10.5:

A dual-scale chart created from two charts

shows a dual-scale chart created from two separate charts. Note that the Tons scale has been altered to use the same number of steps as the $MM scale, which simplifies the chart. You can also use colored text to clarify which scale belongs to which line.

Keep Scale Figures and Steps Readable

The text size of your scale figures should be at least half the size of the average body text used in your slides. For example, if the body text in your text slides ranges from 24 to 30 points, the scale figures should be at least 12 to 16 points. If the scale figures are cramped, instead of reducing the size of the type, reduce the number of steps in the scale, as shown in Figure 10.6.

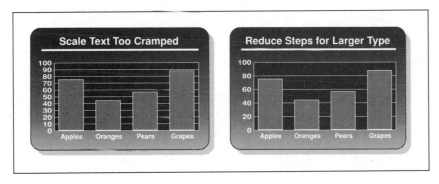

Figure 10.6:

Reduce scale steps for readable type

To make room for readable scale figures, use no more than ten steps in any scale on a slide. However, a scale with fewer than four steps will not provide a useful ruler for the audience. Figure 10.7 illustrates scale step parameters.

GRIDS AND TICK MARKS

Grids and tick marks are used to define exact divisions of the frame into sections that correspond to the scale. A *grid line* extends across the entire chart frame. A *tick mark* is a shorter line that indicates a scale division. Grids and tick marks can also be combined.

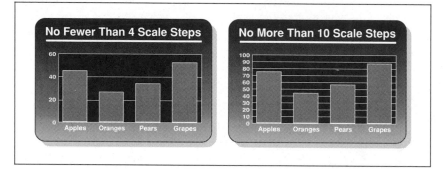

Figure 10.7:

Scale steps should range between four and ten

For charts with full frames, there are a wide variety of ways to lay out grids and tick marks. Figure 10.8 shows some of the variations. Charts with a half frame, baseline-only frame, or no frame support fewer variations, as shown in Figure 10.9.

The *staff grid* (so called because it looks like a musical staff) is a useful variation that can be used in combination with a baseline-only frame. You can create column charts using only a baseline, and then switch to a staff grid for line and area charts that need a y-axis scale. Figure 10.10 shows an example of a baseline-only frame plus staff grid.

OTHER CHART TEXT

There are several kinds of text other than scale values used in charts. Axis titles, axis labels, data values, and callouts all contribute to the clarity of your charts and graphs. The type size for all these elements should be at least as large as your scale figures.

Axis Titles

An axis title identifies the units of a scale or a larger category describing axis labels. Axis titles are especially useful for clarifying scales that have

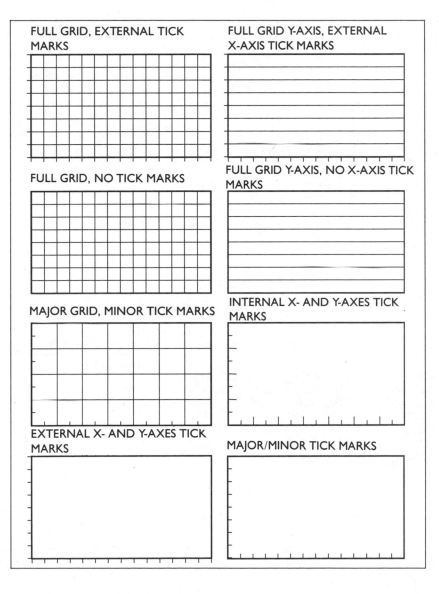

FULL GRID, EXTERNAL TICK MARKS

FULL GRID Y-AXIS, EXTERNAL X-AXIS TICK MARKS

FULL GRID, NO TICK MARKS

FULL GRID Y-AXIS, NO X-AXIS TICK MARKS

MAJOR GRID, MINOR TICK MARKS

INTERNAL X- AND Y-AXES TICK MARKS

EXTERNAL X- AND Y-AXES TICK MARKS

MAJOR/MINOR TICK MARKS

Figure 10.8:

Grid and tick mark variations for full-frame charts

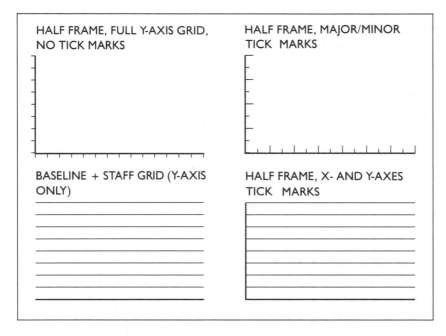

Figure 10.9:

Grid and tick mark variations for half-frame, baseline-only, and no-frame charts

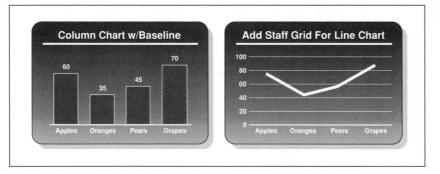

Figure 10.10:

Staff grid as baseline-only variation

large values. For example, a column chart scale ranging from zero to 10 million dollars could be difficult to read with so many zeros. Adding *$ Millions* as the axis title and eliminating the zeros will make the scale much easier to read and comprehend, as shown in Figure 10.11.

Keep your axis titles short and to the point; don't use *Thousands of Dollars* where *$000's* will do. You can use abbreviations such as M or MM for

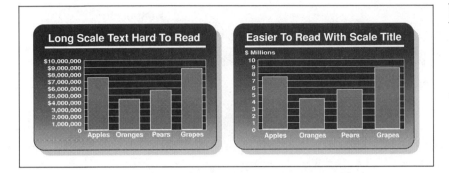

millions, K or 000's for thousands, and /Yr for per year. Abbreviations can save a great deal of space on your charts and graphs.

Axis Labels

On some charts, such as column charts, an *axis label* is placed under each graphic on the x-axis to identify the category being plotted. Labels should be spaced evenly along the axis, just like scale values. There are two ways of setting up axis labels:

- *Object-aligned labels* are usually associated with a graphic object such as a bar or column. This type of label should be used with bar, column, and pictograph charts. An object-aligned label does not need any sort of grid or tick mark.

- *Grid-aligned labels* should be used with line and area charts when it is necessary to line up labels at the bottom of the chart frame with data points some distance away.

Figure 10.12 illustrates both object-aligned labels and grid-aligned labels.

Data Values

Data values show the actual value of a chart item, such as column values or pie percentages. Data values should be placed either inside or directly adjacent to the corresponding chart graphic, as shown in Figure 10.13.

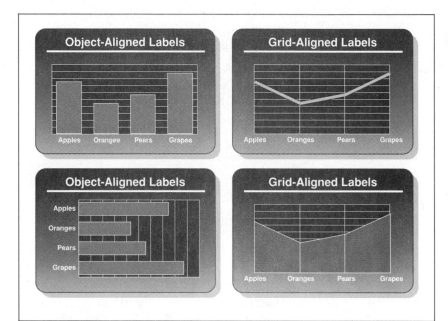

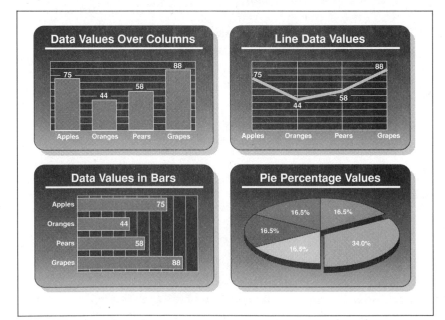

Keep your data-value text short. Large numbers should be rounded to three or four significant figures. Use abbreviations if necessary. Be sure to key the accuracy of your data values to what is being said in the speech. If the speaker is saying "Acme profits soared to nearly 31 million dollars in 1993, the data value on the accompanying chart should read $30.6 M, not $30,609,784.23.

Callouts

A *callout* is descriptive text in a chart that is not data or part of the axes. The most common use of a callout is to identify plotted lines in a line chart when there are more than one. Other callouts identify categories in stacked column charts. A callout can also serve as a notation for a particular data point. Figure 10.14 shows how callouts can be used in charts.

Keep callouts as simple as possible. Remember, you are creating a chart to take the place of text. Don't clutter your charts with more words than you need.

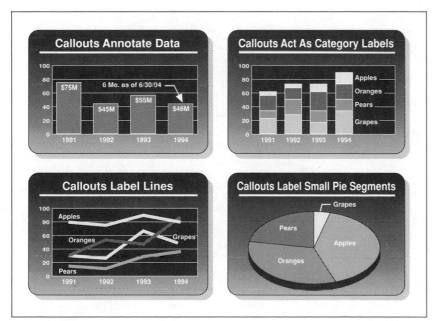

Figure 10.14:

Callouts serve several purposes in charts

LEGENDS

When there is not enough room on a chart for a callout, or if you need to identify several categories within a single chart, you may need to add a *legend*. A legend is a visual key that identifies chart segments when labels and callouts are inadequate. Legends are mainly used for charts that have multiple sets of data points. Most charts complicated enough to require a legend are too complicated for a slide.

Never use a legend where you can use labels or callouts. Legends can be hard to read for the audience, who have to switch their attention back and forth from chart segments to the legend to make sense of the graph.

The most important part of a chart is the plotted data, not the legend. Place your legends inside the plotting area. Legends placed outside the plotting area usually cause the actual chart to be much smaller, giving too much weight to the legend. Figure 10.15 shows some examples of chart legends.

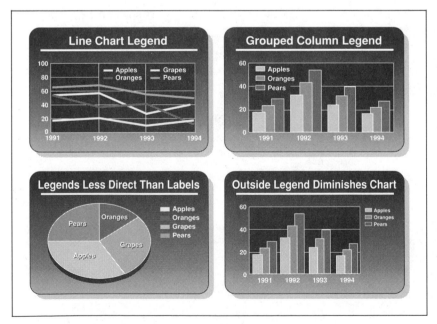

Figure 10.15:

Chart legends

Some presentation graphics programs automatically create a legend, even for a chart with a single set of data points. Delete the legend, and put the name of the set in your slide title or a subtitle.

CREATING COLUMN CHARTS

The column chart is one of the most common and useful types of charts. Column charts are best suited to displaying the relative size or volume of tangible, physical things. Use them to compare weights, dollar values, and object quantities.

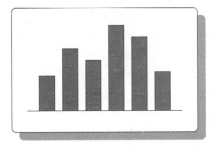

Since it is common to read passing time from left to right, a column chart is ideal for showing the change in size or volume of a single item over a period of time. This type of column chart actually has two scales. The y-axis scale (vertical) measures the data values; the x-axis scale (horizontal) measures the passing of time.

A column chart can also show the relative quantities of several different items at a particular time. The main limitation for this use is that x-axis labels are often quite long compared with date or time labels. Bar charts are usually more appropriate for this type of data. However, if your x-axis labels are short, you can use a column chart for this purpose. Figure 10.16 shows examples of column charts that plot change over time and between categories.

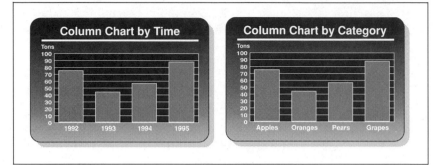

COLUMN CHART LAYOUT

A column chart is made of rectangles that represent an item or series of items. Labels placed under the baseline along the x-axis identify each column. The y-axis consists of a scale to measure the relative height of each column.

The columns in the chart should be evenly spaced and should use most of the width of the plotting area. The space between columns should be no less than 25 percent of the column width and no more than 100 percent, as illustrated in Figure 10.17. However, if you have a large number of closely spaced narrow columns, they will look better with the columns touching (similar to a histogram, described later in the chapter).

Your tallest column should also use as much of the full height of the plotting area as possible. For example, if the largest data value in your chart is 72, make your scale 0 to 75 or 0 to 80. The columns should use at least 75 percent of the plotting area height.

You can use virtually any grid/tick mark combination with a column chart; the complexity of the data should guide your decision. A single set of columns needs little in the way of a scale or grid, especially if you are showing data values on top of the column. Other variations on the

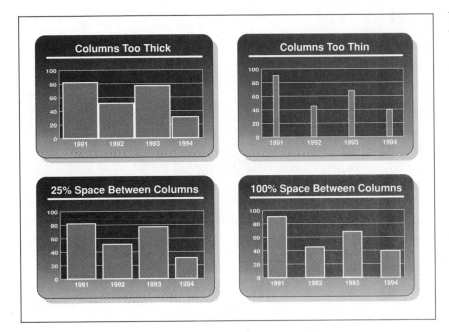

Figure 10.17:

Columns should be evenly spaced

column chart may require more complicated scales and grids. Use only the grid lines and tick marks that are necessary for clear, accurate communication.

You can place data values above your columns, eliminating the need for a grid entirely. By including data values, all you really need is a baseline. Remember to keep your data values short; they should not exceed the width of a column. If necessary, round off data values to three or four significant figures.

COLUMN CHART VARIATIONS

The column chart is one of the most versatile chart types. It can be adapted to provide a wide variety of information and even substitute for a pie chart. The following sections describe some useful variations for presentations.

Stacked Column Charts

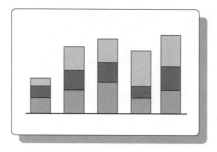

A stacked column chart shows how a series of components adds up to a whole. Each column is composed of segments that represent a series of data values, which add up to a total value.

Limit yourself to a maximum of six segments per column. If you have more than six series of data, combine leftover data into a single data value and label it *Other*. The most important data series should be placed on the baseline, since only those segments can be easily compared.

There are two ways to determine the height of each column:

- *Cumulative segments* are used to show parts of a whole. Each segment adds its value to the total height of the column. For example, three cumulative segments of 20, 25, and 30 show the contributions in the first, second, and third quarters, which add up to a year-to-date total of 75.

- *Incremental values* show a series of steps toward a total. For example, using the same three segments, you can show totals of 20, 45, and 75 at the end of the first, second, and third quarters.

Figure 10.18 illustrates both of these systems for determining column height in a stacked column chart. Although the graphic on both charts is

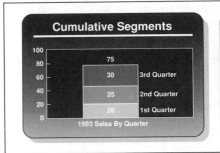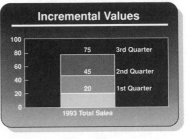

Figure 10.18:

Column height represents cumulative segments or incremental values

identical, the data values used to define the graphic are different, and they should be treated differently. Cumulative segment values should be placed in the center of their respective column segment. Incremental values should be placed on top of their respective column segment. Category labels should align with the data value text. In both cases, the total should be placed above the entire column.

Don't use a legend as a key to your segments. Place callouts to the right of the last column aligning with and identifying the corresponding segments, as shown in Figure 10.19.

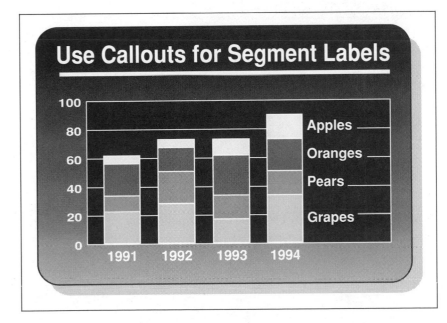

Figure 10.19:

Stacked segment labels

If you need to emphasize the change between segments of a stacked column chart, use connecting lines to make the relationships clearer. You can also fill in the connecting areas, creating a variation similar to an area chart. Filled connectors should be a darker shade of your segment color so they are not mistaken for actual data values. Figure 10.20 shows how connectors can be used on stacked column charts.

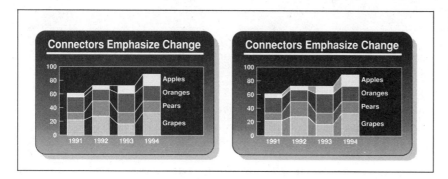

Figure 10.20:

Connectors on stacked column charts

Grouped Column Charts

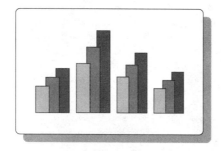

A grouped column chart compares the components of several data value series in relationship to each other. Each group is composed of several columns, each of which represents a different data series.

Keep your grouped column charts as simple as possible. Column groups should have no more than three to four columns or data series. Avoid putting data values at the top of the columns, since too many figures will be hard to read. Use a good, clear scale and grid instead.

Groups can be arranged with the columns either touching or slightly overlapping. Use overlapping columns only if each set is consistently larger or smaller than the others, forming a stairstep effect. The tallest column should be in the back, with shorter columns ranked in front of it. Columns should not overlap more than one-third of their total width.

You will usually need a legend or callouts to identify the series being plotted. Use callouts only if there is a clear area somewhere in the chart for the text and there are no other bars to get in the way. A legend can be set off in a box within the plotting area to help isolate it from the columns and text in the chart.

Figure 10.21 shows several examples of charts with grouped columns to illustrate the variations.

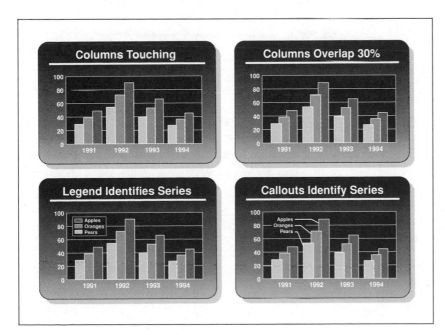

Figure 10.21:

Grouped column charts

Histograms

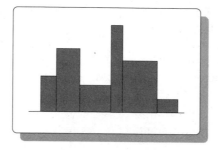

Histograms are a special category of column chart which use a variable scale for both axes. In the examples of column charts you've seen in this chapter, the columns have been evenly spaced and represent specific points in time or individual items, and the width of each bar is irrelevant to the data being presented.

In a histogram, the width of a column also carries information. Typically, the y-axis scale of a histogram measures the relative value of the columns, as in other column charts. The x-axis, however, serves as another scale in which the width represents a span of time or other variable. In Figure 10.22, the column width shows the age range of the sample data, and the height shows the percentage of rock and roll fans in that age range.

The columns in a histogram should always touch, since they act as a continuous data measurement along the x-axis. The labels should be aligned with the center of the column they identify, just as in other types of column charts. You can also use a graduated scale along the x-axis, similar to one used in a bar chart.

DEPTH IN COLUMN CHARTS

The most common enhancement used with any chart is to add depth to your graphics, giving them a more solid and substantial feel.

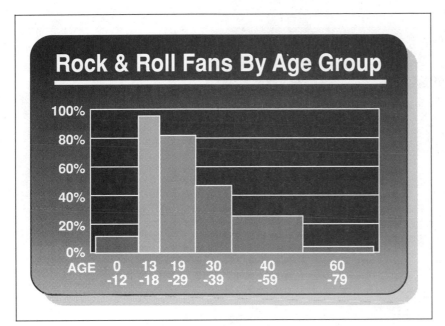

One way to add depth to a column chart is by using the *true perspective* method. As illustrated in Figure 10.23, this type of depth makes the columns appear as if they are true solid objects floating in the slide space. The column surface is extruded backwards into the field of the slide and scaled, making it appear farther away than the front. True perspective depth is not supported in most presentation programs, and it is difficult to get right, since the audience is usually viewing the graphic from different angles, diminishing the effect. True perspective does not work well with any type of y-axis scale because the depth distorts the columns' relationship with the scale.

Oblique depth, the type commonly used in most presentation and charting software, is a simulation of perspective and depth. The surface of the column is extruded, usually up and to the right, but the back is not scaled. Oblique depth is simpler to create than true perspective depth,

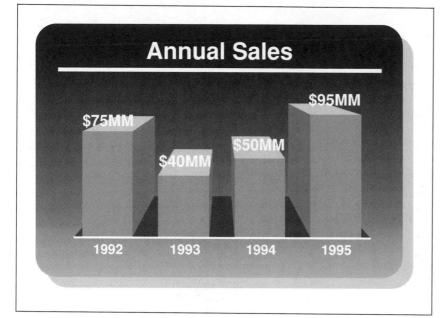

True perspective column chart

and it is compatible with y-axis scales. However, when using depth with a scale, it is very easy to misrepresent data.

Figure 10.24 shows two examples of the same oblique depth column chart, with the scale set up differently in each one. In the chart on the left side of the figure, the scale figures are in the same plane as the front of the columns. Because the natural tendency is to measure the front of the column against the scale, the 1992 column looks like it has a data value of 69. Actually, the grid and scale are keyed to the back plane of the columns, where the height of the 1992 column is read as 75.

The chart on the right side of Figure 10.24 has the scale figures in the back plane, which improves the readability of the chart. However, the values are still not completely clear. On any type of three-dimensional chart, you should include the data values to avoid ambiguity.

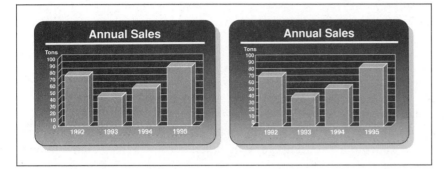

Figure 10.24:

Oblique depth column charts

An alternative way to add depth is by using a *pseudo-3D* chart, as shown in Figure 10.25. This type of chart represents the data more accurately than true perspective or oblique depth charts. In a pseudo-3D chart, the chart frame acts as a window, and the depth is shown extruding down and to the right. The scale and grid refer to the front of the column, and

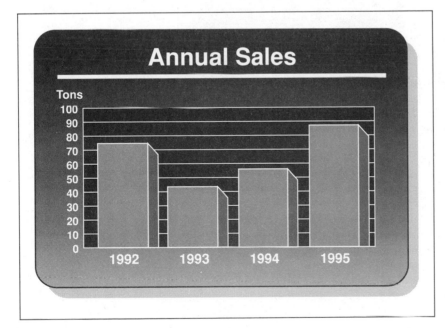

Figure 10.25:

Pseudo-3D column chart

the top of the column reflects a true data value in relation to the grid. This is the only type of three-dimensional chart that works well without data values.

COLUMN CHART BUILDS AND REVEALS

Builds on column charts can be created along the x-axis or y-axis. A regular column chart build reveals each column or group of columns in sequence from left to right along the x-axis. You can also highlight and tone back the columns as they are revealed, as shown in Figure 10.26.

On a stacked column chart, you can also reveal each category in sequence from bottom to top along the y-axis. This variation can be used

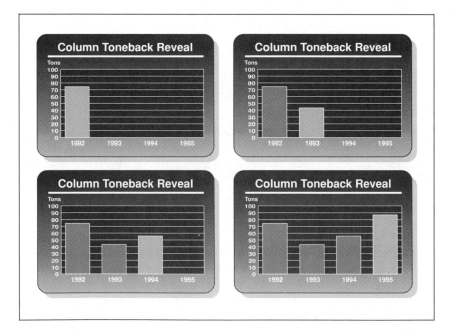

Figure 10.26:

Column chart build series

effectively to clarify complex stacked columns, allowing the speaker to address each category separately. Figure 10.27 illustrates a stacked column chart build series.

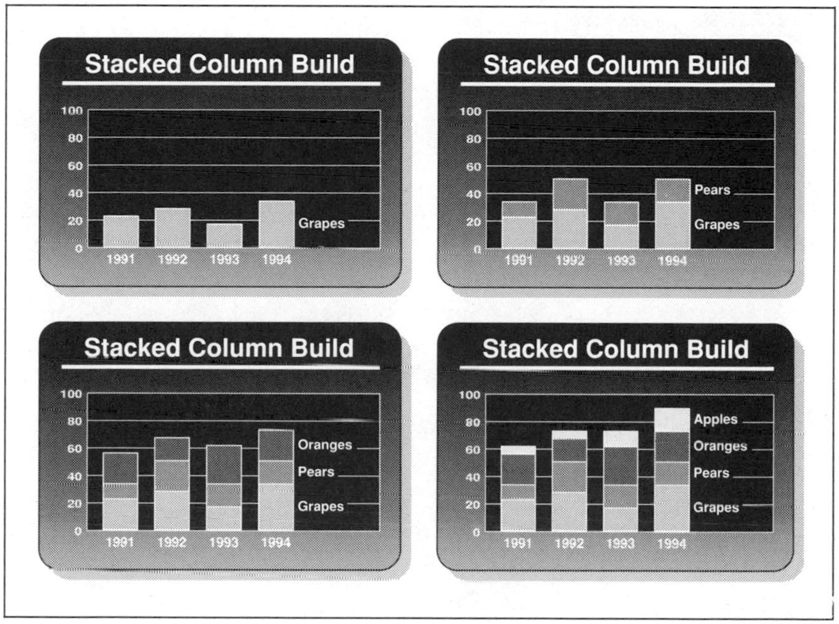

Figure 10.27:

Stacked column chart build

CREATING BAR CHARTS

Similar to a column chart, a bar chart is used to compare the relative size of items. The bar chart is a rotated version of the column chart, with the vertical y-axis becoming the baseline and the horizontal x-axis becoming the scale. This arrangement makes it possible to have longer labels for bars than would be practical for the columns in a column chart.

Bar charts are particularly good for showing the rankings of several items. In fact, arrangements other than by rank are often awkward and should be avoided. For example, Figure 10.28 shows two charts that plot monthly sales data for several salesmen. Notice that the longer names would be too wide to use in a column chart, but they are readable on a bar chart. The chart on the left side of the figure also ranks the data from top to bottom according to sales. The same chart organized in alphabetical order (on the right side of the figure) looks much more disorganized and is less effective.

BAR CHART LAYOUT

Like a column chart, a bar chart is made of rectangles that represent an item or series of items. The axes of a bar chart are the reverse of a

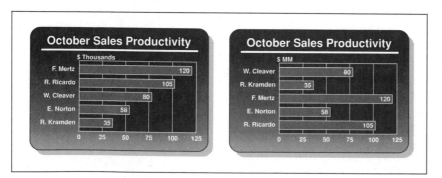

Figure 10.28:

Bar arrangement affects chart readability

column chart. Labels placed to the left of a baseline along the y-axis identify the bars. The x-axis consists of a scale to measure the relative length of each bar.

Traditionally, the scale for a bar chart is placed at the top of the plotting area. However, the top position, directly under the slide title, is strong and can make the slide look top heavy. It is usually better to place your scale at the bottom of the plotting area, as illustrated in Figure 10.29.

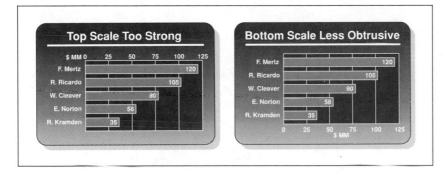

Figure 10.29:

Top and bottom bar chart scales

Your bars should be evenly spaced and should use most of the height of the plotting area. The space between bars should be no less than 25 percent and no more than 100 percent of the bar thickness. One exception to this rule is when you have many closely spaced narrow bars. In this case, have the bars touch (similar to a column chart histogram).

The longest bar should use as much of the full width of the plotting area as possible. The bars in the chart should use at least 75 percent of the width of the plotting area.

Place the data values either inside or outside the end of the bars, as shown in Figure 10.30. Data values inside the bar emphasize the graphic over the text; data values outside the bar put more (but not all) the emphasis on the text.

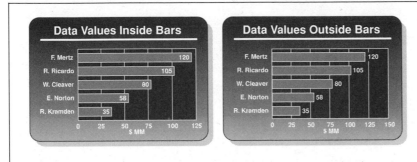

As with column charts, use the minimum number of grid lines and tick marks to clarify your bar charts. If you are showing data values, you may need only a baseline on the y-axis. However, for long bars, a full grid along the x-axis will help the audience measure their length.

Keep the bar labels as brief as possible to give the chart itself plenty of room. If you can't avoid long bar labels, divide them into two or more lines, as shown in Figure 10.31.

Figure 10.31:

Avoid wide bar chart labels

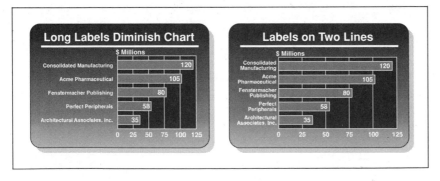

BAR CHART VARIATIONS

Bar chart variations include stacked, grouped, and histogram charts. The guidelines for laying out these types of charts with columns, described earlier in the chapter, also apply to bar charts. The variations described in the following sections are unique to bar charts.

Paired Bar Charts

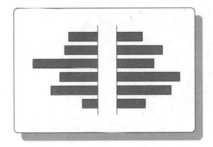

Paired bar charts are useful for making relative comparisons based on different criteria. A paired bar chart plots two sets of bars for the same item and can use different scales and grids for each set.

The chart consists of two separate plotting areas, with the same set of labels for both y-axes placed between the plotting areas. In the left plotting area, the x-axis scale reads from right to left. In the right plotting area, the x-axis scale reads from left to right. Using the same number of steps in both x-axis scales will make the chart more attractive. In Figure 10.32, the left scale is in increments of three years to match the number of steps in the right scale.

You will need to place a title above each plotting area to identify the item being charted. Scales should be at the bottom of the plotting area, with the scale titles below the scale figures.

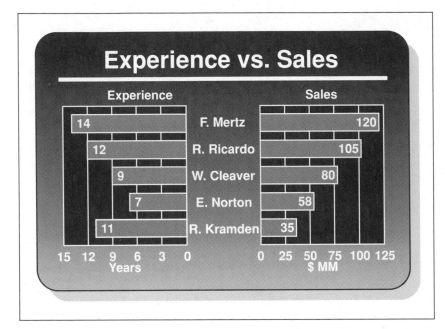

Gantt Charts and Timelines

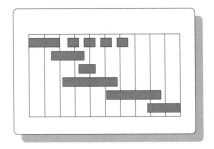

Another excellent use of bar charts is to demonstrate a series of inter-related processes over a period of time. Steps in a process are plotted as bars against a timeline on the x-axis. When it represents a manufacturing or construction process, this type of bar chart is called a *Gantt chart*. The production schedule illustrated in Chapter 1 is a modified Gantt chart.

The Gantt chart is a method of planning and scheduling the steps in a complicated project. Each step is a label on the y-axis and is represented on the chart with a bar, which may not connect to the baseline. Each bar has a separate starting and ending point on the scale.

A Gantt chart scale can range from a few days to many years. Very fine scales, however, will not be readable on slides. Keep your scales simple on the slide and use an audience handout for a more detailed chart.

In the advertising industry, timeline bar charts are used as media buying charts, showing when commercials and other promotions are scheduled. As shown in the example in Figure 10.33, each label may have several

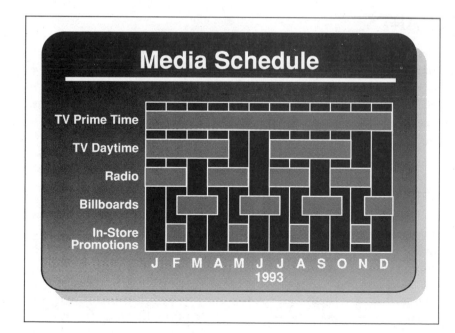

Figure 10.33:

A timeline for a media buying chart

bars associated with it, beginning and ending at different periods within the chart's time frame.

The timeline scale is always continuous. Your scale figures should fall between your grid lines or tick marks, not on them. This designates the space between the tick marks as blocks of time rather than particular moments.

Timeline charts tend to be complicated and difficult to read on slides. Use them sparingly and edit them mercilessly to make them clear, readable, and informative. As a general rule, do not use more than five or six bars per slide. If you must provide more detailed data, put it in audience handouts. Consider dividing large timeline charts into smaller sections (as in a build series) and talking about the individual parts, letting your audience refer to handouts for the big picture.

DEPTH IN BAR CHARTS

The guidelines for adding depth in column charts also applies to bar charts. As when you add depth to column charts, there is a tradeoff between dramatic graphics and accuracy in three-dimensional bar charts. The main consideration is that the chart should reflect the same level of accuracy that the speaker is using in his or her speech. The pseudo-3D method is the best one for showing depth in bar charts.

BAR CHART BUILDS AND REVEALS

You can often make complex timeline charts more readable and understandable by creating them as build or highlight reveal series. Guidelines for bar chart build and reveal series are essentially the same as those for column charts.

One method of dealing with complex information on a Gantt chart is to selectively reveal information on each slide in the build series, similar to the way a stepback reveal is created with text slides. In the sample series in Figure 10.34, when a bar is highlighted, an annotation is added to clarify the chart. As each bar is revealed, the previous annotation is removed and a new one appears.

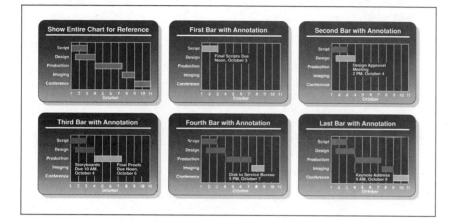

Figure 10.34:

A timeline build series

CREATING LINE CHARTS

Line charts can plot many of the same types of data sets as column and bar charts, but they are particularly useful for showing trends, displaying increases and decreases, and illustrating relationships between several different data series. A line chart has two scales: the y-axis scale measures the data values, and the x-axis scale measures the passing of time or some other variable.

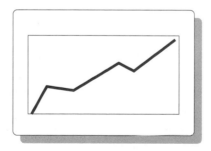

A line chart can give a smoother, more detailed comparison of time-oriented data than is possible in a bar chart, in which the time intervals are limited by the width of the bars. Figure 10.35 shows a line chart and column chart that both plot monthly sales figures for a salesperson. Treated as a column chart, this data is too cluttered. As a line chart, it gives a clean, accurate picture of growth.

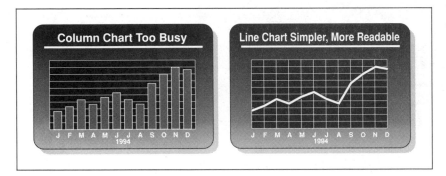

Figure 10.35:

A line chart can show more time intervals than a column chart

LINE CHART LAYOUT

The line in a line chart is plotted against both the x-axis and y-axis scales. A half or full frame (including a staff grid, which serves as a full frame) for the plotting area is essential.

The plot line should be fairly thick and easy to see relative to the grid. Choose a line thickness at least three to four times thicker than your grid lines.

For charts with more than one plot line, choose bright, contrasting line colors and label each line to identify it. Avoid placing more than four plot lines on a chart; any more will be confusing and uninformative, even if you use build or reveal series.

Almost any type of grid and tick mark combination can be used with a line chart. As with any other chart, choose your grid based on the amount of accuracy required. If you show data values, or if extreme accuracy isn't important, a simple frame with tick marks will be adequate. But if you need accuracy, use a full grid.

Any line chart requires at least an x-axis and y-axis scale (see Figure 10.35). Scale labels for line charts should be aligned with the grid; data points should align *on* the grid lines, not *between* them.

Generally, including data values on a line chart will clutter it because you still need the grid. Line charts are best for showing trends, not numerical data. If you must show all the data values, consider using a table.

LINE CHART VARIATIONS

Line chart variations include step lines, line gaps, and standard deviation charts. The variations and their uses are described in the following sections.

Step Line Charts

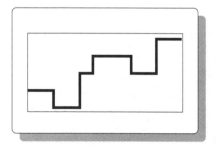

Step line charts plot abrupt rather than gradual change. Their purpose is to show "plateaus" of values related to time. For example, Figure 10.36 shows a step line chart of bus fares over a 35-year period. There is a vertical change wherever a fare increase occurs.

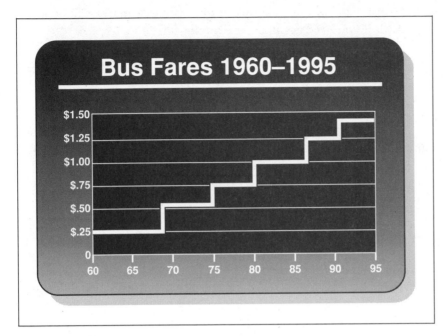

Line Gap Charts

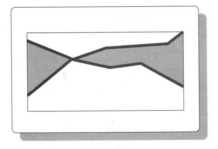

A line gap chart indicates the relationship and difference between two data sets. It plots two separate line series, with the area between them shaded to show the specific relationship between the lines. The line gap chart shown in Figure 10.37 plots sales and costs, and the area between the lines is shaded to represent profit and loss.

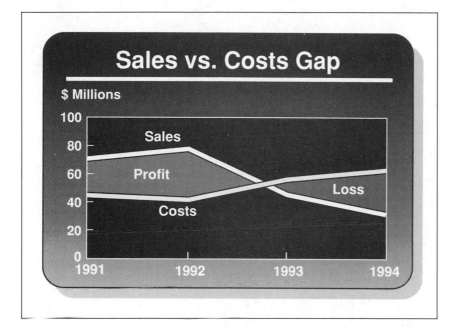

Figure 10.37:

A line gap chart shows the relationship between lines

Standard Deviation Charts

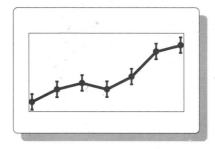

Standard deviation charts, which are used for statistical analyses, are common in scientific presentations. As shown in Figure 10.38, a standard deviation chart indicates the margin of error involved in the calculations used to determine the plotted data points. Each dot on the line indicates a main data point. An I-shaped line extends above the dot to indicate the maximum margin of error, and below the dot to show the minimum margin of error.

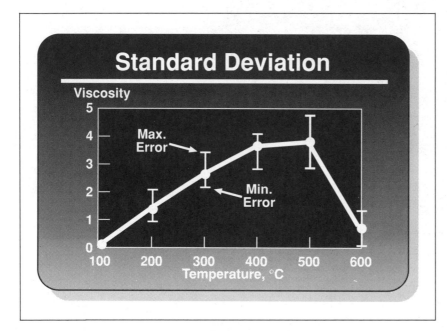

Figure 10.38:

A standard deviation shows the margin of error in calculations

DEPTH IN LINE CHARTS

When it comes to adding depth or three-dimensional effects to line charts, the best advice is *don't*! Even if your column, bar, and pie charts have depth, keep your line charts on one plane.

Adding depth to a line chart creates a ribbon effect. This is usually confusing and unattractive.

LINE CHART BUILDS AND REVEALS

A build series with a single plot line is uncommon in line charts, except as an animation effect in a screen show. The slope and shape of a line are usually a single message, and therefore a single line doesn't require a step-by-step approach.

For a chart that plots several lines, a build series allows individual messages to be communicated and can show clear comparisons between lines. Figure 10.39 shows a reveal series in which a reference category is left highlighted throughout, while three lines are successively revealed for comparison to the reference line and then toned back.

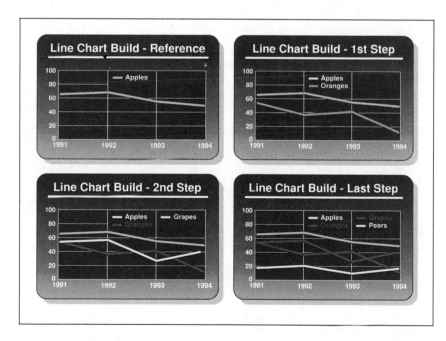

Figure 10.39:

Line chart reveal series

CREATING AREA CHARTS

An area chart is a plotted line with the area between the line and the baseline shaded, giving a more graphic look to the chart. The large shaded surface indicates volume, similar to a column chart.

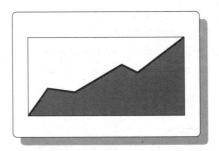

An area chart that plots a single data set is more decorative than a line chart but provides the same information. The most useful type of area chart shows several data sets in a stacked format, as described in the section about area chart variations.

AREA CHART LAYOUT

The basic design guidelines for creating area charts are the same as those for creating line and column charts. However, you should not overlay the grid on top of the plotted areas or your chart will have a checkerboard look. Use external tick marks for your x-axis, since the internal grid will be hidden by the plotted areas.

AREA CHART VARIATIONS

Area chart variations include stacked and photo charts. You can also add depth to an area chart, which can cause the same scale and accuracy problems encountered in adding depth to column charts.

Stacked Area Charts

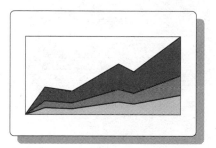

When it is used to plot multiple data sets, an area chart can clearly show the comparison between component parts of a total amount, similar to a stacked column chart. Figure 10.40 shows the amount of information that can be relayed in a stacked area chart compared with a standard area chart.

Avoid using more than four or five areas in the chart. If you have several small areas to plot, combine them into a category called Other and plot them as a single segment.

The largest or most important area of your chart should sit on the baseline. This enables the audience to determine the absolute data values of the most vital information. Once an area has been plotted on top of another, without a straight baseline, it becomes difficult to assess the actual values.

Place the labels for each plotted area directly in the area. If a plotted area is too small for text, use a callout to identify it.

Photo Area Charts

A dramatic effect can be achieved by placing a photograph in the plotted area. The picture should have a direct relation to the data being plotted and

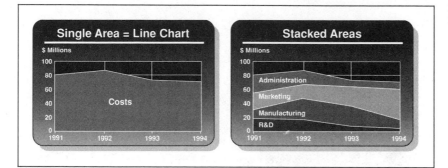

Figure 10.40:

Stacked area charts compare parts of a whole

not just decorate the chart. Figure 10.41 shows an area chart that plots cat food sales with an appropriate photograph.

AREA CHART BUILDS AND REVEALS

There are two methods of creating build series for area charts and they are strongly message-related. Your choice depends on the way your speech and message are structured.

In an *add-on build*, the largest segment is plotted first, and then each new category is added on top of it, as shown in Figure 10.42. This is the type of stacked area chart generated by most presentation and charting programs, and it is the simplest. This approach requires you to talk about the baseline item first. The disadvantage of an add-on build is that only the first segment displays a true picture of its individual data because each new area is plotted on top of the original, making the actual data values for the new segments difficult to determine.

If you have the time, and it suits the content of your speech, the *push-up build* is a dramatic way of creating an area chart build. In a push-up build, each new segment is plotted *under* the previous segment, as shown

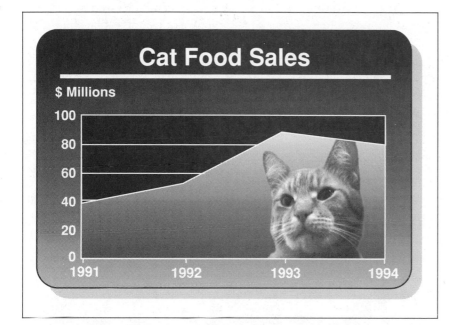

Figure 10.41:

A photo area chart

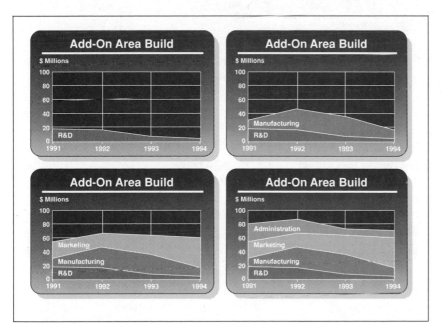

Figure 10.42:

Add-on area chart build series

in Figure 10.43. In this way, the new segment can be viewed in relation to the straight baseline, giving a truer picture of its data. The older segment is pushed up and becomes distorted by the new segment. In this build, your most important bottom segment appears last in the sequence, allowing you to build your speech to the most important topic.

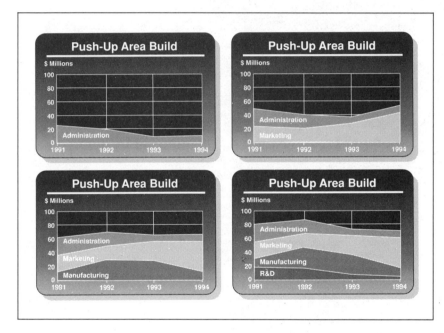

Figure 10.43:

Push-up area chart build series

Both of these build series types can also work as reveal series by toning back the color of older segments when a new segment is revealed.

CREATING SCATTER CHARTS

The scatter chart is a tool for plotting coordinate points on two scales when there is no direct trend or relation between the individual data.

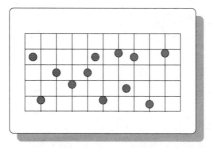

Each dot or other mark on the chart represents two data values along the x- and y-axes. Both axes are usually continuous scales. A common use for the scatter chart is to graph price performance.

SCATTER CHART LAYOUT

The design guidelines for laying out scatter charts are similar to those for line charts. Use a full grid, but don't space the grid too tightly or it will conflict with the plot point labels.

Plotting single points for each category involves attaching a label to each dot as an identifier. Try to limit your plot points to less than ten on this type of scatter chart or the chart will be too cluttered.

Use a legend when plotting multiple points from single or multiple categories. You can plot quite a few points with this method, since individual points usually aren't labeled. Many programs allow you to use different shapes for scatter chart points, but at a distance, shapes become difficult to tell apart. The chart will be more legible if you use color to differentiate your categories. Choose high contrast colors such as yellow, green, and light blue so that closely spaced dots won't be mistaken for each other.

Figure 10.44 shows a single-point scatter chart with data point labels and a multiple-point scatter chart with a legend.

BUBBLE CHART VARIATION

A *bubble chart* is a variation of a scatter chart that adds a third dimension, as illustrated in Figure 10.45. In addition to the position of the dot, its

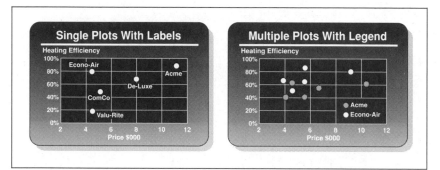

Figure 10.44:

Scatter charts

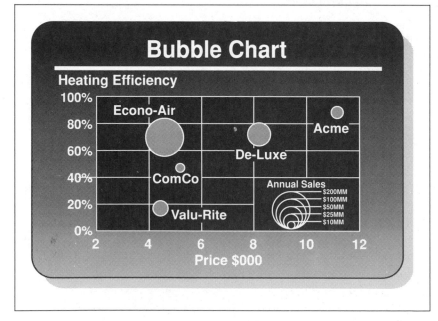

Figure 10.45:

A bubble chart

size also represents a data value. An important thing to remember when creating bubble charts is that your data should be reflected in the *area* of the circle, not its radius or diameter.

CREATING PICTOGRAPH CHARTS

A pictograph is a chart in which appropriate graphic icons are substituted for the traditional graphics of bar and column charts. All the design guidelines that apply to bar and column charts also apply to their pictograph equivalents.

The following are other guidelines for creating pictograph charts:

- Keep your graphic symbols simple.
- Choose symbols that are appropriate to the topic of the chart.
- Represent data value changes by more or fewer symbols, not by the size of the symbols.
- Because pictographs are often visually inaccurate, include data values for precision.

Figure 10.46 shows examples of two pictograph charts: one uses people figures to represent numbers of employees and the other has car symbols showing imported vehicle data.

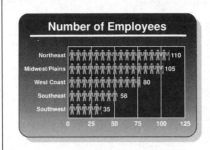

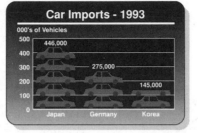

Pictographs use appropriate symbols

CREATING PIE CHARTS

The circle has always been a symbol of the whole. A pie chart's main function is to show the relationship between the parts of that whole.

In business presentations, a pie chart is most often used to show the share or percentage of individual categories in relation to a whole, such as market shares or the distribution of budget expenditures.

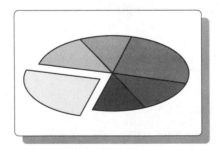

PIE CHART LAYOUT

Of all the chart types, pie charts are the simplest to design. The scale of a pie chart is always 0 to 100 percent, and your data must always total 100 percent. All your data, no matter what its original form, needs to be converted into percentages of the pie. Many charting programs allow you to enter raw data in any type of unit and then automatically convert your data into percentages. Limit your pie charts to no more than six pie segments to maintain clarity.

Avoid using a legend with pie charts because it is difficult to visually connect the legend colors to the pie segments. Instead, use labels placed inside or directly adjacent to your pie sections.

Since people read clockwise, the most important pie segment should begin at the 12 o'clock position of a flat pie chart (in three-dimensional pie charts, the bottom segments are emphasized).

You can highlight a segment of a pie chart by pulling it out of the complete circle, as shown in Figure 10.47. The *exploded* segment can also be highlighted with a brighter color for further emphasis.

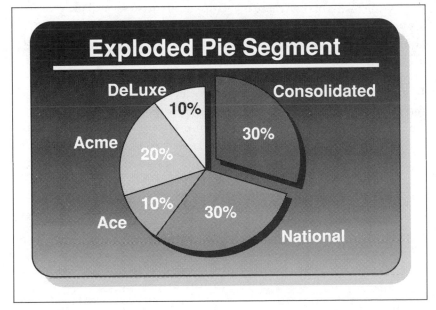

Figure 10.47:

An exploded pie segment

PIE CHART VARIATIONS

There are a few interesting variations on pie charts, including one that isn't a pie at all. Your data may be suitable for a 100 percent stacked column chart or a proportional pie chart.

100 Percent Stacked Column Charts

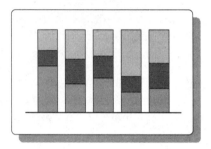

With some forms of data there is a temptation to use several pie charts on a single slide. However, multiple pies are often confusing and unreadable. The best alternative to multiple pies is a 100 percent stacked column chart.

In a 100 percent stacked column chart, illustrated in Figure 10.48, all the columns are the same height, representing a value of 100 percent. The individual segments of each column represent percentages of the 100 percent total. A 100 percent stacked column chart should conform to the same basic design and layout guidelines as other column charts.

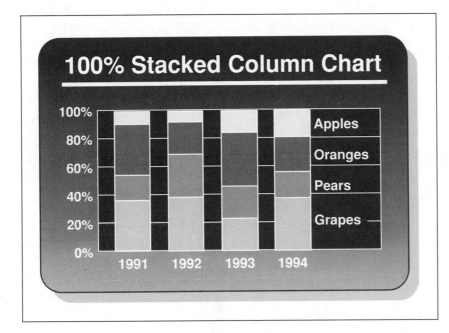

Figure 10.48:

A 100 percent stacked column chart

Proportional Pie Charts

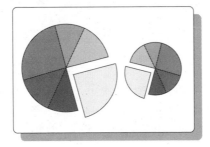

Use a proportional pie chart when you need to compare the relative size of two pies (never more than two!) to convey important information. *Proportional* pie charts can compare size and volume as well as share. As shown in Figure 10.49, in a proportional pie chart, each pie has a data value represented by the area of the circle and segment percentages that represent portions of the whole pie. Use the *area* of the circle, not the diameter or radius, to determine the proportions of your pies or you will greatly exaggerate the difference in their sizes.

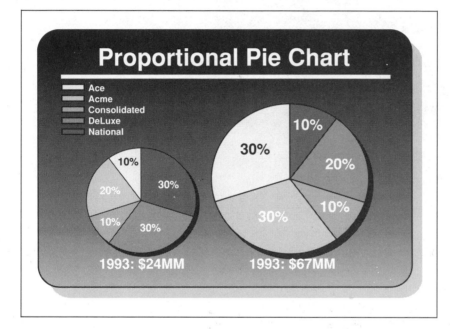

Figure 10.49:

A proportional pie chart

In Figure 10.49, a legend is used to label the segments. With proportional pies, you may have very small segments that are impossible to label properly. In this case, a legend is the best solution.

DEPTH IN PIE CHARTS

The most common form of a three-dimensional pie chart is simply a thick disk tilted back, showing the front edge of the pie.

The main disadvantage of three-dimensional pie charts is that they tend to distort the data. Pie segments at the top of the chart are diminished because they seem further away from the viewer. Pie segments at the bottom are overemphasized because they seem closer. Bottom segments also seem larger because the edge adds to the size of the segment. You can use this effect to your advantage by placing a segment you want to emphasize at the bottom of the chart. Even if the segment is smaller than some others, it will appear larger and more important because of its position, as shown in Figure 10.50.

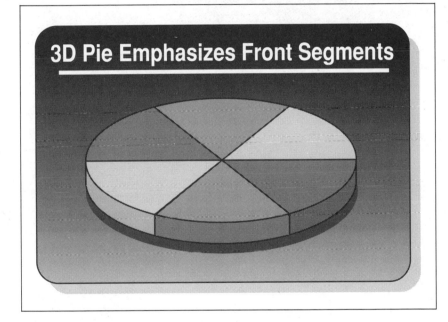

Figure 10.50:

A three-dimensional pie chart

Rotated Pies

You can add variety and style to a presentation by rotating and tilting a three-dimensional pie chart, as shown in Figure 10.51 (if your software can do this). A rotated and tilted pie chart can seriously distort your pie sections, so be sure to include data values to prevent your audience from misinterpreting the charts.

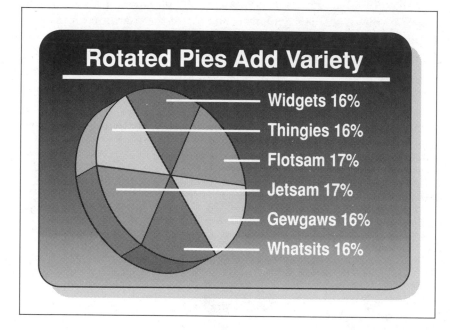

PIE CHART BUILDS AND REVEALS

There are several ways to create build and reveal series for pie charts. The simplest is to add each segment in order to the pie. You can achieve more dramatic effects by combining exploded segments and toneback colors with builds, as shown in Figure 10.52.

CREATING COMBINATION CHARTS

A single type of chart may not convey the message you need for your slide. A combination chart merges two different chart types into a single, coherent message.

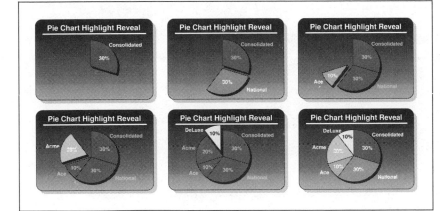

Figure 10.52:

Pie chart highlight reveal series

Since the possible combinations of column, bar, line, area, and pie charts are endless, you must first decide if a combination chart is appropriate for your information. The chart should be a comparison between two separate conflicting or corroborating messages. Figure 10.53 shows two effective combination charts.

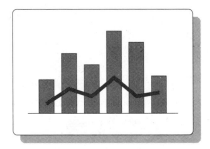

Your information should be based on two separate measurement systems, such as percentage *and* amount or dollars *and* volume. If you are using two scales, make sure it is clear which scale belongs to which chart graphic by keying the color of the scale text to the color of the chart graphic.

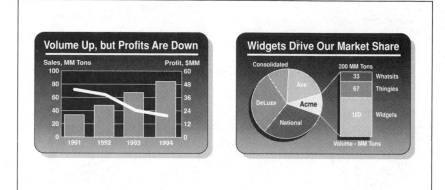

Combination charts compare messages

Above all, keep things simple. Whenever you combine two types of charts, you double the need to eliminate extraneous information and graphic clutter. A combination chart should be no more difficult to read than any other type of chart.

CREATING FLOW AND PROCESS CHARTS

Flow and process charts are intended to show relationships between people and processes rather than numbers. The most common flow charts in business presentations are the organization chart, the PERT chart, and decision trees.

No matter which type of flow chart you use, it's important to organize your chart to fit the available space on the slide.

Here are some guidelines for creating flow charts:

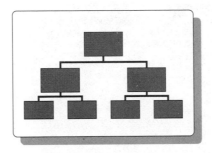

■ Keep your type as large as possible, but don't crowd the edges of your boxes.

■ Abbreviate wherever possible. Use only first initials for names in organization charts.

■ Keep connecting lines short; use the space for boxes and text.

■ Always supply printed handouts when presenting complex charts.

ORGANIZATION CHARTS

Organization charts show the relationships between people in a business or other group. The normal layout for an organization chart is to place the highest ranked person at the top, with subordinates layered underneath, as shown in Figure 10.54. Each person's name, sometimes with a title or job description, is placed in a box. Lines connecting the boxes define reporting and authority connections. The level of the person's box indicates rank and authority.

When creating an organization chart, try to maintain the look of a grid, with same size boxes (especially at each level) and even spacing. To keep the text readable, limit the number of boxes in the organization chart to four rows down by six boxes across. If you need more detail, divide the chart into separate slides. Use straight vertical and horizontal lines to connect boxes, not diagonal lines.

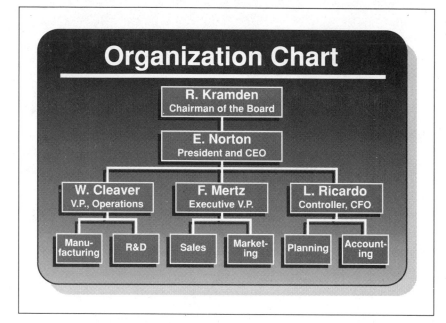

PERT CHARTS

A PERT (Process Evaluation Review Technique) chart diagrams the process of manufacturing a product or completing a task. As shown in Figure 10.55, each step in the process is represented by a box, with connecting arrows showing the process paths.

You can conserve space by changing the direction of the steps. In Figure 10.55, the straight line of the flow chart has been "bent" (arrows going left and right when they should be straight up and down) to make the chart more horizontal.

DECISION TREES

A decision tree, shown in Figure 10.56, is a visual tool for making choices between various options. Questions are posed, and the answers

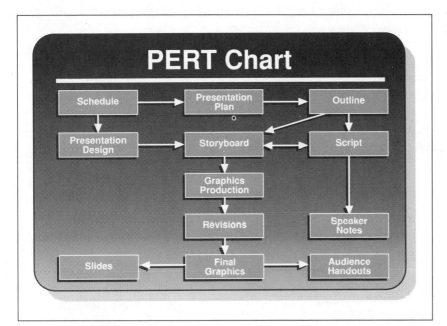

Figure 10.55:

A PERT chart

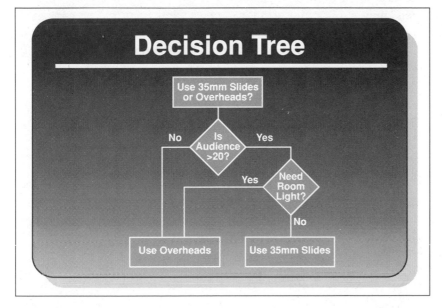

Figure 10.56:

A decision tree

determine the direction to follow in the chart. Eventually, the path leads to a final decision.

Decision trees are seldom simple enough for slide use. The diamonds used for decision forks don't hold a lot of text, so the questions and answers must be short. If you decide to present a decision tree, supply printed handouts of the chart and use your slide as a reference while speaking.

USING COLOR IN CHARTS AND GRAPHS

Color is an essential part of communicating with charts and graphs. The complex data presented in charts is made more understandable by the effective use of color.

The basic color guidelines explained in Chapter 7 are also appropriate when applied to the use of color in charts and graphs. The colors you choose for highlight colors in your palette should also be appropriate as chart colors. Here are some additional guidelines for using color in charts:

- Use warm, cool, and neutral colors to guide audience reactions. Use warm, bright colors to accentuate chart elements, cool and neutral colors to de-emphasize them.

- Use familiar color associations to reinforce your message, such as green for profit and red for loss.

- Color contrast is essential to communication. Choose chart colors for maximum contrast with the background and other chart elements.

- Link related chart elements by assigning signature colors to frequently used chart categories or topics, as described in the next section.

- Use moving highlights to clarify complex charts and graphs and to pace the audience's attention.

SIGNATURE COLORS IN CHARTS

During the course of a presentation, you might deal with the same categories or topics in several charts and graphs. For consistency and as an aid to audience understanding, choose signature colors for each different category and use that same color throughout your presentation. Figure 10.57 shows three different categories represented in four different charts, with the same color used for each category.

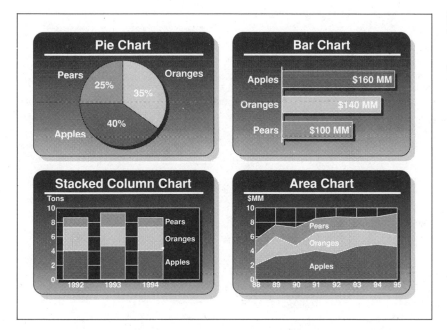

Figure 10.57:

Color coding makes charts easier to understand

THE
REAL
WORLD   LIES, DAMNED LIES, AND STATISTICS

Wednesday, October 10, 11:00 am: Jim Gonzalez starts his rounds of the executive offices, looking for answers and making suggestions on the presentations. His first stop is Victoria's office.

"Morning, Victoria. I've got a few questions about this chart you added last night. I think it needs some work." He places her storyboard sketch on the desk.

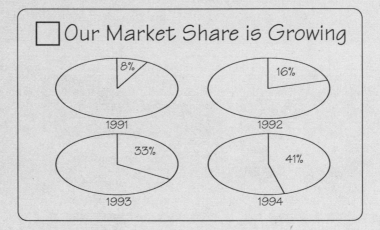

"Four pie charts are a little too busy for one slide," he says. "Why don't we do this as a 100 percent column chart?"

"Do you have an example?" asks Victoria.

"Here, take a look at this," he says as he hands her the rough of his idea.

"I don't know, Jim. Somehow that doesn't look quite as impressive as the four charts."

"True, but it will be easier to read."

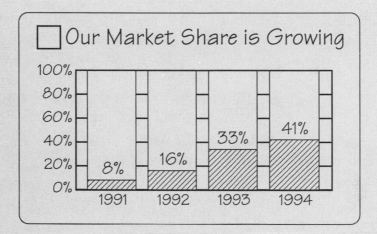

Victoria looks at Jim's rough again. "The main problem I have with this is that our share looks too small in column form."

"Well, we could just do this as a straight column chart, treating the percents as raw figures. It's not exactly kosher because we should be showing the whole market if we're going to be showing our share."

"What do you mean?" she asks. Jim sketches on his pad again.

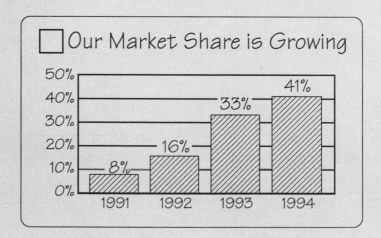

"This way makes the columns twice as high and more impressive, but doesn't misrepresent the figures."

"OK, Jim. I think that will work. Thanks."

Jim heads down the hall to Alan's office. Alan had given him a table to be turned into a slide, but Jim wants to turn it into a chart.

"Good morning, Jim. How are you doing on the slides?"

"Fine, Alan. Almost done. I'd like to talk to you about this table."

"What about it?"

"I'd like to try doing this as an area chart instead of as a table. I think it will look a lot better."

"What did you have in mind?"

"Here's your original table.

▢ Our Product Mix Is In Flux
Units, 000

	1991	1992	1993	1994	1995	1996
Widgets	10	40	98	70	65	89
Flotsam	20	55	40	31	25	30
Thingies	20	55	50	69	85	50
Total	50	150	188	170	175	169

"The three rows of figures for widgets, flotsam, and thingies add up to the total on the fourth line, so I thought it might make a good area chart like this." Jim shows Alan the sketch he made earlier.

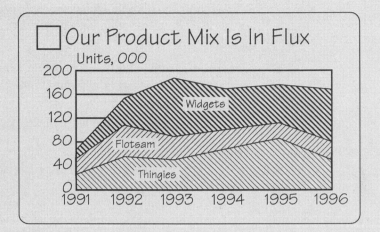

"That's perfect, Jim. The chart shows the fluctuations in our unit sales much more dramatically. Go with it."

"Thanks Alan. I'll have final proofs for your show this afternoon."

SUMMARY

If text slides are the heart of a presentation, then charts and graphs are the brains. The accuracy, clarity, and effectiveness of your charts can make the difference between a disinterested audience and one that understands and acts on your message. Use charts and graphs to clarify complex numerical relationships. A chart is almost always easier to read than tabular data. Here's a summary of things to keep in mind when creating your charts and graphs:

- Remember, only one message and one chart per slide.
- Choose the chart type that best suits your message and data.
- Your chart title should reflect the message of the chart.
- Design a standard chart frame for all the charts in your presentation. Create templates and masters for slides containing different chart types.

■ Keep your charts simple. Make the text readable, use a simple grid, round off data values, and use only the figures that support your message.

■ Divide complex flow and organizational charts into easy-to-understand segments to be presented in several slides. Use audience handouts for clarity.

■ Use depth and three-dimensional effects to give your charts more impact.

■ Use build series, highlights, and color to pace and clarify your charts.

chapter 11

Using Illustrations in Your Presentation

Even in business presentations, the old adage "a picture is worth a thousand words" holds true. You can increase your level of communication by *showing* rather than *telling*. A difficult concept is easier to explain when it is accompanied by a clear, concise illustration. An audience can identify and relate to people and places that are shown in photographs.

You can incorporate illustrations into your presentations in a variety of ways. This chapter describes graphic styles and file types, as well as how to integrate photographs into a presentation.

CHOOSING MESSAGE-DRIVEN GRAPHICS

Like everything else in your presentation, the graphics you include should be message-driven. This means that each illustration and photograph should enhance and clarify your message. A picture that looks nice but doesn't have anything to do with the message will distract the audience from the point the speaker is making.

When an illustration is the subject of a slide, it is an addition to the speech, not a substitute for it. When referring to the slide, the speaker should describe what the audience sees in the illustration, not just introduce it. For example, Figure 11.1 shows a slide with a labeled picture of a baseball field. When this slide is shown, saying "This slide shows a typical baseball field," will not help the audience understand the parts of a baseball field. Even though the parts are labeled in the slide, the speaker should also verbally describe them. The speech should reinforce the illustration, and vice versa.

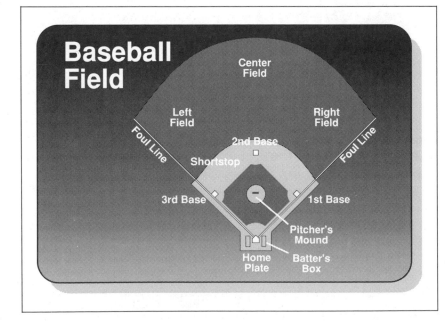

Figure 11.1:

A labeled illustration still needs a verbal description of its parts

CHOOSING ILLUSTRATION STYLES

You should choose an illustration style that is appropriate to your message and maintain that style consistently throughout the presentation. Like the colors and type styles you use in the presentation design, the illustration styles in your presentation influence the mood and perceptions of your audience.

After you select an appropriate style, you should avoid using extremely different styles within the presentation. Don't mix graphics from many different sources, such as several different clip-art collections. A "kitchen sink" approach to illustrations looks haphazard and amateurish. All the pictures in your presentation should look as if they were drawn by the same hand.

The style of a particular illustration is determined by the use of lines, color, and shading. The basic categories of computer art styles are icons, cartoons, graphic illustrations, and maps.

ICONS

Icons are the most basic form of illustration, often consisting of just an outline of the object. They are drawn with basic geometric shapes and minimal line work, as shown in the examples in Figure 11.2.

You don't need special drawing software to create icons. The simple drawing tools available in most presentation graphics software are adequate for this purpose. Creating an icon is an exercise in "less is more." Draw the basic outline of an object with just enough detail to make the idea clear. Use only one or two solid, flat colors to fill the shapes. The effect of an icon should be two-dimensional; avoid graduated fills or textures, which may add depth or excessive detail.

In presentations, icons are useful for identifying general ideas and concepts. For example, you could discuss the idea of a personal computer without specifying a particular type or manufacturer, as shown in Figure 11.3.

Figure 11.2:

Icons consist of simple shapes with little detail

FROM ART OF PERSUASION

Figure 11.3:

Use icons to represent generic concepts

PCs Make A Difference!

- Information Access
- Corporate Communications
- Personal Productivity
- Employee Skills

You can also use icons in charts and graphs to visually communicate ideas and categories. For example, to plot computer sales, you could use a computer icon in a pictograph, as illustrated in Figure 11.4.

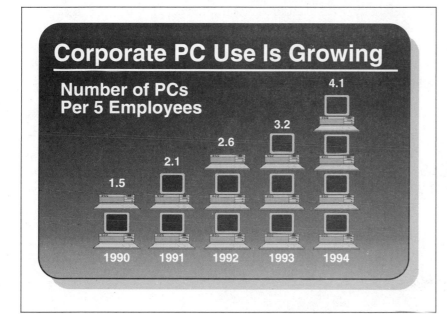

Figure 11.4:

Use icons in pictograph charts

Icons simplify artwork that would be overly complex in the form of a detailed illustration. For example, in a computer networking diagram, the fine details of an illustration would be lost if it were reduced in size. As shown in Figure 11.5, an icon loses little detail.

Because of their general nature, icons are easy to reuse from one presentation to the next. You can keep a library of appropriate icons and use them in many presentations.

CARTOONS

Cartoons are created with a loose, freehand style of line work, with simple color fills. Usually, cartoons are intended to be humorous. The subject is visually exaggerated, colors are bright, and inanimate objects are often humanized. Figure 11.6 shows some examples of cartoon illustrations.

The suitability of cartoons in a presentation depends on the subject matter. For example, cartoons and other funny illustrations are not appropriate in a serious financial presentation. However, a sales or marketing presentation that is intended to uplift and excite an audience might benefit from an occasional amusing cartoon.

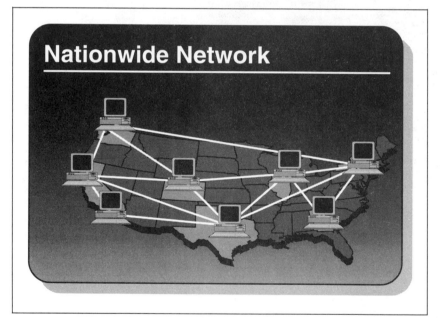

Figure 11.5:

Use icons when a more complex drawing would lose detail

Use cartoons sparingly in presentations. Avoid cute pictures that contribute little to the message. Cartoons can trivialize important information. Limit your use of cartoons to "light" topics and the occasional humorous aside in your speech. Compare the cartoon computer shown in Figure 11.7 to the computer icon in Figures 11.3, 11.4, and 11.5.

FROM ARTS & LETTERS

Figure 11.6:

Cartoons are freehand style, exaggerated drawings

Figure 11.7:

Use cartoons for "light" topics

GRAPHIC ILLUSTRATIONS

The general category of graphic illustrations includes a wide range of styles, from technical drawings to finely detailed artwork.

The most important element of any illustration is clarity. A graphic in a presentation is like going by a highway billboard at 55 miles per hour. Its effectiveness can be judged by how quickly the viewer sees and understands its message. Don't get carried away trying to create a masterpiece; it will probably be on the screen a total of 20 seconds.

Fine lines often will be lost during the slide-imaging process, especially if the illustration is reduced to fit in a small area of the frame. The best illustrations for presentation graphics are those that use detailed *areas* of color to create realistic effects. Figure 11.8 shows some examples of area-based artwork.

Use illustrations to describe things that are difficult to explain verbally. You can show the internal workings of devices, processes, and items that are very small or large. The limits are your imagination and drawing

FROM CORPORATE IMAGES

Figure 11.8:

Graphic illustrations for slides should emphasize areas rather than line work

abilities. Figure 11.9 shows how a graphic illustration of a computer differs from an icon or cartoon.

MAPS

Showing a map is usually the best way to present a list of geographical locations. Unlike a simple text slide listing the names of places, a labeled map slide shows locations in a visual context. This makes it easier for the audience to see where each location is in relation to the others and the distances involved. Figure 11.10 shows an example of a map slide with sales office locations.

Here are some guidelines for using maps in your presentations:

- The basic presentation design rules also apply to maps: keep things simple, use contrasting colors, and make sure the text is readable.

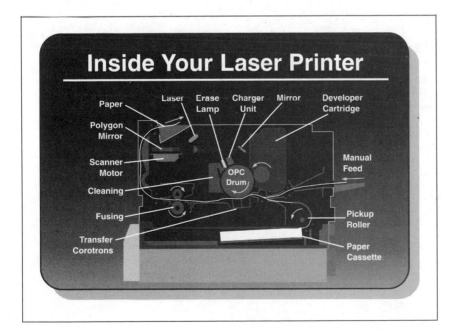

Figure 11.9:

Illustrations can help explain structure

Strive to create as accurate a map as possible. Highlight the correct states or countries and place the cities properly. Placing New York City in New Jersey may insult the citizens of both places.

Use only the level of detail necessary for your message. For example, if you need to identify cities on the West Coast, create a map showing only the western states, not the entire country. Omit state boundaries if you don't need them.

Three-dimensional maps are attractive and easy to create. Since a map has an irregular shape, true perspective drawing isn't necessary to give the illusion of depth. To create a three-dimensional map, simply shrink the map vertically. You can add a drop shadow below it to enhance the three-dimensional effect.

A three-dimensional map can be combined with a simple column chart to show data for each location, as in the example shown in Figure 11.11. Because this type of slide doesn't have a scale for comparing the height of

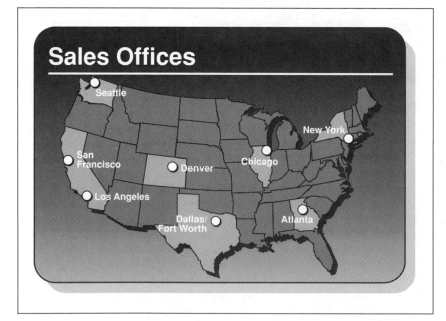

Figure 11.10:

A sample map slide

the columns, you should include the data values with the columns. To keep the slide readable, limit the number of columns. The number of columns you will be able to fit on the map depends on the locations of the columns and their relative heights. If the map-column combination isn't as easy to read as it should be, use a regular column chart instead.

Figure 11.11:

A three-dimensional map combined with a column chart plots data against location

USING ELECTRONIC CLIP ART

You don't have to be a good artist or hire one to include quality illustrations in your presentations. Ready-made computer graphics are available in the form of clip art. Many companies sell clip-art disks, and most presentation and graphics software packages come with their own collections of clip art. Figure 11.12 shows clip-art samples from several desktop presentation programs.

Figure 11.12:

Most desktop presentation packages come with clip art

You can select from millions of clip-art drawings, covering every possible subject, from aerospace to zoology. Prices for clip-art disks are usually reasonable, especially those distributed on CD-ROM disks.

Here are some guidelines for selecting clip art for your presentation:

■ Choose clip art that you can edit and recolor. This will allow you to adjust the illustration so that it conforms with your presentation design.

■ Make sure the clip art is appropriate for presentation graphics. Many clip-art collections are black-and-white PostScript illustrations with very fine lines, which are designed to be printed, not projected on slides.

■ Don't buy an entire clip-art collection for a single illustration. Get a collection that has many illustrations suitable for your business or subject matter.

In your presentation, use clip-art images that are similar in design and drawing style. The illustrations should look like they were produced by the same person.

UNDERSTANDING GRAPHIC FILE TYPES

Computer art falls into two main categories: bitmap graphics and vector graphics. Every form of computer graphics output is based on a bit map. A *bitmap* is a grid of small dots, called *pixels* (from *pic*ture *el*ements), which define the image. Your computer monitor displays its information in the form of color or black-and-white pixels. A laser printer's dots are also a grid of black-and-white pixels. A film recorder creates slides by projecting color pixels on to 35mm film.

Bitmap graphics are files in which the image is made directly of individual pixels. The sharpness and realism of the image are determined by the number of pixels, not by the output device. Figure 11.13 shows the pixels in a bitmap image.

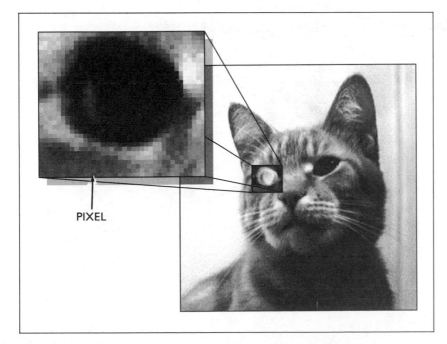

PIXEL

Figure 11.13:

Bitmap graphics are made up of pixels

Vector, or *object-oriented*, *graphics* are created by defining the shapes used in the image with mathematical descriptions. For example, a circle is defined by a certain diameter, with its centerpoint at a particular place in the artwork; a rectangle is defined by its corners at four particular points.

Vector graphics are just a means of getting the best possible bitmap representation on your final output device, whether it is a monitor, laser printer, or film recorder. The vector description tells the output device to turn its pixels on and off (or to make them a certain color) based on how closely each individual pixel fits inside the described shape. Figure 11.14 illustrates how vector graphics are formed.

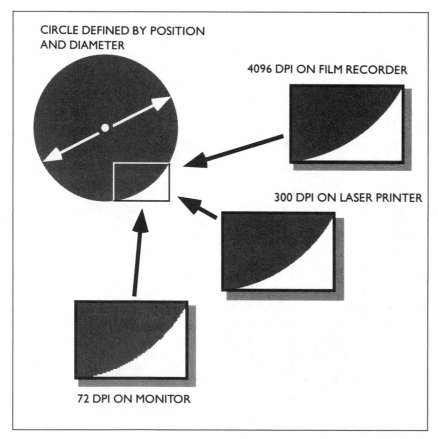

Figure 11.14:

Vector graphics are defined by mathematical descriptions

Illustration style is independent of the graphic file format. A cartoon can be a bitmap or vector graphics file. However, illustrations are more likely to be in vector graphics format than in bitmap file format.

WORKING WITH BITMAP GRAPHICS

For presentations, the use of bitmap graphics is usually restricted to incorporating photographs and other scanned images into slides. File sizes for full color bitmaps can easily reach the multimegabyte range, creating storage, handling, and imaging problems. (Some ways to deal with large bitmap files are suggested in the section about digital photocomposites, later in the chapter).

BITMAP RESOLUTION

Bitmaps are described in terms of their *resolution*, which is the number of pixels they contain. Any bitmap file consists of an exact number of pixels, measured on x and y axes. For example, standard VGA and Macintosh monitors have a resolution of 640 by 480 pixels (640 across by 480 from the top to the bottom), for a total of 307,200 pixels.

Resolution is also described in terms of *dots per inch (dpi)*, especially when referring to laser printers and typesetting equipment. A standard laser printer has a resolution of 300 dpi.

COLOR DEPTH IN BITMAPS

The bitmap grid is also described in terms of its *color depth*, which is the amount of data used to determine the color of each pixel. A black-and-white image has a color depth of 1 bit; that is, each pixel is either on or off, black or white. An 8-bit color image uses eight data bits, yielding 2 to the eighth power, or 256 possible colors. A 24-bit color image uses 24 data bits, for 2 to the twenty-fourth power, or 16.8 million possible colors.

For normal computer graphics, 256 colors are more than enough to create attractive illustrations. Even with a graduated background, most presentation graphics programs will create a file with fewer than 256 colors.

When you are dealing with realistic photographs, however, 256 colors are not nearly enough to render a scene without some undesirable effects. The most common effect is called *posterization*, in which areas that should be smoothly shaded appear to be made up of bands of solid color. To properly display and image the colors in a photograph, 24-bit color is necessary.

BITMAP GRAPHICS SOFTWARE

There are two main types of software that produce bitmap graphics: photo enhancement and paint.

Photo enhancement software is designed to enhance, retouch, and alter scanned photographs. Adobe Photoshop, Letraset ColorStudio on the Mac, and Aldus Photostyler for PCs are examples of photo enhancement programs.

Paint software is designed to create artwork using tools that simulate traditional painter's tools, such as paintbrushes, charcoal, and airbrushes. Supermac's PixelPaint Pro, Electronic Arts' Studio/32 on the Mac, and ZSoft's PC Paintbrush for PCs are paint programs.

BITMAP FILE FORMATS

The basic form of a bitmap graphics file is a listing of each pixel along with its colors. As you can imagine, such a list would be huge, even for a relatively small bitmap such as a computer screen image. In fact, a 640 by 480 pixel, 24-bit image weighs in at well over a megabyte of information.

Bitmap file formats organize and, in some cases, compress the pixel data to keep the file sizes manageable. Graphics can be in one of the bitmap file formats described below.

TIFF Files

TIFF (Tagged Image File Format) is one of the oldest and most universal bitmap file formats. It is a standard method of exchanging bitmap files between Macintosh and PC applications.

TIFF has developed from a 1-bit black-and-white format to a format that supports full 24-bit color and optional data compression. Unfortunately, not all software packages have kept up with the TIFF standard, so some applications produce variations of TIFF formats that are not compatible with other software.

PICT Files

The Macintosh PICT bitmap format is a part of the Macintosh system software and is supported by all Macintosh programs. Some PC programs also support the PICT format.

The PICT format supports full 24-bit color, plus an additional 8 bits for special effects, such as transparency and masking, for a total of 32 bits. PICT data files are automatically compressed when they are saved. Because the 32-bit PICT format is part of the system software, even a Macintosh computer with an 8-bit color monitor can view and edit full-color images.

PCX Files

The early popularity of ZSoft's PC Paintbrush made its native file format, PCX, the standard for DOS-based graphics. It is supported by most presentation graphics and drawing software. Like TIFF, the PCX format has been upgraded many times and now supports full 24-bit color.

TARGA Files

Like the PCX format, the TARGA (.TGA) file format became popular because of a single product: the Truevision TARGA video board. The

TARGA board was the most popular hardware for high-end PC graphics (especially paint) applications because it could display 24-bit graphics on large monitors. Many software applications were designed specifically for the TARGA file format. The TARGA format supports 32-bit color and data compression.

Windows Bitmap Files

The Windows Bitmap (.BMP) file format is used by Microsoft Windows to exchange bitmap graphics between Windows applications. Most Windows-based paint programs can save files in BMP format, and most Windows-based presentation graphics programs can import BMP files. The BMP format supports up to 24-bit color.

WORKING WITH VECTOR GRAPHICS FILES

Vector graphics are called *resolution-independent* because the description of the artwork is independent of the output device. The image you see on your monitor may be jagged because the monitor's resolution is low (about 72 dpi). When you print your graphics on a laser printer, the edges become smoother because the laser printer has a higher resolution (about 300 dpi) than a monitor. When vector graphics are imaged on a film recorder, which has a high resolution (up to 8000 dpi), the edges become very smooth, even though the actual size of the image on the film is only 1 by 1½ inches.

VECTOR GRAPHICS SOFTWARE

Each vector graphics program uses its own internal system for drawing illustrations. The quality of a vector-based drawing program depends on the variety of tools it provides and the accuracy of those tools.

Popular Macintosh drawing programs include Adobe Illustrator, Aldus Freehand, Claris MacDraw Pro, and Deneba Canvas. The best PC drawing programs are Windows-based. They include CorelDRAW!,

Micrografx Designer, and Arts & Letters. Also, all the presentation graphics programs mentioned in this book are vector-based.

VECTOR GRAPHICS FILE FORMATS

There are several universal vector graphics file formats that are supported by drawing and presentation programs. Each file format has a unique way of describing the shape and position of objects. The most common formats are described below.

PostScript Files

PostScript was developed by Adobe Systems in the mid-1980s as a tool for creating typefaces, drawing graphics, and laying out pages. Originally intended for black-and-white laser printer output, PostScript has grown to encompass color and work with virtually any medium. Color printers, film recorders, plotters, computer displays, even color copiers now have PostScript interpreters, which provide an enormous variety of output options for PostScript files.

The most well-known products of PostScript are the thousands of Type 1 PostScript fonts. PostScript's powerful drawing tools enable the artist to create very detailed pictures. PostScript supports bitmap graphics, but the files can be large because they are not compressed.

PostScript has become the standard for exchanging vector graphics files between different computer systems because most Macintosh and PC drawing and illustration programs support the original Adobe Illustrator format (Illustrator 1.1). Normally, PostScript files imported into presentation graphics programs are in the form of Encapsulated PostScript (EPS), a special form of PostScript file that includes a small, low-resolution bitmap preview of the graphic. EPS files are not usually interchangeable between Macintosh and PC systems because of the incompatibility of the bitmap preview.

Quickdraw Files

The Apple Quickdraw graphics description language made the Macintosh the most popular computer among graphic designers and artists.

The Quickdraw (PICT) format allows graphics files to be exchanged between any Macintosh programs through the Clipboard. This makes graphics transfer a simple cut or copy and paste operation.

Quickdraw supports both vector and bitmap image descriptions. All Macintosh-based drawing and presentation programs can import and export PICT files.

Computer Graphics Metafiles

The Computer Graphics Metafile (.CGM) format is the most common graphics language and interchange format used by DOS-based graphics software, including Harvard Graphics, Lotus Freelance Plus, and many other programs. The CGM format can support quite detailed graphics. However, the implementation in early versions of many programs is often only fair, and CGM files produced by those programs may be distorted or have other problems when transferred to another program.

Windows Metafiles

The Windows Metafile Format (.WMF) is similar to the Macintosh PICT format in that it is designed for the easy exchange of graphics files between Windows applications through the Clipboard. Most Windows graphics applications will also save files in the Windows Metafile Format so they can be imported into other programs.

INTEGRATING PHOTOGRAPHY INTO YOUR PRESENTATION

Photographs are an integral part of our lives. We accept photographs as windows on reality: family snapshots, news photography, even photographs in advertising act as a link to real life. Placing photographs in your presentation provides a depth and realism that can't be achieved by even the best computer graphics.

The simplest way to incorporate photography in your presentation is to include full-frame photographic slides. This method is inexpensive and convenient. The only costs are for film processing and mounting, and your local one-hour photo store can produce the slides. The only drawback is that a full-frame photograph will not have the formatting and design of the rest of the slides, so it will disrupt the graphic look of your presentation.

Integrating photography into an overall presentation design is a little more complicated, but the rewards in design and format consistency are great. The process of combining photography and computer graphics is called *compositing*, and the end result is called a *photocomposite*. Figure 11.15 shows an example of a photocomposite.

There are two ways to produce photocomposites for presentations:

- *Conventional photocomposites* are created with conventional photographic techniques, using special equipment.

Figure 11.15:

A photocomposite

■   *Digital photocomposites* are created with a computer, using a scanner or electronic photography to incorporate the photographic image into the presentation program.

The following sections describe these methods and their advantages and disadvantages.

CONVENTIONAL PHOTOCOMPOSITES

Before the advent of scanners, all photographs were inserted into slides via optical processes similar to those used to create movie special effects. In many cases, this is still the best and most economical method of combining computer-created graphics and photography. It enables you to include artwork that requires special photographic treatment or is too large to place on a scanner. Using conventional photographic techniques, anything that can be photographed can be placed in your slides.

Creating conventional photocomposites is not a do-it-yourself project. This method requires sophisticated photographic equipment and in-house film processing. Many service bureaus and photo labs offer photocomposite and other photographic services in addition to computer graphics imaging, and they are your best source for photocomposite work.

You can, however, reduce your costs by using your presentation graphics software to create the basic elements that the service bureau's photographer needs to produce the final product. The process of compositing involves creating a *window* in your computer graphics file where the photograph will be inserted. The instructions that follow are general; your service bureau may have slightly different requirements. Always check with your service bureau before you prepare your own photocomposite graphics.

Photocomposite Preparation

A photocomposite with a single photograph inset into a computer graphic background requires three main elements:

■   A *color computer element*, which consists of the background, title, and any other text or graphics, plus a black window in the exact size and position where the photograph is to be inserted, as shown in Figure 11.16. The window must be exactly the same shape as the photograph. Place a light-colored line around the window to cover any small alignment errors in the final composite.

■   A *black-and-white mask*, which consists of a single clear area defining where the photograph will appear, as shown in Figure 11.17. The mask is created from a *copy* of the color computer element, with all the unnecessary artwork removed, and all the colors changed to black (including the line around the window), except the window, which is changed to white. Some service bureaus ask you to reverse this color scheme, with a white background and a black window.

Figure 11.16:

Color computer element

■ Your *original slide* or *photo print*, with crop marks if you do not want the entire image to be inserted, as shown in Figure 11.18. On 35mm slides, cropping should be indicated on the slide mount with short lines defining the top, bottom, and sides of the area to be used. On large transparencies (4 by 5 inches or bigger) or prints, use a tissue paper overlay with a box drawn around the area to indicate cropping.

Send your disk, along with your original slide or print, to the service bureau. Documentation is very important at this stage. Clearly indicate (using a sketch or a printout of your computer graphics) which original

Figure 11.17:

Black-and-white mask

slide belongs to which computer file. Keep in mind that many vendors' production schedules require two to three days for turnaround on photo-composites, so allow extra time or create and send in your composites for imaging before the rest of your presentation.

The service bureau will image and process your computer files. On a special copy camera, your original photograph is rephotographed so it is cropped, sized, and positioned as closely as possible to the window position, and then this film is processed. Your mask and the resized photograph are sandwiched together and placed on alignment pins in a special-effects camera. The mask allows only the window area to be exposed. Without advancing the film in the special effects camera, your original color computer graphics element is photographed. The color element exposes the areas that were black on the mask; the black window is unexposed.

The resulting "double-exposure" is your final photocomposite, which is then processed and mounted for your final slide. Figure 11.19 illustrates the photocomposite production process.

Figure 11.18:

Cropping shows which part of the image to include

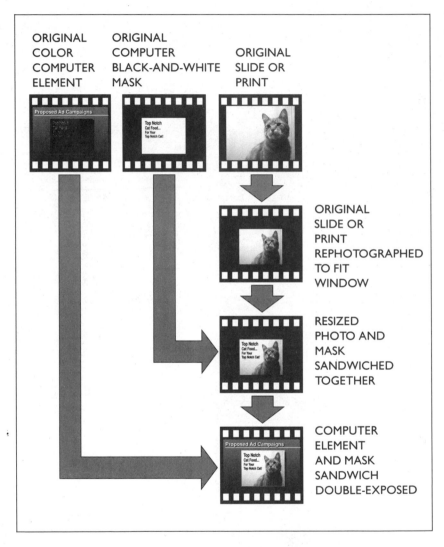

The quality of a conventional photocomposite depends on the accuracy of the mask, the quality of the original photograph, and the skill of the photographer. There is very little margin for error in this process, so consult your service bureau and be sure to do a trial run before diving into a big project involving conventional photocomposites.

DIGITAL PHOTOCOMPOSITES

Digital photocomposites are created entirely in your computer. Using scanners or electronic photography, color bitmap images are stored on disk, where they can be viewed, cropped, altered, and then combined with vector graphics to create an electronic version of the photocomposite.

The first step in creating digital photocomposites is to get the photographic image into your computer.

Scanners

Scanners have become an integral part of creating professional-looking presentations. In addition to scanning photographs for composites, you can also scan logos and other artwork for tracing in a drawing program. There are three types of scanners: flatbed, slide, and hand-held.

A *flatbed scanner* works like a copy machine. You place the artwork to be scanned face down on a glass plate, which is moved in small increments. A bright light allows an optical system to project the image onto an electronic sensor, which converts the reflected light into signals that are interpreted by your computer to create the final bitmap image. Figure 11.20 shows how a flatbed scanner works.

Flatbed scanners are rated according to the maximum resolving power of the sensor. Resolution is measured in dots per inch (dpi), which is the smallest area that can be detected by the sensor. Consumer models range from 300 to 600 dpi; professional scanners designed for high-end publishing can scan thousands of dots per inch.

Flatbed scanners come in both gray-scale and color models. The gray-scale machines will usually scan up to 256 levels of gray (8-bit); the color machines scan up to 16.7 million colors (24-bit).

A *slide scanner* performs the same task for 35mm slides, except that the light is projected through the slide rather than reflected. Resolution on a slide scanner is measured in *line resolution*; the maximum number of individual rows of pixels that can be scanned from a slide. Most consumer

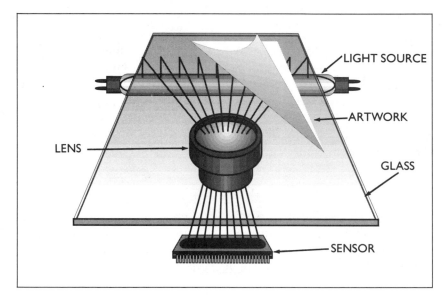

Figure 11.20:

A flatbed scanner

slide scanners work at resolutions from 1500 to 3000 lines. All slide scanners have a 24-bit color depth. Figure 11.21 illustrates how a slide scanner works.

A *hand-held scanner* is a flatbed scanner turned inside out. The optical system is located behind a glass window in the unit. Holding the scanner in your hand, you pass it over the artwork to create the computer data. Generally, hand-held scanners are not accurate enough for scanning photographs to be used in presentations.

Electronic Photography

Unfortunately, you can't tuck a flatbed or slide scanner under your arm, take it out to the branch office, and take snapshots of the winner of the monthly sales contest. But you can take an electronic camera.

An electronic camera is essentially a video camera that records a still image in digital form, just like a scanner. Products such as the Sony Mavica system and the Canon Xapshot store digital images on a small

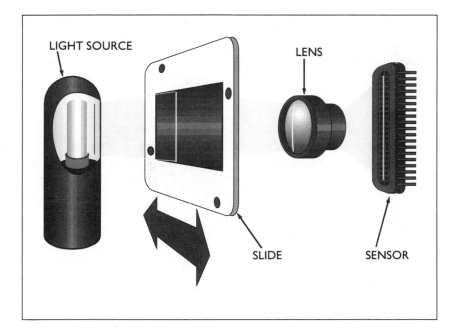

Figure 11.21:

A slide scanner

diskette, which can then be accessed by your computer. You can transfer your best photographs to your hard disk for storage, and then reuse the camera diskette for your next photographic session.

Electronic photography's main drawback is that the images have a fairly low resolution of 1000 pixels square or less. However, several companies are planning to introduce models that produce high-resolution digital photographs.

The Data Storage Dilemma

The biggest drawback to using any sort of digital photographic image is the sheer size of the file created. A 24-bit scan of an 8-by-10-inch photograph at 300 dpi creates a file of up to *22 megabytes*!

One way to avoid wasting disk space (and time) is to *not* scan your materials at the highest possible resolution. When you are going to place the scanned images in 35mm slides, you should not be thinking in terms of dots per inch, but rather of the total number of pixels being created. The maximum number of pixels necessary to create a clear, full-frame, photographic image of a natural scene on 35mm film is about 1200 pixels wide by 800 pixels high. Photographs to be placed in windows may need even fewer pixels to be usable.

When you need a photograph for compositing in a slide, scan at a resolution that will give you the appropriate number of pixels. For example, an 8-by-10-inch photograph scanned at only 120 dpi will have more than enough pixels to be sharp on a slide (8 inches by 10 inches by 120 dpi = 960 pixels x 1200 pixels).

Keep in mind that to fully fill a slide frame, a bitmap graphic needs to have its pixels in the same 2 to 3 proportion as the slide. Different proportions will leave gaps in the slide frame, as if you used the wrong page setup in formatting your slides.

Storing even medium-resolution photographic files can add up to a lot of disk space. If you are planning to use electronic photography and create photocomposites, be prepared to spend a lot of money on image storage. Here are some tips on storing your large image files:

- Invest in a large hard drive (at least 150 megabyte) to handle currently active files. You will quickly run out of disk space with anything smaller.

- Large bitmap files can often be reduced to 20 percent or less of their original size by using image compression or archiving software. Save valuable disk space with PC archiving software such as ARC and PKZIP, or Macintosh compression software such as Stuffit, DiskDoubler, and CompactPro.

- Use removable storage such as Bernoulli, Syquest, or tape backup to store files that are no longer current. Prices on removable storage devices have dropped radically in recent years, and they now compete with floppy disks on price per megabyte.

THE
REAL
WORLD   THE 64,000 KILOBYTE PRESENTATION

Thursday, October 11, 10:00 am: Jim Gonzalez is on the phone with Larry Thomas at Slides R Us, talking about a small problem with the files he is preparing to send over for imaging.

"Well, Larry, some of these files are pretty big. I have some slides with photos of the bigshots, and they're all about 6 megabytes apiece. How should I send them over to you?"

"That sounds awfully big for simple photocomposites, Jim. How did you scan them?"

"We got some black-and-white prints from personnel and scanned them on our ScanBoss 600, then imported them into our presentation file."

"How big were the photos?"

"8 by 10's," says Jim.

"And I'll bet you scanned them at 300 dpi, or thereabouts, right?"

"Right."

Larry winces. Fortunately, Jim was a good client who could handle a bit of last-minute advice. "Jim, I think you may have to rework those photo slides. It sounds like your scans are much too big. I could image them as they are, but it would take much longer than a standard image and that will slow down delivery *and* cost you extra."

Jim is dubious. "You mean I should redo all four slides?"

"Absolutely. You don't need such large files to have a good-looking photocomposite. I'd rescan all four of the photos at 100 dpi. At that rate, your files will come in under a megabyte apiece and you can just toss them on floppies."

"Will that be enough for a sharp photo? It sounds like pretty low resolution."

"Don't worry. Even at 100 dpi, you'll have an 800 by 1000 pixel file. That's plenty sharp, enough if you're not filling the frame. I assume these photos are going in windows on the slide?"

"Yes," says Jim.

"Then don't worry. They'll be fine. Why don't you go ahead and send me the rest of your files? When the four composites are ready, send them over and I'll put them on the schedule with no rush charges, since the rework is my idea."

"OK, Larry," Jim replies. "I'll have those four to you by the end of the day. By the way, it looks like we're going to need two each of these shows after all. Can we fit that into the shooting schedule?"

"That's no problem, Jim. Make sure you mark two each on your order form."

"Will do. Thanks a lot, Larry. I'll talk to you later this afternoon. Bye."

"Bye, Jim."

SUMMARY

You can enliven your presentation and improve your communication with the audience by incorporating illustrations and photography into your slides. Here are some of the guidelines for using illustrations in presentations:

■ Illustrations should be message-driven and in a style that is appropriate to your speech and message. Never include a picture just because it looks nice.

■ The speech should give a verbal guide to what the audience is seeing. Never assume an illustration is self-explanatory.

■ Maintain a consistent illustration style throughout your presentation. Avoid the "kitchen sink" approach to illustration.

■ Bitmap or pixel-based graphics are described by their resolution and their color depth. Output resolution is limited to the actual number of pixels in the file.

■ Vector, or object-oriented, graphics are resolution-independent. They will print at the maximum resolution of the output device.

■ Integrate photography into your presentation using photocomposites, produced by a service bureau or with a computer. Check with your service bureau for advice on combining photographs with presentation graphics.

■ When you create digital photocomposites, keep your file sizes under control by limiting scans to less than 1200 by 800 pixels. Use compression software to save disk space.

chapter 12

Producing Your Final Output

The final step in preparing a presentation is creating the 35mm slides or overhead transparencies and producing your speaker notes and handouts. Your output equipment options range from $1,000 laser printers to $50,000 film recorders to $80,000 color copiers. The method you choose to produce your final output should be based on three main factors: the nature of your audience, your presentation goals, and your budget.

The level of quality required for your output depends on the type of presentation you are producing. As you would expect, the higher the quality of the output, the higher the price you pay for it.

MATCHING THE OUTPUT QUALITY TO THE TYPE OF PRESENTATION

Presentations generally fall into two major types: peer presentations and public presentations.

In a *peer presentation,* a speaker presents information to a small group of people within his or her organization. For example, it may be a presentation to fellow employees or immediate superiors regarding a budget, proposal, or another project. The relationship between the speaker and his audience is usually casual, with the emphasis on cooperation and dialogue rather than showmanship.

Peer presentations don't call for sophisticated graphics or high-quality output. Their main purpose is nuts-and-bolts communication, and they often involve group interaction. Most companies wisely discourage any wasteful extravagance when it comes to in-house presentations, preferring to save their money for more image-oriented public presentations. Overhead transparencies or 35mm slides produced in-house using a desktop film recorder are suitable for peer presentations. Computer screen shows, which allow last-minute alterations to slides, are also a good choice for these "shirt-sleeve" presentations.

A *public presentation* is one in which the speaker attempts to inform, motivate, and persuade an audience composed mostly of outsiders. Whenever a presentation is given to strangers, the relationship between the speaker and the audience is more formal. The speaker presents information to the audience, and any interaction between the speaker and audience occurs during a question-and-answer period at the end of the presentation.

A public audience can be unpredictable; your audience members might be receptive, neutral, or actively hostile. Such presentations rely much more on showmanship and image than do peer presentations, simply because an unknown audience must be *involved* before they are *convinced*.

Public presentations demand more attention to the quality of the final output. In addition to informing the audience, your graphics must also perform public relations functions. Today's audiences have had a lifetime of exposure to high-quality presentation graphics, from billboards to television advertising. In a public forum, your images must compete in quality with graphics produced by professional designers (not to mention MTV!).

The most common output option for a public presentation is 35mm slides. For presentations that involve group interaction, overhead transparencies are a good choice. Screen shows, animation, and even live video, output on high-quality video projection units, are other options for public presentations.

It never pays to cut corners when you are preparing your final slides, overhead transparencies, and handouts for public presentations. Use professional-quality film recorders and color printers for your output. Use high-quality projection equipment and, if possible, have an experienced operator on hand to handle projection problems.

PRODUCING 35MM SLIDES

Getting your presentation graphics from disk to final slide is an exacting process, which starts with producing the right type of files to send to a film recorder and ends with processed and mounted slides. You can produce 35mm slides in-house with your own film recorder or send your files to a service bureau for final output.

FILM RECORDERS

A film recorder is a device for interpreting graphics information and imaging it onto standard color slide film. Film recorders produce much higher density information than most other computer output devices. Typically, slides are imaged at a resolution of 4096 by 2730 pixels (4K, or 4000 lines), for a total of more than 11 million pixels packed into a film area of $1\frac{1}{2}$ square inches. Some film recorders will also image at a resolution of 8192 by 5460 pixels (8K, or 8000 lines), although this is beyond the resolving capacity of most 35mm film. By comparison, a full-page, letter-size graphic from a laser printer displays about 3200 by 2200 pixels in an area 50 times larger than a slide.

Imaging Software

A film recorder, like all other computer devices, is controlled by software. The process of preparing the vector and bit map graphics in your file for use by the film recorder is called *rasterizing*. The imaging software that controls the film recorder analyzes your graphics file and converts it to a series of pixels in a grid matching the area of the slide.

Each pixel is analyzed for color and is broken down into components of red, green, and blue in a process that is similar to the way color separations are created for print media. The data for each of the three color components is then temporarily stored on the hard disk of the computer controlling the film recorder.

Most service bureaus use special imaging software packages to send files to a film recorder. All require that graphic files be saved in a limited number of file formats. The most common file formats are PostScript, Macintosh PICT, and Matrix SCODL. (The SCODL format is specific to Agfa-Matrix Corporation's film recorders.) Your service bureau may require you to save your graphics in one of these formats.

Some desktop film recorders also come with drivers that allow direct printing to slides from within applications. Most consumer models use this method for imaging.

Film Recorder Operation

All film recorders use the same basic method for converting your graphics files into slides. The speed and quality of a film recorder depend on the quality of its parts. Every film recorder consists of three main components—the camera, the filter assembly, and the CRT (cathode-ray tube)—all encased in a lightproof cabinet to prevent reflections (see the color illustration at the end of Chapter 7).

The camera portion of the film recorder advances an unexposed frame of film into position and then opens the shutter to start the exposure. The filter assembly rotates the filter wheel to place the red filter into position in front of the camera lens. (The usual order of exposure in film recorders is red, then green, then blue.)

The red exposure data is sent by the computer to the CRT in the form of a scan line of up to 8000 pixels. Each pixel can have up to 256 levels of gray which, when photographed through the red filter, yield the same number of reds. The scan line moves across the face of the CRT until the red data is completely exposed to the film. The filter assembly then rotates the green filter into position, and the green data is sent to the CRT. The blue data is treated similarly. When the blue data is exposed, the camera closes the shutter and advances the film for the next slide.

This explanation oversimplifies the amazing fact that a professional high-resolution (8000-line) film recorder processes almost 128 *million* pixels in less than one minute to expose a single frame of film. Most standard 35mm slides are imaged at 4000 lines, not 8000, but even that is quite a feat.

Types of Film Recorders

Slides can be created with a desktop film recorder or a professional film recorder. Desktop film recorders are generally purchased by individual and small in-house operations. Professional film recorders are designed for high-volume users, such as service bureaus and large corporate graphics departments.

Desktop film recorders (usually priced under $12,000) trade off speed and quality for price. The quality of the slides they produce is acceptable for peer presentations, but it is much lower than the quality of the images created by their more powerful professional counterparts. These types of film recorders have the following disadvantages:

■ Their cameras are usually modified consumer 35mm models, not specially designed for imaging. Only 36 frames can be imaged before the camera must be reloaded with film.

■ The size restrictions necessary to make a compact consumer device limit the size and power of the CRT.

■ Imaging times can be up to 15 minutes for some slides, especially those with complex gradient color.

■ Color rendition and brightness can vary unpredictably.

Professional film recorders (which range in price from $25,000 to more than $100,000) deliver much higher quality for their higher price. Slides imaged on these film recorders are suitable for the most sophisticated presentations. These types of film recorders have the following advantages:

■ They use special high-quality optics, which eliminate distortion and improve image sharpness.

■ Large-capacity film transports allow imaging of hundreds of frames without reloading.

■ Large, industrial-strength CRTs are brighter and sharper, yielding more saturated color and faster imaging times.

■ Special automatic calibration systems maintain color quality and consistency.

SLIDE PRODUCTION WITH IN-HOUSE FILM RECORDERS

How do you decide whether to invest in your own film recorder? There are several good reasons to do your own imaging:

■ Security: If you deal in confidential information, imaging your own slides keeps it behind closed doors.

- Convenience: An in-house film recorder works on your schedule and never closes or goes on vacation.

- Fast turnaround: In an emergency, slides can be imaged immediately.

One reason you should not use to justify an in-house film recorder is the cost of slides. Despite manufacturers' advertising claims, the cost benefits of an in-house film recorder are marginal compared with using a service bureau. Equipment, supplies, processing, and staff costs will be only slightly less per slide than service bureau charges, especially if you need high-quality slides.

Here are some factors to consider before purchasing a film recorder for in-house use:

- Output quality: Determine what sort of presentations you are doing and the quality of the images you desire. Check the output from different film recorders, comparing sharpness, color saturation and contrast, and smoothness of gradients.

- Volume: You should be producing at least 100 slides per month to justify the trouble and expense of even the most inexpensive desktop film recorder.

- Hidden expenses: In addition to the cost of the film recorder, take into account the costs of film, processing, mounting, delivery charges to a photo lab, and staff time (and overtime!) required for in-house imaging.

- Staff commitment: Like any output device, a film recorder requires someone to operate, maintain, and purchase supplies for it. Even moderate production volumes (600 slides per month and up) may require at least a part-time employee. If the necessary manpower isn't already available, you'll need to add staff.

SLIDE PRODUCTION WITH IMAGING SERVICE BUREAUS

Most people who produce presentation graphics send their files to a service bureau for imaging. Service bureaus come in all shapes and sizes, ranging from large nationwide chains to small mom-and-pop operations.

All service bureaus will take your files, image them onto 35mm film, process the images, and mount your slides. Which one you choose depends on your budget, the amount of support you need, and your turnaround time requirements.

National Service Bureaus

At the large end of the scale are the nationwide imaging service bureau chains: Genigraphics, Autographix, and Magicorp. All three of these companies offer high-quality slides at competitive prices. Many presentation graphics software packages include special drivers or communications modules to prepare files for one or more of these service bureaus. The driver software allows you to send your files to the service bureau via modem, which is especially useful if you live outside a major metropolitan area and do not have access to a local bureau.

Using a national service bureau is like sending your vacation snapshots to Kodak. The turnaround time is excellent and the quality is high. What you don't get is a lot of individual attention and service. National service bureaus have very specific delivery and turnaround schedules; you must send your files by a particular time of day if you want delivery within 24 hours. If you do not have much experience with presentation graphics, you may need more help than a national service bureau can provide.

Local and Regional Service Bureaus

Local service bureau operations can range from a local copy shop with a desktop film recorder to a full-service audiovisual provider with the same sophisticated equipment and capabilities as a national service bureau. Here are some guidelines for selecting the right service bureau for your slide imaging:

■ Do the employees have experience with your software? Is the staff knowledgeable and professional? Your service bureau should be a source of advice and troubleshooting, not just slides and overhead transparencies.

■ What kind of equipment does the service bureau use? A service bureau should use professional equipment, for both its quality and reliability.

■ What sort of film processing is used? Many smaller bureaus use a local photo lab for processing, which slows turnaround time. Others process their own film by hand, which leads to processing inconsistencies. A top-notch service bureau has full professional film-processing capabilities in-house.

■ Does the service bureau offer a variety of services beyond slides, including training or other support services? The experience and success of a service bureau are often reflected in the variety of services it provides. A service bureau with the confidence to offer training and support usually has the expertise required to produce high-quality slides.

■ Can the service bureau work with your deadlines? Within reasonable technical limitations (such as imaging and developing times), a service bureau should do everything in its power to meet your deadlines.

You may notice that price wasn't mentioned in the list above. It was omitted because it should be the last and least important criterion for selecting a service bureau. Service bureaus must compete in their local areas. Most charge from $9 to $15 per slide. The cost of film and processing varies little from one operation to another. The real differences are the service and quality you receive.

The most important thing is to develop a relationship with your service bureau. Let them get familiar with you and your special imaging requirements. For example, if the service bureau staff knows which colors and typefaces you normally use, they will be able to detect missing fonts or color problems earlier in the process, saving you time and money.

Local service bureaus in your area should be listed in your telephone book Yellow Pages, under Audio-Visual Services or Slides. You can also refer to Appendix B in this book for a list of local and regional service bureaus.

SLIDE MOUNTING AND HANDLING

After your film is imaged and developed, it needs to be mounted and placed in slide trays for projection. You can mount your own slides, but generally you should leave it to the service bureau or photo lab. There are several different types of mounts for your slides, as shown in Figure 12.1, and trays in which to place them. The slides should be numbered and inserted into the tray in the proper orientation.

Figure 12.1:

Types of mounts for 35mm slides

Plastic and Cardboard Mounts

If you send your computer files to be imaged by a service bureau or you send your self-imaged film to be processed by a photo lab, you will probably receive them in a standard plastic or cardboard mount. Cardboard mounts are used by mass-market photo processors like Kodak. The majority of service bureaus and small photo labs use plastic mounts.

For either plastic or cardboard mounts, a frame of film is cut from the processed strip of film, and the film chip is placed in the slide mount, where a small amount of adhesive holds it in place. The mount is then sealed by pressure or heat to hold the film firmly. Some slippage of the film within the mount may occur, so make sure you allow for it by maintaining a 5 percent margin in your format design, as described in Chapter 6.

Glass and Glassless Pin-Registered Mounts

Glass pin-registered mounts are the standard type used by the audiovisual industry. The glass protects the film from dust and scratches. Molded into the mount are small rectangular pins, which fit in the sprocket holes of the film. When imaged on a pin-registered film recorder, the elements of each slide will line up perfectly from one slide to the next.

This type of mount is essential if you are using multiple projectors to create smooth fades from one slide to another. The main disadvantage of glass mounts is that they are very heavy and prone to breakage (if a slide tray is dropped).

Glassless pin-registered mounts offer the same tight registration as those with glass, but with considerably less weight. Service bureaus charge a premium for pin-registered slide mounts.

Black Duplication Mounts

If you are planning to distribute many copies of your show (such as to your company's sales force around the country), it is often not economical to create many copies of it directly on a film recorder. The most cost-effective method is to have each slide of your show duplicated photographically.

For this type of reproduction, you need to image only one master set of slides for the photo lab to copy. Your master set of slides should be mounted in black pin-registered duplication mounts. The black color prevents reflections, and pin-registration ensures accurate framing for the best possible duplicates. Your duplicate sets can be in any type of mount.

Slide Trays

The largest supplier of slide trays is Eastman Kodak, who developed the Carousel projector and slide tray. Kodak manufactures three types of trays, which all have equivalents in other manufacturers' product lines:

- Kodak B80T, the standard Carousel tray, holds 80 slides in any type of mount.

- Kodak AV780, a special slide tray with a dust cover, also holds 80 slides in any type of mount. This tray is very useful if you are going to be traveling with your presentation. The plastic cover protects the slides from dust and dirt.

- Kodak B140 holds 140 slides, but only those with unregistered plastic or cardboard mounts. Pin-registered mounts are usually too thick to fit in the narrow slots of this tray.

Figure 12.2 shows the different types of slide trays.

Figure 12.2:

Types of slide trays

Placement of Slides in Trays

The orientation in which your slides should be placed in a slide tray depends on how they are to be projected.

Front projection is the most common method of projecting slides. The projector is placed at the rear of the audience, and it projects slides over the heads of the viewers onto the screen in front of them. For front projection, your slides should be placed in the tray upside down and with the right-reading side facing away from the screen when it is projected. The right-reading side is the side of the mount facing you when you can read the slide correctly.

Rear projection is used in some corporate conference rooms, as well as in large auditoriums. The projector is placed behind a translucent screen, and the slides are projected onto it. For rear projection, slides should be placed in the tray upside down and with the right-reading side facing toward the screen.

If you are making a presentation in an unfamiliar setting, call ahead and find out what sort of projection setup is being used. Then tray your slides accordingly.

Slide Numbering

One of the biggest disasters to befall a presenter is dropping the slide tray just before the presentation and having to reconstruct the slide order in a hurry. Numbering your slides will make disaster recovery a lot easier. Using a permanent marker, place a number, corresponding to the slide's place in the presentation, on the slide mount. The number should be placed in the "thumb" position: where you would normally hold the slide when placing it in a slide tray from behind the projector, as shown in Figure 12.3.

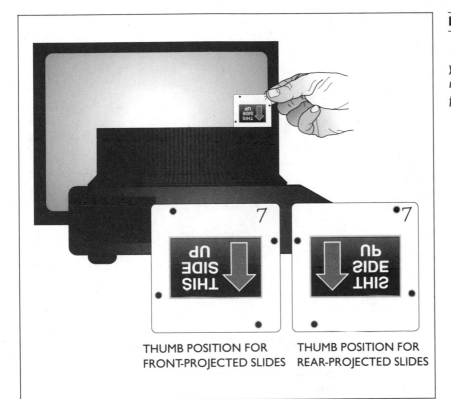

Figure 12.3:

Place slides in trays to match your projection setup, and number them in the "thumb" position

THUMB POSITION FOR
FRONT-PROJECTED SLIDES

THUMB POSITION FOR
REAR-PROJECTED SLIDES

PRODUCING OVERHEAD TRANSPARENCIES

Overhead transparencies are especially useful for presentations that include audience interaction. The speaker can write on the projection surface to respond to a question or comment visually as well as verbally.

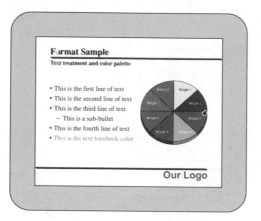

There are a variety of ways to produce overhead transparencies. Because your output choices range from low-cost, black-and-white laser printer transparencies to relatively expensive photo-quality transparencies, your budget is a prime consideration.

PRINTED OVERHEAD TRANSPARENCIES

You can produce overhead transparencies with several types of printers. The most common printers used for presentation-quality transparencies are laser, color wax thermal, color inkjet, and dye sublimation printers.

Laser Printers

Laser printer transparencies are the lowest cost presentation medium. Average costs are less than $1 per transparency. If you design a black-and-white presentation with the laser printer in mind, the final output can be attractive. Keep the design very simple, avoid large filled areas, use patterns sparingly, and use black copy and graphics on a clear (white) background.

Use overhead transparency film designed for laser printers, which is available from several manufacturers. Other types of transparency material may melt in the heat of the printer's fusing unit, causing severe damage to the printer. Place the material in the paper tray of your printer and print each frame of your presentation.

Color Wax Thermal and Color Inkjet Printers

Color wax thermal printers work on the same principle as standard four-color printing. However, they use a special wax-based ink, which is melted onto the paper in separate cyan, magenta, yellow, and black (CMYK) dots. The dots are printed in a tight pattern, which the viewer's eye interprets as a single color dot.

The process of creating other colors through the mixture of these four secondary colors is called *dithering*. The dithering process can produce many colors, but often at the expense of creating a textured look in certain colors due to the arrangement of the CMYK dots.

Color is applied by pressing a very thin sheet of plastic material against the paper or transparency material and passing it through the printer. The plastic is coated with wax-based ink in one of the CMYK colors. As the two sheets pass through the printer, a thermal print head melts small areas of the ink sheet, causing them to stick to the paper. The process is repeated for each of the four colors.

Initially very expensive, color wax thermal printers are now competitive in price with high-end laser printers (in the $5,000 range). This is the best type of printer to use if you create a lot of color overhead transparencies. Service bureau charges are from $5 to $16 per transparency.

Like color wax thermal printers, color inkjet printers produce colors through the application of small color dots, except that the color dots are sprayed onto the paper. Because the ink used in most color inkjet printers is more opaque than the wax-based ink used in thermal printers, these types of printers produce low-quality overhead transparencies. The exception is the IRIS color inkjet printer, a very high-end device that produces output similar to that of a dye sublimation printer.

Dye Sublimation Printers

In a dye sublimation printer, the image is formed by layering dots of a translucent dye (cyan, magenta, and yellow) on top of each other, rather than side by side. This effect creates a dot of pure mixed color, which blends with its neighbor to create a true continuous field of color. Images produced on dye sublimation printers are virtually indistinguishable from true color photographs and transparencies.

The major drawback to these printers is their rather astronomical cost, both for equipment and supplies. Printers range from $24,000 to $60,000, and supplies can cost up to $12 per page. But for many applications, the price is worth the high quality. Service bureaus charge from $15 to $50 for each dye sublimation transparency.

PHOTO PROCESS TRANSPARENCIES

Another method for producing high-quality transparencies is photographic processing. To create a photo process transparency, your file is first imaged as a 35mm slide, and then the slide is photographically enlarged to fill an 8-inch-by-10-inch sheet of color film. The image quality is almost as good as 35mm slides, although type will often be a little blurry due to the extreme enlargement. The transparencies are resistant to scratches and easy to clean.

Photo process transparency material costs can be high, due to the cost of film and processing. However, there are a few photo transparency systems, such as the CibaCopy process, which produce affordable high-quality transparencies from slides. The best idea is to have your photo process transparencies produced by a photo lab or service bureau. Large-format film processing requires exact procedures and lots of chemicals that aren't appropriate in most offices. Service bureaus charge from $8 to $25 per photo process transparency, depending on the process used.

OVERHEAD TRANSPARENCY MOUNTING AND HANDLING

The light backgrounds frequently used in overhead transparencies are particularly susceptible to dust and fingerprints. Color wax thermal materials also scratch easily. Because of the great amount of moving, shuffling, stacking, and general abuse that they suffer during their lifetime, overhead transparencies must be mounted and stored properly to preserve maximum image quality. Here are some tips for extending the life of your transparencies:

- To prevent damage during storage, handling, and projection, overhead transparencies should be mounted in cardboard or plastic frames (available from most office or photographic supply stores).

- Store and transport the transparencies in a box, with paper slipsheets between the transparencies to prevent scratching.

- Handle transparencies by their frames to prevent fingerprints and scratches.

- Store transparencies, especially those created using the color wax thermal process, away from heat.

Always number your overhead transparencies! One slip of the hand can knock over a whole stack at the last moment, causing a frantic scramble to figure out their proper order.

If you want to write on your preprinted overhead transparencies, don't waste money having them reprinted every time you give a speech. Tape a clear acetate sheet to the top of the overhead transparency frame, covering the preprinted transparency. Write on it during the presentation and simply discard and replace it with a fresh sheet for your next presentation, as shown in Figure 12.4.

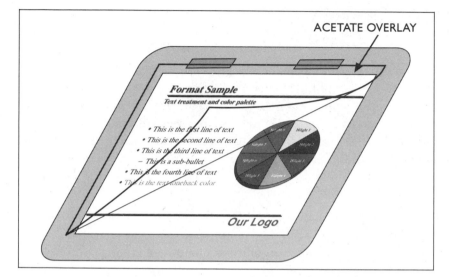

ACETATE OVERLAY

Figure 12.4:

Write on the acetate overlay, not directly on the preprinted transparency

PRODUCING SPEAKER NOTES AND HANDOUTS

In addition to your slides or overhead transparencies, you may want to create speaker notes and handouts for your presentation. Some presentation graphics packages have built-in capabilities for creating notes and handouts. You can also use word processing, drawing, or page layout software to produce these presentation materials.

SPEAKER NOTES

Speaker notes are the final text for the speech along with copies of the graphics. The speaker can refer to the printed version of each slide instead of looking at the screen.

The best layout for speaker notes is to place a large image of the current slide at the top of the page with the speech directly below it, as shown in Figure 12.5. Here are some guidelines for creating speaker notes.

- Create a separate notes page for each slide in the presentation. For your build or reveal series, show only the final version of the slide.

- Set the speech text in at least 14-point type (18 is better), double spaced, with left justification.

- Each page should end with a slide-change cue to move on to the next slide and notes page. On build slides, use a colored marker to mark each slide change in the text.

- Include page numbers below the text or adjacent to the graphic. This will make it easier to reassemble the script if it gets out of order.

- To make the speaker's job as easy as possible, place the speaker notes in a loose-leaf binder so that the pages will lie flat and be easy to turn.

If someone other than the speaker is operating the projector, make a duplicate of the speaker notes for the operator to follow. All cues and text changes should be marked in this copy as well.

AUDIENCE HANDOUTS

Many presenters are tempted to load the audience with tons of paper to take home after a presentation. These "souvenir" handouts usually end up in the wastepaper basket unread, no doubt contributing to the destruction of our forests and global warming. Handouts are often misused in this way, but there are some very good reasons for using them:

- When your slides present very complex data, a handout enables the audience to study the information more closely, both during and after the presentation.

- If your audience needs detailed information from your speech to pass on to others, handouts containing your entire slide show will free them from taking copious notes.

- In training presentations, a complete set of handouts can be a visual manual that provides space for students to take notes.

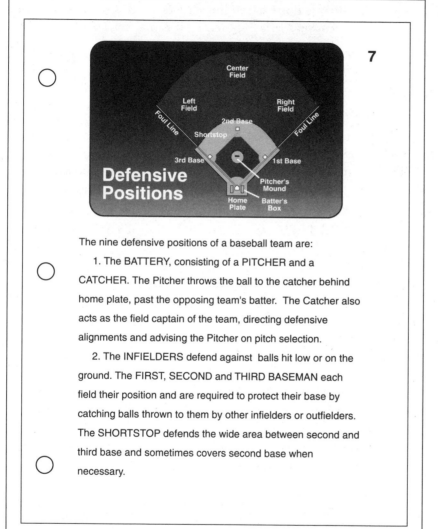

The best format for your audience handout depends on your purpose for distributing them. The following sections provide general guidelines for creating handouts and specific suggestions for the three main types of handouts: complex slide data, presentation summaries, and training materials.

General Guidelines for Audience Handouts

Most presentation graphics programs will automatically create some form of audience handout. However, you may have to modify the format to ensure a professional look. Here are some tips:

- Don't crowd the page. Place comfortable margins around your graphics. Leave room for three-hole punching even if you aren't punching the paper yourself.

- Always include the speaker's name, company, and the title of the presentation on every handout page.

- Print only the final step, which contains all the information, in a build series (except for stepback reveal series).

- Use the best printer available in your office for a master copy, preferably a laser printer. The copies you distribute should be clean and professional in appearance.

- If you have several pages, number them. In handouts with several slides on a slide page, you can also number each page.

- If you have more than 20 pages in the handout, put them in a binder for easy handling.

- Refer to handout pages by number in the speech. Don't let the audience guess what they're supposed to be viewing.

Handouts for Complex Slide Data

The most common use of handouts is when the data on your slides is too complex to follow. Tables, complex charts, timelines, and other graphics may require a handout to make the audience's job easier. Create handouts only for the slides that need clarification. Print one slide per page in landscape orientation to match the slide or overhead transparency format, as shown in the example in Figure 12.6.

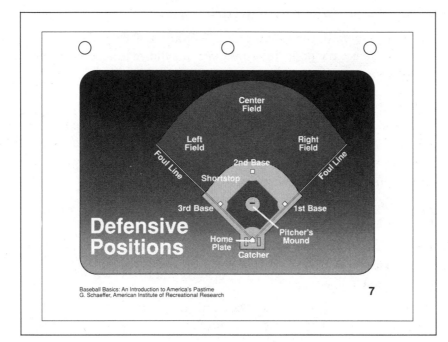

Figure 12.6:

An audience handout for a complex slide

The handouts should be given to the audience members before the beginning of the presentation. Even though reading ahead might be a problem, interrupting a presentation to pass out handouts would be worse.

Handouts for Presentation Summaries

If it is necessary to give your audience handouts containing your entire slide show, the most important thing is to keep the audience from getting ahead of the speaker by reading the handouts in advance. If possible, give the handouts to the audience at the end of the presentation.

To conserve printing costs and create a manageable document, place multiple slides on a page. You can place from two to six frames on a page, either in portrait or landscape mode, as shown in Figure 12.7.

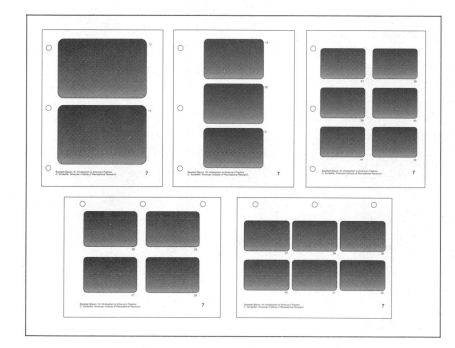

Figure 12.7:

Formats for presentation summary handouts

Make sure all the copy on the handouts is readable. Adjust the number of frames per page for readability if necessary. Number each frame as well as each page in the handout.

Handouts for Training Presentations

For training presentations, handouts can serve as a quick and easy training manual. Training handouts should be distributed before the presentation.

Create handouts with plenty of room for notes next to the slide graphics. The best orientation is a column of three or four frames per page, as shown in Figure 12.8. Use a cover page for the presentation title and include a blank page or two at the end for extra notes.

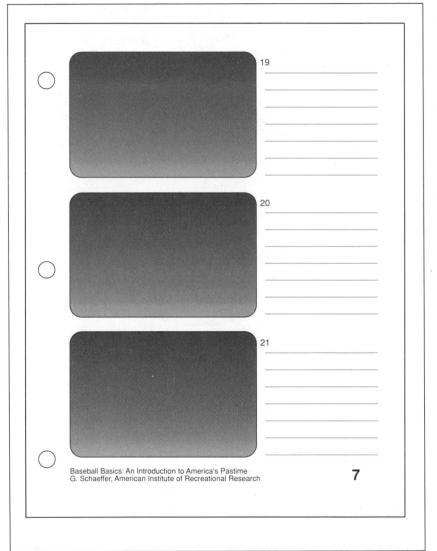

Baseball Basics: An Introduction to America's Pastime
G. Schaeffer, American Institute of Recreational Research

Figure 12.8:

A page of a handout for a training presentation

THE REAL WORLD   THE PAPER CHASE

Thursday, October 11, 1:00 pm: Jim Gonzalez breathes a sigh of relief as he ships out the final disk to the service bureau for imaging. The last two weeks have been amazingly busy. In addition to the slide shows he has been creating, he also had to lay out the corporate newsletter, an employee benefits brochure, and charts for the press release about the Billie Bob Boone stock transaction. He is just about to go out for lunch when George Spelvin walks into his office.

"Good afternoon, Jim. I just wanted to thank you for the fine job you've done. We all think this is going to be a terrific presentation, and you were a big factor in making it that way."

"Thanks, Mr. Spelvin."

"There's just one more thing we need to finish up this project."

Cold chills run down Jim's spine. "What's that?"

"I need 40 sets of handouts of the presentation to give to the analysts."

Remaining outwardly calm, Jim replies, "No problem. But I don't think the company copy center can handle that job in a single day on such short notice. I may have to farm it out to a copy service."

"That's fine. Do what's necessary. Thanks again."

"By the way, how many slides do you want on a page?"

"Can we do more than one?" George asks.

"Sure. In fact, I think we'd better. There are almost 110 slides in all three shows. That's a lot of paper."

"What do you suggest?"

"Let's put four slides on a page. That will cut the number of pages down to less than 30 per book."

"Good. That will be fine. Thanks, Jim."

Jim's hand reaches for the phone before George is out of the office. He's soon on the line with Tom Freeman of the Copy Shoppe.

"Hi, Tom. This is Jim Gonzalez at Hypothetical. I've got a bit of an emergency here, and I hope you can help me out."

"Afternoon, Jim. What's up?"

"I've got a rush copy job for some booklets we need to put together, 40 copies, about 30 pages each. I'll also need them bound with a cover. By tomorrow, end of day."

"That's no problem, Jim. When can I have copy to work with?"

"Probably not until the end of the day today. I'll start printing it on the laser printer right now. I'll also have to do a cover for it. I'll talk to you later about details."

"OK. Call me when you have more information."

Jim fires up his presentation graphics software to set up his handouts. He sets up a page with four slides on it and a short header with the Hypothetical logo and the title.

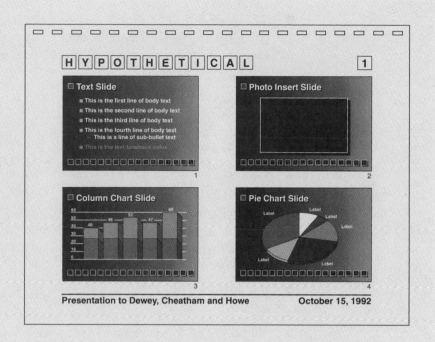

He starts the file printing and goes to lunch.

SUMMARY

The way that you produce your presentation depends on your audience, your presentation goals, and your budget. Here is a review of your output options and the factors to consider:

■ Peer presentations are given to small groups of people within an organization. They are simpler and more casual, so they require less expensive output. Overhead transparencies are the most common medium for peer presentations.

■ Public presentations are given to inform, motivate, and persuade an audience of outsiders. Quality and graphic sophistication are more important. The most common medium for public presentations is 35mm slides.

- The quality of a film recorder is determined by the quality of its parts, such as its CRT and the optics in the camera. Film recorders range from inexpensive desktop models to professional systems costing up to $100,000.

- An in-house film recorder offers security, convenience, and fast turnaround. It requires a firm commitment to support costs and staff. Producing slides in-house provides no significant cost savings compared with using a service bureau.

- Choose a service bureau based on service, reliability, and expertise. Make cost your last consideration.

- Methods for producing overhead transparencies range from using a laser printer to print black-and-white transparencies to photo processing high-quality color transparencies. Choose the one that best suits your needs and budget.

- Speaker notes include slide graphics with the speech to aid the speaker.

- Audience handouts are useful for showing complex slide data, summarizing the presentation, and serving as training materials. The best layout for audience handouts and the best time to distribute them depend on how they will be used by the audience.

chapter 13

Presentation Day

After you have produced your presentation materials, your final tasks are to polish your delivery and arrange your setting. If you are the speaker, the most important thing you can do to guarantee a successful presentation is to practice.

In a perfect world, any good-sized corporate office or hotel conference center would have a completely equipped theater, with professional projection equipment, clear sight lines, good microphones, proper amplification, and a full-time electrical engineer to keep it all running smoothly. In the real world, a presenter has to work with the space he or she is given. Turning an empty room into a suitable place for a presentation is called *staging*, and it involves everything from setting up chairs in the meeting room to distributing handouts to audience members as they leave.

REHEARSING YOUR WAY TO A SUCCESSFUL PRESENTATION

Rehearse your speech several times with the completed slides, overhead transparencies, or screen show visuals, using the same type of projection equipment you will have for the presentation. Practice in front of friends or co-workers, and ask for their opinions and advice about your presentation. Here are some things to work on during your practice sessions:

- Adjust your pacing and vocal inflection to enhance your audience's interest. Change the speed of your delivery for variety. Vary the pitch and volume of your voice to emphasize points. Strategic pauses project confidence; stop talking occasionally to let the audience members catch up to what you are saying and gather their thoughts.

- Be aware of your posture and hand gestures. Don't just stand stiffly, clutching your speaker notes; relax and communicate with your entire body.

- Practice making eye contact with audience members. As you move from point to point in your speech, switch to another person. Maintaining eye contact personalizes your presentation and can help alleviate any nervousness you may feel.

■ Practice displaying each visual at the appropriate moment in your script. Get accustomed to changing your overhead transparencies, operating the slide projector's remote control, or clicking the mouse for a screen show.

■ Mark slide-change cues and other comments clearly on your speaker notes.

And when you think you've got your presentation perfected, don't stop; practice some more.

STAGING YOUR PRESENTATION

The best planned and most beautifully designed presentation is useless if the audience can't hear the speaker or see the graphics. Your goal in staging any presentation is to make it as easy as possible for the audience to get your message.

For staging considerations, the two categories of presentation audiences are large, formal audiences in a theater-style arrangement and small, informal audiences in a conference room. Each category presents different problems for different presentation methods. Here are some factors to consider when staging a presentation:

■ Projection setup and sight lines: Positioning the projector, the screen, and audience seating for maximum visibility.

■ Speaker position: Where the speaker is in relation to the audience and the graphics.

■ Audibility: Making sure the speaker can be heard by everyone in the audience.

■ Room lighting: Adjusting the room lighting to suit the presentation medium and audience needs.

■ Handout distribution: Controlling how the audience receives printed materials.

A great deal of the work involved in staging a presentation can often be turned over to a professional audiovisual staging company (look in the Yellow Pages under Audio-Visual Equipment - Renting & Leasing). These companies can handle everything from single slide projector setup to large multispeaker, multiprojector presentations, complete with equipment operators.

If you do not hire a professional to do the job, you should be aware of the challenges of meeting room setup. No meeting room is perfect, so stay flexible, plan ahead, and take a few precautions against disaster. The following sections provide some guidelines for staging 35mm slide, overhead transparency, and screen show presentations.

35MM SLIDE PRESENTATION SETUP

When you are staging a 35mm slide presentation, you need to consider the best position for the projector, the level of room lighting, and the equipment to have on hand.

Slide Presentations in a Large Meeting Room

It is often difficult to maintain clear lines of sight when projecting slides for a large group. As shown in Figure 13.1, the projector is positioned behind the audience. It should be placed high enough to ensure that the cone of light from the projector to the screen isn't blocked by the heads of seated audience members. Audiovisual and photographic supply stores carry projector stands with telescopic legs that can raise a projector up to six feet. The ideal height for the projector is at the same level as the center of the screen, but this is difficult to achieve outside a fully equipped theater.

A proper projection screen will give better image quality, but a blank, white wall can serve as a screen. Remember, if you project onto a colored wall, it will tint your slides, possibly resulting in some strange color effects.

You should stand to one side of the screen (with or without a podium), close enough for the audience to see you peripherally while looking at the screen.

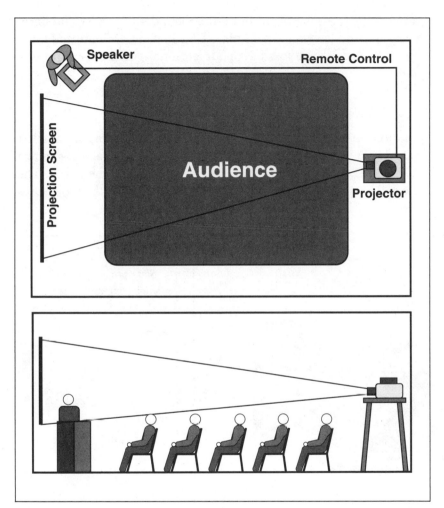

Figure 13.1:

Slide projection setup for a large meeting room

Make sure the remote-control cord is long enough to reach the podium from the projector. There should also be a reading light on the podium to illuminate the script, as well as your face if no other light is available.

When presenting in a large room, you should make sure the audience will be able to hear you. Most conference centers, hotels, and other meeting places provide microphones and amplification in any room large enough to require them. But if the room does not have amplification equipment, have someone sit in the back of the audience and listen to you. You may have to adjust your personal volume control to be heard.

Slide Presentations in a Conference Room

To project slides for a smaller group in a conference room, the simplest arrangement is to place the projector on the conference table, as shown in Figure 13.2, or on a separate table at the end opposite the screen. The projected image will clear the seated group easily, even if the projector is placed directly on the conference table.

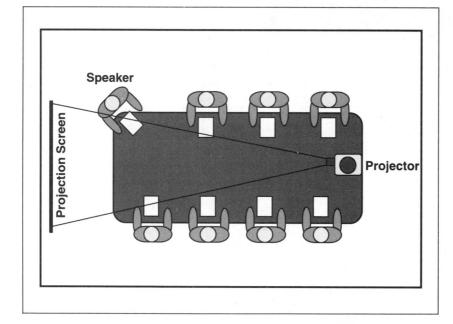

Figure 13.2:

Slide projection setup for a small conference room

You should either sit off to one side at the screen end of the table, facing the group, or stand next to the screen. Run the remote-control cord for the projector under the table.

The cooling fan on slide projectors can be quite noisy. In a small conference room, you may have to speak up to be heard by those sitting closest to the projector.

Room Lighting for Slides

The rich colors and predominantly dark backgrounds used for 35mm slides require that the overall room lighting be kept fairly low. Bright lights in the room, especially if they shine directly on the projection screen, will cause the colors of the slides to wash out. Text will be difficult to read, and color contrast in graphics will disappear. But don't leave yourself in the dark. A separate light on the speaker will greatly increase audience attention, if it can be done without washing out the screen.

Arrange to have a room-lighting control available at the podium. If this is not possible, agree on a lighting-change signal between the speaker and whoever has access to the controls.

Disaster-Avoidance Equipment for Slide Presentations

If you are taking your own projector to a meeting, don't count on having everything you need available. Be prepared for the worst possible scenario; pack some insurance along with your projector and slides:

- A 25-foot extension cord, because the nearest outlet may not be within reach of the projector's power cord. Also include a three-prong adapter in case you need to project in an older building that doesn't have modern wiring.

- A spare bulb for the projector, because your projector's bulb may blow out at the worst possible time. Make sure the replacement you buy matches the type for your projector. Learn how to change the bulb quickly.

- An extension cord for your projector's remote control. They come in lengths of up to 200 feet; 50 feet should be more than enough for most meeting and conference rooms.

- If you are using glass pin-registered mounts, some spare mounts wrapped in tissue or a plastic bubble pack. Dropping a tray can crack the glass mounts.

- A clean, lintless cloth for wiping slides and projector lenses. Kodak Film Cleaner (available from photographic supply stores) will remove dust and fingerprints from slides.

- A small roll of aluminized duct tape (also called *gaffer's tape*, after the head electrician on a movie crew) for taping cords to the floor to prevent audience members from tripping on them and destroying your projector (not to mention breaking their necks).

OVERHEAD TRANSPARENCY PRESENTATION SETUP

Usually, overhead transparency presentations are given to small, informal groups and are relatively easy to stage. However, if you are presenting transparencies in a large room, there are several factors to consider in your arrangement.

Overhead Presentations in a Large Meeting Room

In a large room, because of the relatively short projection distance (called the *throw*) required for overhead projection, it is usually necessary to place the overhead projector at the front of the audience, as shown in Figure 13.3. This arrangement eliminates the possibility of an audience member getting in the way of the projected image, but it also places the speaker and projector directly between the audience and the screen. The image should be projected high enough on the screen so that the speaker doesn't block the image. The first row of the audience should be set far enough away from the speaker and the projector to be able to see the screen above.

You should stand at the side of the projector, with your writing hand closest to the projector. That way, when you need to write on a transparency, your body won't block the projector's light.

Make sure there is a surface next to the projector large enough to hold two stacks of transparency frames: one stack as a supply and one for those already used. The supply stack should be in the order of the presentation, top to bottom. As you remove a transparency from the projector, place it *face down* on the used stack so the transparencies will be in the proper order when you are finished.

If you are using a portable LCD display screen with a laptop computer, connect it with a long cable and change the speaker's position to the left or right of the screen, as for a slide presentation.

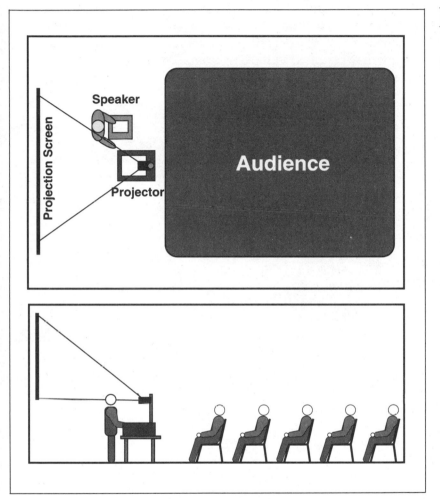

If the room does not have any amplification equipment, check to see if you are audible from the back of the audience. You may have to speak louder to be heard.

Overhead Presentations in a Conference Room

A conference room is the natural place for an overhead transparency presentation to a small group. The projector can be set up at the end of the conference table opposite the projection screen, as shown in Figure 13.4. You should stand next to the projector, with the transparencies on the conference table. The only drawback to this arrangement is that your audience may resemble a crowd at a tennis match, looking back and forth between you and the screen.

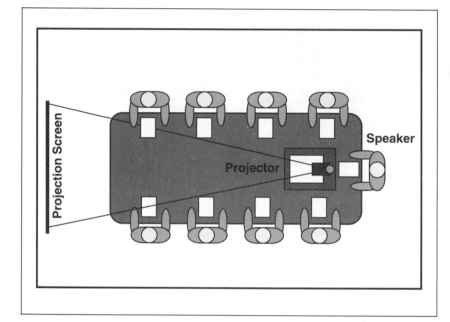

Figure 13.4:

Overhead projection setup for a small conference room

Room Lighting for Overhead Transparencies

Overhead transparencies are perfect for use in a partially lighted room. When designed with light backgrounds and dark text, they will be readable even under full light (although not in a brightly sunlit area).

Disaster-Avoidance Equipment for Overhead Presentations

If you are taking your own projector to the presentation, you should also bring most of the items recommended for 35mm slide presentations: a 25-foot extension cord for the projector, a three-prong adapter, a spare bulb for the projector, aluminized duct tape for taping cords to the floor, and a few blank transparencies in case you want to improvise during the presentation.

SCREEN SHOW SETUP

Connecting a computer directly to a large video monitor or to a video projection system makes it possible to change your visuals moments before beginning your speech. You can also field complex financial questions from audience members and show them your answers directly in a spreadsheet or by creating a chart on the fly. The catch is that video systems are still not as standardized as other presentation media.

If you walk into a conference room with a carousel full of slides, the odds are extremely good that your slide tray will fit on someone else's projector. If you walk into a meeting with a laptop computer, there is very little assurance that you will be able to just plug it into the monitor in the room and start showing your presentation.

Before getting involved with video and screen shows, you should talk to a reputable computer dealer who has experience in video projection. Some imaging service bureaus also produce screen show presentations and will provide advice.

To produce a screen show in your own conference or meeting room, you need to purchase compatible equipment and software and get a reliable dealer to install it. Taking a laptop computer on the road with the intention of using it for your screen show presents more of a challenge.

A Screen Show on the Road

If you are taking a screen show on the road, it is very difficult to "rely on the kindness of strangers" because of the many different projection systems available. You should determine in advance what sort of projection or display system is available in your intended meeting space and whether it is compatible with the computer you will be using. Of course, you can always tote your own video system around, but you will need a strong back.

Large video projectors generally do not travel well. Apart from their large size and weight, the bumping and jarring that accompanies air or automobile travel can put them out of alignment (causing color problems and ghosting) or shut them down entirely. If you are giving presentations on the road to large audiences, your life will be easier if you contract with a staging company to set up a video projection system in each location.

Some new video projector models are smaller and more portable, but they can't fill as large a screen as the larger units. If you are speaking to audiences of no more than 40 people, one of these units may be suitable.

Video Projection in a Large Meeting Room

Most video projectors have a short throw, similar to overhead projectors, requiring them to be placed close to the front of the room. However, video projectors can usually be placed much lower, greatly improving the sight lines of the audience. Figure 13.5 shows the recommended setup. The speaker and computer can be positioned to the side of the screen, as with slide projection.

Room lighting for any sort of video projection should be kept low (as for slides), since projected video images, which have much lower contrast than projected slides, are easily washed out by ambient light.

Video Monitors in a Conference Room

In a small conference room, a single large-screen monitor (27- to 35-inch diagonal screen) may be adequate for your presentation. A single monitor can be placed at the end of the conference table. The speaker can stand with the computer next to the monitor, as shown in Figure 13.6, or the show can be operated from a seated position at the table (as for slide projection).

You can also use two or three smaller monitors, depending on the layout of the room. Using multiple monitors requires a special video signal

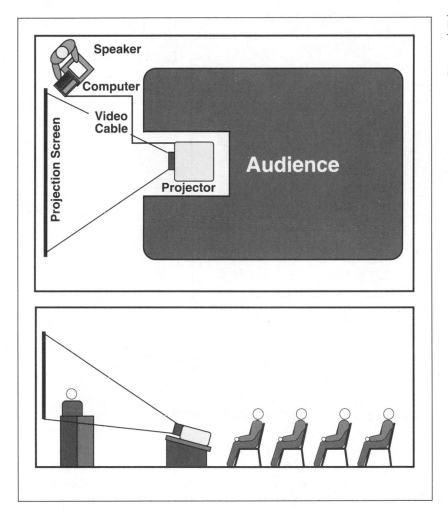

Video projection setup for a large meeting room

enhancer/splitter, which amplifies the video signal and then directs it to several monitors simultaneously.

Room lighting can usually be set much higher when using video monitors instead of video projection. However, be careful that glare and reflections on the monitor screen do not reduce its readability.

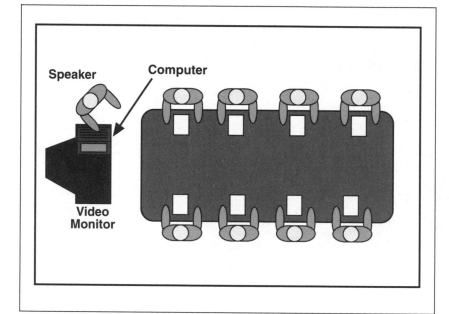

Figure 13.6:

Video monitor setup for a small conference room

DISTRIBUTING AUDIENCE HANDOUTS

Distributing handouts during a presentation is disruptive and distracting to the audience members. Keep their attention focused by distributing handouts either before or after the presentation. The layout and size of the meeting room will determine your handout strategy.

LARGE MEETING ROOM HANDOUTS

If your audience needs the handouts during the presentation, place copies on each seat in the meeting room, face up. Handouts that are intended for distribution after a presentation should be placed on a table or chair at every exit to the meeting room. At the end of the presentation, announce that handouts are available.

The self-service approach does not guarantee that every audience member will get a copy. If you want to ensure that all the audience members receive handouts, station someone at each exit to distribute them.

Multipage handouts should always be bound or corner-stapled. Never use paper clips because they will pop off in the bustle at the door, causing a mess, especially if the audience members are helping themselves to the handouts.

CONFERENCE ROOM HANDOUTS

The informal nature of a conference room makes distribution of handouts easy. Place bound or stapled copies of the handouts at each seat, or distribute them in person immediately after the presentation.

THE
REAL
WORLD   ON THE ROAD

Monday, October 15, 10:00 am: "Good morning, ladies and gentlemen. I'm George Spelvin, Chairman of Hypothetical International. It's a pleasure to be here today at Dewey, Cheatham and Howe to talk about the future of Hypothetical and your role in making it happen. With me today are Alan Smithee, our President, and Victoria Regina, our Chief Financial Officer.

"A journey of a thousand miles begins with a single step. In the past 15 years, Hypothetical has taken many steps in growing to the company it is today. But the time for walking is over. And the time has come to fly..."

The journey for this presentation has been a long one. But today, standing in front of his audience,

George is confident of success. All the elements of an effective, persuasive presentation are at work:

> A thorough presentation plan covers all the information and arguments needed to persuade the audience.

> The outline is organized for a dramatic pace and tells the Hypothetical story effectively.

> George and his fellow executives have written clear, conversational scripts and have rehearsed them diligently.

> The presentation graphics are well-designed, with concise text slides, message-driven charts, and attractive illustrations and photography.

> High-quality slides illuminate the screen behind him, and professionally printed and bound handouts are in the hands of his audience.

> There is a spare projector bulb in his briefcase.

11:15 am: "And if there are no further questions, I'll take no more of your valuable time. Thank you."

George steps from the podium and shakes hands with John Doe, president of Dewey, Cheatham and Howe.

"Thanks for the forum, John. I hope we gave your people the information they needed."

"That was a fine presentation, George. Why don't the three of you join me at the University Club for lunch, and we'll discuss some details."

How will the stock issue go? That's not part of our story. Of course, like any cautionary tale, this saga does have a moral: *plan ahead!* Despite the pitfalls encountered during the presentation design and production process, the production team members adhered to a plan that developed a message, focused their creative efforts, and guided them through the rough spots.

SUMMARY

When the production work for your presentation is finished, you need to practice your speech and stage the show. Set up your meeting room to provide the best possible projection environment for your slides, overhead transparencies, or screen show:

- The projector should be positioned so the audience doesn't block the projected image.

- The speaker should be positioned facing the audience and not blocking the projector or the audience's view of the screen.

- Pay special attention to the volume of the speaker's voice. Use microphones and amplification where necessary.

- Adjust the room lighting to the presentation medium (and vice versa). Don't try to project slides or video in bright room light.

- Be prepared! If you don't know the conditions in which you'll be presenting, pack extension cords and other accessories to prevent disaster. And if you think you do know the meeting conditions, pack your accessories anyway.

- Distribute your handouts in a way appropriate to their use in the meeting. Always staple or bind handouts; never use paper clips.

- For large presentations or video projection presentations, contract with a staging company to ensure a professional setup.

When all is said and done, a presentation is a lone speaker in front of an audience. Everything that comes before—the planning, the production, the practice—affect the persuasiveness of the speaker's message. Take the time to master your presentation graphics software, learn to plan and organize, and make your next presentation fly.

appendix A

Choosing the Right Desktop Presentation Software for the Job

Your presentation software should provide the tools you need to develop your message and create an attractive, effective presentation:

- Outlining and organizational tools
- Design and formatting options
- Typography and text control
- Color options

- Charting and graphing capabilities
- Slide, overhead transparency, and printed output

All these features are important considerations in choosing software for creating presentations. In addition, there are a few other items to consider when evaluating a program:

- Ease of use
- Predesigned templates and formats
- Clip-art libraries

Before shopping for presentation software, decide what is most important to you. Do you need outlining and organizational tools, or do you just need outline importing capability? Do you need lots of fonts? Do you need preformatted templates? Go to your local software store and get demonstrations of programs that interest you. Read the product reviews in computer magazines, such as *PC World, PC Magazine, MacWorld,* and *MacUser.*

DOS-BASED SOFTWARE

While vastly improved over the years, DOS-based presentation graphics software has always lacked certain features that make the Windows and Macintosh programs so easy to use. None of the DOS-based programs allow you to view an entire presentation for slide sorting, and all of them make the creation of master slide formats difficult at best. DOS software exports files in either SCODL or EPS format for imaging.

APPLAUSE II 1.5

Ashton-Tate Corporation
20101 Hamilton Avenue
Torrance, CA 90509 (213) 329-9989

Applause II is the easiest to learn of the DOS-based programs. It has excellent color options, a wide range of charts and graphs, master backgrounds, and good screen show capabilities. However, it lacks outlining, organizing, and speaker notes features. The acquisition of Ashton-Tate by Borland may affect the support for Applause II.

FREELANCE GRAPHICS 4.0

Lotus Development Corporation
55 Cambridge Parkway
Cambridge, MA 02142
(617) 577-8500

Freelance Graphics 4.0 has some major improvements over previous versions. Its main strength is in charting, with hot links connecting to Lotus 1-2-3 spreadsheets. The drawing interface has been upgraded, and it includes an outliner. But a limit of 13 colors per slide (and no graduated color) makes Freelance a poor choice for presentation graphics.

HARVARD GRAPHICS 3.0

Software Publishing Corporation
3165 Kifer Road
Santa Clara, CA 95056
(408) 986-8000

Harvard Graphics is the granddaddy of DOS-based presentation graphics software, and it has always had strong charting capabilities. New version 3.0 is a significant improvement over earlier versions. Its additions include improved drawing tools, more color and font support, and interactive screen show capabilities. Harvard Graphics 3.0 is the most versatile presentation package for DOS.

SLIDEWRITE PLUS

Advanced Graphics Software, Inc.
333 W. Maude Avenue, Suite 105
Sunnyvale, CA 94086
(408) 749-8620

SlideWrite Plus has one special advantage over the other DOS-based
(and even most Windows- and Macintosh-based) presentation graphics
packages: sophisticated scientific charting tools. It also includes special
scientific fonts for creating complex formulas. Its main weaknesses are in
color support and organizational tools.

MACINTOSH SOFTWARE

The graphics orientation of the Apple Macintosh
has made it the tool of choice for many desktop
presentation producers. Most service bureaus
report that they image more slides created on the
Macintosh than on PCs. Macintosh software for
presentations usually offers several advantages
over DOS products: integrated outlining and presentation management, automated creation of handouts and speaker
notes, and multiple slide masters. The Macintosh interface makes these
programs much easier to learn than DOS programs. Macintosh presentation software exports files in either PICT or EPS format for imaging.

CA-CRICKET PRESENTS 2.01

Computer Associates
711 Stewart Avenue
Garden City, NY 11530
800) 645-3003

CA-Cricket Presents is a strong presentation program that emphasizes
graphics and charting. It comes with a separate outlining program
(ACTA), but does not link the outline and presentation graphics. Early

versions offered imaging only via Autographix, with no export capabilities; version 2.01 supports PICT output for imaging by independent service bureaus.

MORE 3.0

Symantec Corporation
10201 Torre Avenue
Cupertino, CA 95014
408) 253-9600

MORE is ideal for those who need an outliner with presentation capabilities instead of presentation software with an outliner. Master slide templates, good drawing tools, and excellent charting and graphing capabilities all contribute to a complete presentation graphics package.

PERSUASION 2.1

Aldus Corporation
411 First Avenue S.
Seattle, WA 98104
(206) 628-2320

Persuasion is the current king of the hill in desktop presentation software. Its integrated outliner is linked directly to slide text, so changes in one are reflected in the other. It provides superb handling of master templates, color, and slide organization. The software package includes a stand-alone player program, which allows Persuasion screen shows to be presented on Macintosh or Windows systems.

POWERPOINT 2.01

Microsoft Corporation
One Microsoft Way
Redmond, WA 98052
(206) 882-8080

PowerPoint, though it was the first and most popular presentation program for the Macintosh, lacks many of the tools now considered essential for creating presentations. It has very limited drawing tools and does not have an integrated outliner or charting and graphing capabilities. Its strong point is excellent automated color palettes, which make color selection easy for the novice.

WINDOWS 3.0 SOFTWARE

The graphic user interface of Microsoft Windows 3.0 has made it possible for PC users to have the same control and power over their presentation graphics as Macintosh owners. Along with a few familiar names from the Macintosh world, there are a few newcomers, as well as some old standbys reborn under Windows. Windows-based presentation software features many of the advantages of Macintosh software, including integrated outlining, slide sorting, and automated creation of speaker notes and handouts. The Windows environment also has more color support, giving you a better idea of what your slides will look like on the screen.

CA-CRICKET PRESENTS 2.01

Computer Associates
711 Stewart Avenue
Garden City, NY 11530
(800) 645-3003

CA-Cricket Presents is the weakest of the Windows presentation graphics programs. It comes with a separate outlining program (CA-Cricket Abstract), but does not link the outline and presentation graphics. Charting and drawing are not as well implemented as in other Windows-based programs, and it has a limited number of templates.

CHARISMA

Micrografx Inc.
1303 Arapaho
Richardson, TX 75081
(214) 234-1769

Charisma is the flip side of many other Windows-based presentation packages. Its charting and drawing features are very powerful, with a wide range of chart styles, excellent drawing tools, and an extensive clip-art library. On the other hand, it lacks both an outliner and a slide sorter, making planning and organization difficult. Speaker note creation is also weak.

HARVARD GRAPHICS FOR WINDOWS

Software Publishing Corporation
3165 Kifer Road
Santa Clara, CA 95056
(408) 986-8000

Harvard Graphics for Windows takes full advantage of the Windows environment. It includes an integrated outliner, hot links to Excel and 1-2-3 spreadsheets, a slide sorter, automatic creation of audience handouts (but not speaker notes), and excellent charting tools. The program can import charts created with the DOS version.

HOLLYWOOD

Claris Corporation
5201 Patrick Henry Drive
Santa Clara, CA 95052
(408) 727-8227

Hollywood is a strong contender for the best of the Windows presentation graphics packages. It has excellent outlining and organizational tools, powerful formatting and color control, text-manipulation tools similar to those found in high-end illustration software, and automated speaker notes and handouts. There are even paint and airbrush tools for creating simple bitmap graphics.

PERSUASION 2.1 FOR WINDOWS

Aldus Corporation
411 First Avenue S.
Seattle, WA 98104
(206) 628-2320

Persuasion for Windows is a top-notch presentation program. Its integrated outliner is linked directly to slide text, so changes in one are reflected in the other. It provides superb handling of master templates, color, and slide organization. It also has a stand-alone screen show player program, which allows you to present screen shows on Macintosh or Windows systems.

POWERPOINT FOR WINDOWS

Microsoft Corporation
One Microsoft Way
Redmond, WA 98052
(206) 882-8080

The Windows version of PowerPoint is an improvement over the Macintosh version. Although it lacks an integrated outliner and has very limited drawing tools, the program includes a charting module. Like the Macintosh version, its strong points are excellent automated color palettes and ease of use.

Making Do With What You Have

If you're planning to produce a lot of slides, it pays to use one of the programs above. The powerful tools a true presentation graphics program provides make the process of organizing and creating a presentation much simpler. But if you don't have the need (or the budget) for dedicated presentation software, you don't have to purchase a high-end presentation graphics program. You may already have the tools you need on your computer. With a little extra work, and doing without some features such as outlining and slide sorting, desktop publishing and illustration programs can create high-quality graphics for slides and overhead transparencies.

You should contact your local service bureau to find out which programs it supports, and what special setup may be required to create slides from different programs.

DESKTOP PUBLISHING PROGRAMS

Desktop publishing software, such as Aldus PageMaker, Ventura Publisher, FrameMaker, and Quark Xpress, offers a solution to creating slides in a pinch. Many independent service bureaus can image PostScript files to slides and overhead transparencies from page layout software packages. You can create master pages, enter text, and import charts, graphs, and illustrations, just as you would with a presentation program.

ILLUSTRATION/DRAWING PROGRAMS

Another source for slides is an illustration or drawing program, such as Adobe Illustrator, Aldus Freehand, CorelDRAW!, Deneba Canvas, Micrografx Designer, and MacDraw Pro. Drawing programs can create PostScript or PICT files, which can be imaged on film recorders. In many cases, the superior drawing abilities of these programs can be an advantage.

If you need to create very detailed illustrations, you should consider having slides made directly from the program, rather than importing graphics files into a presentation program before imaging them.

GRAPHIC SPREADSHEETS

Graphic spreadsheet programs can be used to create charts and graphs for presentations, but they lack the text, drawing, and organizational tools to stand on their own. PC-based spreadsheets Lotus 1-2-3/G, Microsoft Excel, and Borland Quattro Pro output file formats that can be imaged to a film recorder. All Macintosh spreadsheets will export charts and graphs as PICT files, which can also be imaged.

PHOTO ENHANCEMENT/PAINT PROGRAMS

If you want to include photographs or other scanned images in your slides, you may want to invest in photo enhancement software, such as Adobe Photoshop or Letraset ColorStudio for the Macintosh and Aldus PhotoStyler or Image-In for Windows. Placing scanned images in a presentation usually requires the precise cropping and image enhancement available with these programs.

Paint programs, such as PixelPaint Pro, Studio/32, PC Paintbrush, and Lumena, usually produce a low-resolution bitmap image, which limits their usefulness for creating slides or overhead transparencies. However, the low resolution is acceptable for video or screen shows. Paint programs are also useful for creating presentation backgrounds, where resolution isn't as important as it is for text and graphics.

appendix B

Guide to Imaging
Service Bureaus

You can have your presentation files imaged by a national or a local, independent service bureau. See Chapter 12 of this book for the factors you should consider in selecting an imaging service bureau.

NATIONAL COMPANIES

The three most popular national service bureaus, Autographix, Genigraphics, and MAGICorp supply special drivers that come with a variety of presentation programs. The drivers include file export and communications modules, which allow you to call toll-free numbers to transmit your files via modem.

Because of the large volume of business they do, national bureaus concentrate on the most popular presentation programs, such as Power-Point, Persuasion, and Harvard Graphics. Font support is usually limited to a few dozen typefaces.

Most of the local sites for the national service bureaus also offer photographic and other services in addition to imaging. To find the local center nearest you, call the toll-free numbers provided in this appendix.

AUTOGRAPHIX

Autographix
63 Third Avenue
Burlington, MA 01830-9661
(800) 548-8558

Autographix operates more than 20 corporate-owned and affiliated locations that use the Autographix imaging hardware and software. Autographix has been particularly diligent in providing drivers for DOS-based presentation software, such as Harvard Graphics and Lotus Freelance.

GENIGRAPHICS

Genigraphics Corporation
2 Corporate Drive, Suite 340
Shelton, CT 06484
(800) 638-7348

Genigraphics operates more than two dozen regional service bureau locations throughout the United States and Canada. Modem orders are processed through a central location and then dispatched to your local Genigraphics center for imaging and delivery. Genigraphics pioneered the audiovisual computer graphics industry in the middle 1970s, with a series of innovative workstations that were the predecessors of today's desktop presentation software.

MAGICORP

MAGICorp, Ltd.
777 Old Saw Mill River Road, Suite 222
Tarrytown, NY 10591
(800) 367-6244

MAGICorp operates from a central location in New York, offering modem service to the United States and Canada.

INDEPENDENT IMAGING SERVICE BUREAUS

The services offered by independent service bureaus depend on their equipment and experience. Unlike national service bureaus, independent service bureaus are not committed to a particular driver-based hardware arrangement, so they can often provide support for a wider range of software and fonts. Some of the imaging service bureaus in the United States and Canada are listed below. Contact the one nearest you for specific information about its services and requirements. Check your local Yellow Pages (under Slides & Filmstrips, Computer Graphics, or Audio-Visual Production Services) for other independent service bureaus in your area.

ARIZONA

Data Imaging Center
2450 South 24th Street
Phoenix, AZ 85034
(602) 275-6565

CALIFORNIA

Accent Presentations, Inc.
12780 High Bluff Drive, Suite 250
San Diego, CA 92130
(619) 755-1158

Corporate Images, Inc.
10 Jackson Street
San Francisco, CA 94111
(415) 421-9900

Graphic Presentation Services
1102 Broadway, Suite 104
Santa Monica, CA 90401
(213) 451-1307

Icon West
7961 West 3rd Street
Los Angeles, CA 90048
(213) 938-3822

Panorama Productions
2353 De La Cruz Boulevard
Santa Clara, CA 95050
(408) 727-7500

Slide Master
1111 Town & Country Road, Suite 22
Orange, CA 94301
(714) 541-5753

COLORADO

Avenir Corporation
1100 Bannock Street
Denver, CO 80204
(303) 623-4600

CONNECTICUT

Chromakers, Inc.
880 Canal Street
Stamford, CT 06902
(203) 323-7277

DISTRICT OF COLUMBIA

Corporate Visions, Inc.
1835 K Street NW #510
Washington, DC 20006
(202) 833-4333

GEORGIA

SlideImagers
22 Seventh Street
Atlanta, GA 30308
(404) 873-5353

ILLINOIS

CMI Business Communications
150 East Huron
Chicago, IL 60611
(312) 787-9040

MAINE

Slide Works
94 Commercial Street
Portland, ME 04101
(207) 774-2689

MASSACHUSETTS

Graphics Express
297 Newbury Street, #21
Boston, MA 02115
(617) 267-1441

MICHIGAN

AV Computer Graphics, Inc.
30800 Telegraph Road, Suite 1751
Birmingham, MI 48010
(313) 646-0200

MINNESOTA

Slide Services, Inc.
2537 25th Avenue South
Minneapolis, MN 55406
(612) 721-2434

MISSOURI

Steven Blives & Associates
10131 Old Olive Road
St. Louis, MO 63141
(314) 997-1188

NEW YORK

Brilliant Image
Seven Penn Plaza
New York, NY 10001
(212) 736-9661

Jack Ward Color Service
220 East 23rd Street
New York, NY 10010
(212) 725-5200

Visual Horizons
180 Metro Park
Rochester, NY 14623
(716) 424-5300

NORTH CAROLINA

Image Associates, Inc.
4314 Bland Road
Raleigh, NC 27609
(919) 876-6400

OHIO

EDCOM Productions, Inc.
26991 Tungsten Road
Cleveland, OH 44132
(216) 261-3222

Image Source, Inc.
801 Front Street
Toledo, OH 43605
(419) 697-1111

Photo Lab, Inc.
1026 Redna Terrace
Cincinnati, OH 45215
(513) 771-4400

OKLAHOMA

Communicating Arts
2516A East 71st
Tulsa, OK 74136
(918) 493-5700

OREGON

Slidepro, Inc.
108 NW 9th Street, Suite 202
Portland, OR 97209
(503) 242-0034

TEXAS

Imaging Presentations, Inc.
8150 Brookriver Drive, Suite S-205
Dallas, TX 75247
(214) 638-0292

NPL, Inc.
1926 West Gray
Houston, TX 77019
(713) 527-9300

SlideMasters, Inc.
1100 Business Parkway
Richardson, TX 75081
(214) 437-0542

Stokes Imaging Service
7000 Cameron Road
Austin, TX 78752
(512) 458-2201

UTAH

Replicolor Computer Graphics
236 Edison Street
Salt Lake City, UT 84111
(801) 328-0271

WASHINGTON

Pro Image Resource
123 NW 36th Street
Seattle, WA 98107
(206) 547-5470

CANADA

Digital Presentations
3266 Yonge Street
Toronto, ON M5P 1G4
(416) 537-0161

Graphically Speaking Services, Inc.
210-1161 Melville Street
Vancouver, BC V6E 2X7
(604) 682-5500

Management Graphics, Inc.
20 Martin Ross Avenue
Toronto, ON M3J 2K8
(416) 667-8877

SYGRAF, Inc.
53 Duke, #145
Montreal, QC H3C 2L8
(514) 392-1502

appendix C

Bibliography of Recommended Reading

PRESENTATION PLANNING AND PUBLIC SPEAKING

Effective Business and Technical Presentations, George L. Morrisey (Addison-Wesley Publishing Company).

Effective Presentation Skills, Steve Mandel (Crisp Publications, Inc.).

Making Successful Presentations, George T. Vardaman (American Management Associations).

Presentations for Decision Makers, Marya W. Holcombe and Judith K. Stein (Lifetime Learning Publications).

Speechmaking...More than Words Alone, Eastman Kodak Motion Picture and Audiovisual Markets Division.

STORYBOARDING

Rapid Viz: A New Method for the Rapid Visualization of Ideas, Kurt Hanks and Larry Belliston (William Kaufman, Inc.).

TYPOGRAPHY

The Mac Is Not a Typewriter, Robin Williams (Peachpit Press).

Type Wise, Kit Hinrichs (North Light Books).

CHARTS AND GRAPHS

Say It With Charts, Gene Zelazny (Dow Jones-Irwin).

Statistical Graphics, Calvin F. Schmid (Wiley-Interscience/John Wiley & Sons).

The Visual Display of Quantitative Information, Edward R. Tufte (Graphics Press).

INDEX

Selections from The SYBEX Library

DESKTOP PRESENTATION

Harvard Graphics Instant Reference
Gerald E. Jones
154pp. Ref. 726-6
This handy reference is a quick, non-technical answer manual to questions about Harvard's onscreen menus and help displays. Provides specific information on each of the program's major features, including Draw Partner. A must for business professionals and graphic artists who create charts and graphs for presentation.

Harvard Graphics 3 Instant Reference (Second Edition)
Gerald E. Jones
200pp; ref. 871-8
This handy, compact volume is the single complete source for quick answers on all of Harvard's menu options and features. It's small enough to keep on hand while you work—and fast enough to let you keep working while you look up concise explanations and exact instructions for using Harvard commands.

Mastering Animator
Mitch Gould
300pp. Ref.688-X
A hands-on guide to creating dynamic multimedia presentations. From simple animation to Hollywood-style special effects, from plan-

ning a presentation to bringing it all to life—it's all you need to know, in straightforward, easy-to-follow terms.

Mastering Harvard Graphics (Second Edition)
Glenn H. Larsen
375pp, Ref. 673-1
"The clearest course to begin mastering Harvard Graphics," according to *Computer Currents*. Readers master essential principles of effective graphic communication, as they follow step-by-step instructions to create dozens of charts and graphs; automate and customize the charting process; create slide shows, and more.

Mastering Harvard Graphics 3
**Glenn Larsen
with Kristopher Larsen**
525pp; Ref. 870-X
This highly praised hands-on guide uses engaging tutorials and colorful examples to show exactly how to create effective charts, graphs, presentations, and slide shows. Readers create virtually every kind of chart, including many not covered in Harvard's manual. Companion diskette features over $40 worth of clipart—absolutely free.

Teach Yourself Harvard Graphics 3
Jeff Woodward
450pp; Ref. 801-7
A graphical introduction to the hottest-selling presentation graphics program! This illustrated guide leads newcomers

through the exact steps needed to create all kinds of effective charts and graphs. There are no surprises: what you see in the book is what you will see on your screen.

Up & Running with Harvard Graphics
Rebecca Bridges Altman
148pp. Ref. 736-3

Desktop presentation in 20 steps—the perfect way to evaluate Harvard Graphics for purchase, or to get a fast, hands-on overview of the software's capabilities. The book's 20 concise lessons are time-coded (each takes no more than an hour to complete), and cover everything from installation and startup, to creating specific types of charts, graphs, and slide shows.

Up & Running with Harvard Graphics 3
Rebecca Bridges Altman
140pp; Ref. 884-X

Come up to speed with Harvard Graphics 3—fast. If you're a computer-literate user who needs to start producing professional-looking presentation graphics now, this book is for you. In only 20 lessons (each taking just 15 minutes to an hour), you can cover all the essentials of this perennially popular progam.

DESKTOP PUBLISHING

The ABC's of the New Print Shop
Vivian Dubrovin
340pp. Ref. 640-4

This beginner's guide stresses fun, practicality and original ideas. Hands-on tutorials show how to create greeting cards, invitations, signs, flyers, letterheads, banners, and calendars.

The ABC's of Ventura
Robert Cowart
Steve Cummings
390pp. Ref. 537-9

Created especially for new desktop publishers, this is an easy introduction to a complex program. Cowart provides details on using the mouse, the Ventura side bar, and page layout, with careful explanations of publishing terminology. The new Ventura menus are all carefully explained. For Version 2.

Desktop Publishing with WordPerfect 5.1
Rita Belserene
418pp. Ref. 481-X

A practical guide to using the desktop publishing capabilities of versions 5.0 and 5.1. Topics include graphic design concepts, hardware necessities, installing and using fonts, columns, lines, and boxes, illustrations, multi-page layouts, Style Sheets, and integrating with other software.

Mastering CorelDRAW 2
Steve Rimmer
500pp. Ref. 814-9

This comprehensive tutorial and design guide features complete instruction in creating spectacular graphic effects with CorelDRAW 2. The book also offers a primer on commercial image and page design, including how to use printers and print-house facilities for optimum results.

Mastering Micrografx Designer
Peter Kent
400pp. Ref. 694-4

A complete guide to using this sophisticated illustration package. Readers begin by importing and modifying clip art, and progress to creating original drawings, working with text, printing and plotting, creating slide shows, producing color separations, and exporting art.

SYBEX

FREE BROCHURE!

Complete this form today, and we'll send you a full-color brochure of Sybex bestsellers.

Please supply the name of the Sybex book purchased.

_____

How would you rate it?

_____ Excellent   _____ Very Good   _____ Average   _____ Poor

Why did you select this particular book?

_____ Recommended to me by a friend

_____ Recommended to me by store personnel

_____ Saw an advertisement in _____

_____ Author's reputation

_____ Saw in Sybex catalog

_____ Required textbook

_____ Sybex reputation

_____ Read book review in _____

_____ In-store display

_____ Other _____

Where did you buy it?

_____ Bookstore

_____ Computer Store or Software Store

_____ Catalog (name: _____)

_____ Direct from Sybex

_____ Other: _____

Did you buy this book with your personal funds?

_____ Yes   _____ No

About how many computer books do you buy each year?

_____ 1-3   _____ 3-5   _____ 5-7   _____ 7-9   _____ 10+

About how many Sybex books do you own?

_____ 1-3   _____ 3-5   _____ 5-7   _____ 7-9   _____ 10+

Please indicate your level of experience with the software covered in this book:

_____ Beginner   _____ Intermediate   _____ Advanced

Which types of software packages do you use regularly?

_____ Accounting	_____ Databases	_____ Networks
_____ Amiga	_____ Desktop Publishing	_____ Operating Systems
_____ Apple/Mac	_____ File Utilities	_____ Spreadsheets
_____ CAD	_____ Money Management	_____ Word Processing
_____ Communications	_____ Languages	_____ Other _____

(please specify)

Which of the following best describes your job title?

_____	Administrative/Secretarial	_____	President/CEO
_____	Director	_____	Manager/Supervisor
_____	Engineer/Technician	_____	Other _____

(please specify)

Comments on the weaknesses/strengths of this book: _____

_____

_____

_____

_____

Name _____

Street _____

City/State/Zip _____

Phone _____

PLEASE FOLD, SEAL, AND MAIL TO SYBEX

-- -- -- -- -- -- -- -- -- -- -- -- -- -- -- -- -- -- -- --

SYBEX, INC.
Department M
2021 CHALLENGER DR.
ALAMEDA, CALIFORNIA USA
94501

SYBEX

FROM CORPORATE IMAGES

USING ILLUSTRATIONS AND CLIPART

COMBINING PHOTOGRAPHY AND COMPUTER GRAPHICS